MILLER AND *McFARLANE*: THE IMPLICATIONS FOR MATRIMONIAL LAWYERS

SPECIAL BULLETIN

MILLER AND *McFARLANE*: THE IMPLICATIONS FOR MATRIMONIAL LAWYERS

SPECIAL BULLETIN

Roger Bird

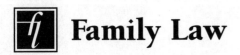 **Family Law**

Published by
Jordan Publishing Limited
21 St Thomas Street
Bristol BS1 6JS

Whilst the publishers and the author have taken every care in preparing the material included in this work, any statements made as to the legal or other implications of particular transactions are made in good faith purely for general guidance and cannot be regarded as a substitute for professional advice. Consequently, no liability can be accepted for loss or expense incurred as a result of relying in particular circumstances on statements made in this work.

British Library Cataloguing-in-Publication Data
A catalogue record for this book is available from the British Library.

ISBN 1 84661 033 8

Typeset by Etica Press Ltd, Malvern, Worcestershire
Printed and bound in Great Britain by Antony Rowe Limited, Chippenham, Wiltshire

CONTENTS

Part A – The background

1 INTRODUCTION

1.1 Very few cases relating to ancillary relief reach the House of Lords. Family cases which get that far usually relate to children, particularly public law issues. When the financial dispute between Mr and Mrs White reached their Lordships in 2000 (*White v White* [2001] 1 AC 596 – hereafter referred to as '*White*') it was thought that this would be the final word on these matters for a considerable time. *White* set out guidelines for the determination of such cases which may be summarised as follows:

- The court must be fair. There can be no discrimination between husband and wife in their respective roles. Whatever the division of labour, fairness dictates that this should not prejudice either party when considering the statutory factors. There should be no bias in favour of the breadwinner as against the homemaker and childcarer.

- When carrying out the statutory exercise, the judge should always check his or her tentative views against the 'yardstick of equality of division'. Equality should only be departed from if, and to the extent that, there is there is good reason for doing so. This does not mean that there is a starting point or presumption of equality.

- The concept of reasonable requirements is erroneous. The statute refers to 'needs' but this is only one of the statutory factors.

1.2 However, this was not to be the last word and certain issues remained to trouble the courts, including the Court of Appeal. These issues may be summarised as essentially the search for fairness, and what fairness means. Given that the court must be fair, and given that the yardstick of equality is overriding but does not amount to a rigid regime of equality, what are the circumstances in which the court may be fair and at the same time depart from equal shares? Would this be appropriate where, for example, the marriage was short? If so, what constitutes a short marriage? Would it be appropriate where one party had created the wealth enjoyed by the couple by his or her exceptional contributions? If so, how exceptional would the contributions have to be? It would be inappropriate to recite the cases in which these issues were discussed and sometimes contradictory answers given; for a detailed account see R Bird 'Dividing Matrimonial Assets after *Lambert v Lambert*' (Family Law 2003) and R Bird *Ancillary Relief Handbook* 5th edn (Family Law, 2005), pp 26–34.

1.3   Running parallel with all of this was academic criticism of the whole approach of the law of England and Wales. This law is based on a discretionary approach, and even in recent times judges in the Court of Appeal have gone out of their way to emphasise that there is no formula which will apply to all cases; these matters have to be considered on a case-by-case basis. The criticism made is that even on that basis, analysis of the cases reveals no rational pattern, and further, that this unpredictable case-by-case approach is unfair, since parties who wish to settle their disputes are given uncertain guidance and often have to risk large sums of money to achieve a result.

1.4   The combined appeals of *Miller v Miller* and *McFarlane v McFarlane* which have now been decided by the House of Lords have therefore attracted widespread interest, both among family lawyers and in the popular press. This Special Bulletin will consider the result of these appeals, and the guidance given, and attempt to answer the question of whether the law is now more clear than it was before.

1.5   First, the facts of both cases and the results in the courts below must be considered.

2 *McFARLANE*

The facts in *McFarlane*

2.1 Both parties were aged 44 and had married in 1984. There were three children, aged 8, 13 and 15. The husband was a partner in a firm of chartered accountants and the wife, who had qualified and practised as a solicitor, had not worked since 1991 by agreement. The capital assets were about £3m and equal division was agreed. The husband's net income was £753,000 per annum. It was agreed that the husband would pay the school fees and £20,000 per annum for each child. The issue before the district judge at first instance was what should be the wife's share. The wife put her income needs at £128,000 per annum and sought an order of £275,000 per annum. The husband declined to specify his income needs and offered £100,000 per annum. He said that he intended to pay off his share of the borrowings incurred on his new house over 5 years, which would require payments of £347,500 per annum.

2.2 At first instance, District Judge Redgrave found that the parties' contributions to this long marriage had been different but of equal value. The wife's contributions had enabled the husband to create a working environment that had produced greater rewards, in respect of which she should have her fair share. It was unreasonable to expect the wife to take steps to improve her earning capacity in the foreseeable future. The district judge was 'far from satisfied' that either party intended to provide for their future years by pension investment.

2.3 The order made was for £250,000 per annum, ie 33.18% of the husband's net income, to be index-linked. In the Court of Appeal, Thorpe LJ commented (at para [23]) that:

> '... implicit within the district judge's reasoning is first the conclusion that the wife should have the same opportunity as the husband to make provision for the years of retirement and second the conclusion that she should have the means with which to insure herself and the children against the risk of premature cessation of the husband's high professional earnings'.

2.4 The husband appealed on several grounds, and the appeal was heard by Bennett J, whose judgment will now be considered.

Bennett J's judgment in *McFarlane*

2.5   Bennett J rejected all but one of the husband's criticisms of the district judge's judgment. The criticism which found favour was Bennett J's finding that:

> '... the district judge had wrongly allowed for the wife to build up a retirement fund and/or to insure herself against the husband's incapacity or premature death'.

2.6   During the course of argument, this had emerged as a submission that the district judge had impermissibly subverted a periodical payments order as a mechanism to provide the wife with additional capital. Bennett J said:

> '... it is my judgment, with all due respect to the district judge, that, having given the wife an award from which she is likely to be able to save large sums of money and thereby accumulate capital, it is no answer to say, as she did, that it is a matter for the wife whether she chooses to make provision for pension and other matters'.

2.7   He therefore chose to exercise his discretion afresh.

2.8   He asked the question: 'what figure should then be substituted for £250,000?' and answered:

> '... the quantification of periodical payments is more an art than a science. The parameters of s 25 are so wide that it might be said that it is almost impossible to be "scientific". In my judgment, I would be doing justice to both parties if I award the wife £180,000 per annum by way of periodical payments'.

2.9   He concluded:

> 'I am sure the parties will understand that no family judge in exercising this jurisdiction can achieve perfection given the width of s 25. He or she can only do his best to get as near to it as possible in the circumstances of any particular case.'

2.10   The wife appealed from that decision. Most readers will remember that this appeal was heard at the same time as the better-known case of *Parlour v Parlour*, which attracted more media attention because of the celebrity status of Mr Ray Parlour. There are therefore matters in the judgments of the Court of Appeal which relate to both cases, and sometimes more to *Parlour* than *McFarlane*. One linking factor to both cases is that both appeals were from Bennett J, who had heard *Parlour* at first instance and *McFarlane* on appeal from District Judge Redgrave, and had directed himself in *Parlour* according to his decision in *McFarlane*.

The issue before the Court of Appeal

2.11   Thorpe LJ observed that:

'... the skeleton arguments prepared for the appeals ... address the very general question: what should be the principles governing an award of periodical payments during joint lives or until remarriage in any case where the net income of the payer significantly exceeds what both parties need in order to meet their outgoings at the standard of living which the court has found to be appropriate'.

2.12   He continued:

'Mr Mostyn [for Mrs Parlour] has repeated the submissions that he advanced unsuccessfully in the court below. He advances this cogent criticism of Bennett J's judgment: in McFarlane were the principle asserted by Bennett J sound, then, as he himself partially recognised, his order breached it, albeit to a lesser extent than that of the district judge. What was the rationalisation for the uplift of over £50,000 that Bennett J allowed the wife above her annual need for expenditure? If there were no need that could be categorised as "income" then the surplusage has to be categorised as capital or as income available for the acquisition of capital.'

2.13   As to the opposing arguments (see paras [47], [48] and [52]):

'Mr Posnansky and Mr Francis [for the husbands] assert that the court's simple task is to order such proportion of the income as will enable the carer to discharge the outgoings on the single parent family home and the other anticipated family expenses.'

2.14   Thorpe LJ made three preliminary points (at paras [54], [55] and [56]). First, the cases before Bennett J had been argued primarily as claims for indefinite and continuing periodical payments – this was a mistaken approach:

'... neither case should have been approached on that basis. In both cases a clean break had been partially achieved and a proper concentration on s 25A both by the parties and by the court would have provided a short answer to the issue of principle so extensively debated'.

2.15   Second:

'... the present appeals are far removed from any norm. In one case the single net income probably exceeds the expenditure of the two households (at a very high standard but excluding housing costs for the husband) by about £550,000 per annum. In the other, the single net income probably exceeds the expenditure of the two households by about £900,000 per annum. It is only the huge excess over need that creates the debate as what are the principles governing the quantification of the payee's award. Only that excess allows the advancement of the appellants' ambitious models. Only that excess renders the respondents' contrary propositions unconvincing'.

2.16   Third:

'... in both cases the past surplus which had been converted into capital assets was divided by agreement. In the one case the division was equal, in the other the earner took about 60%. It was the scale of the contemplated future surplus that prevented the complete agreement, namely the clean break dismissing all claims. In both cases the agreement was seen, or should have been seen, as but the first stage in the progress to clean break. The future surplus could provide the consideration for the dismissal of the wife's outstanding claims. How many years of garnering of surplus would be necessary could not be calculated but only estimated. All depended on the surplus in each of the future years'.

2.17   Those principles run through the judgments of the court (see eg Wall LJ at paras [134] and [143]). The essential point where Thorpe LJ identified error on the part of Bennett J (see paras [66] and [67]) was in his failure to identify the importance of s 25A. In any case in which, despite a substantial capital base available for division, clean break was not presently practicable, the court had a statutory duty to consider the future possibility. That duty assumes particular prominence in cases where there is a certain and substantial surplus of future income over future needs. If the surplus would be predictably short-lived, the first option for consideration should be the planned progress to clean break by means of a substantial term order open to a later application for extension.

2.18   The obligation on the parties to achieve financial independence was mutual. The earner must give proper priority to making payments on account out of the surplus income. The payee must invest the surplus sensibly or risk that her failure to do so might count against her on an application for discharge under s 31(7A) and (7B). Given the mutuality of the obligation, the opportunity and responsibility to invest should be shared. It was discriminatory, and therefore wrong in principle, for the earner to have sole control of the surplus through the years of accumulation. The preferred mechanism by which the surplus is to be divided annually must be periodical payments. They were variable and could therefore reflect fluctuations in the payer's income. They were determined by the court in the event of dispute and terminated on the re-marriage of the recipient. The practicality of such an order will depend upon many factors. Essentially, the completion of the process must be foreseen within a relatively short span. A term of 5 years might be towards the limit of the foreseeable.

The outcome in *McFarlane*

2.19 As far as *McFarlane* was concerned, the Court of Appeal decided that Bennett J had erred in interfering with the district judge's order, which was therefore restored (applying *Cordle v Cordle* [2001] EWCA Civ 1791, [2002] 1 WLR 1441) subject only to the imposition of a 5-year term and removal of the index-linking provision. In *Parlour*, Thorpe LJ observed that Mr Parlour might be nearing the end of his playing career and continued:

> 'These considerations only underline the obvious need for a substantial proportion of the income in the present fat years to be stored up against the future famine. Again I conclude that it would be wrong in principle to leave the responsibility and opportunity to the husband alone. The wife's and the children's needs were put at £150,000 by the judge. To award her the global figure of £444,000 per annum sought by Mr Mostyn allows her and obliges her to lay-up £294,000 per annum as a reserve against the discharge of her periodical payments order. I would in this case order a 4-year extendable term. Hopefully a clean break will be achievable then on an assessment of the husband's earning capacity at 35 years of age and the wife's independent fortune derived from the original capital settlement augmented by the substantial annual surplus built into her periodical payments order in the interim.'

2.20 Both Latham LJ and Wall LJ agreed with Thorpe LJ's proposed orders, but Wall LJ added some words of his own which amount to a less than ringing endorsement (see para [140] et seq). In *McFarlane* he found himself in some difficulty in deciding what was the proper order, but recognised that the only course open to the court was to restore the district judge's order. In *Parlour*, he was clearly unsure about the efficacy of Thorpe LJ's solution but was conscious of the cost implications of a further hearing and was therefore persuaded that he should follow the proposed course.

2.21 Thorpe LJ observed that both the husbands had failed to complete the section of Form E containing their budgets for future needs and had refused requests for information. The court was told that a practice had grown up for substantial earners to decline any statement of their needs. Thorpe LJ said that this practice must stop.

Comment on *McFarlane*

2.22 The Court of Appeal was at pains to emphasise that the two cases before it were exceptional and outside the normal run of ancillary relief applications which come before the court. The exceptional factors were the very large incomes of the parties coupled with the fact that there was insufficient capital to provide a clean break now. One might also add the fact that the wives in both cases had no immediate prospect of improving their earning capacity and had to care for young children. The predominating factor, therefore, became how best to prepare for a clean break in years to come. However, even if the effect of the judgment were limited to that class of case, it still had a significant effect. As Thorpe LJ pointed out, there must be many high-earning professional couples who will find themselves in a similar financial situation.

2.23 Looking beyond those facts, it appeared at the time that the following messages of general importance could be derived from the judgments:

- The importance of s 25A was firmly re-asserted. The underlying policy of the legislature in inserting this section was not open to doubt.

- This must be read with s 31(7A)–(7F) which significantly strengthen the court's powers to bring about a clean break on variation.

- Where a clean break is not immediately possible, the court has a statutory duty to consider the future possibility and, if possible, to make an order which will enable both parties to start to provide for a later clean break.

- Periodical payments cannot be limited to the needs of the receiving party. To do so would be to concentrate on one s 25(2) factor to the exclusion of the others.

2.24 However, it has to be said that the judgments did not assist in deciding what proportion of the payer's income should be taken. In *Parlour* the wife's submission was that the division of income should be in the same proportions as the division of capital and that submission succeeded. The wife had conceded that a departure from equality of capital was appropriate. The question remained, therefore, whether, if that concession had not been made and if the court had divided capital equally, the division of income would also have been equal.

2.25 Little help as to the amount of periodical payments was derived from *McFarlane* because the Court of Appeal merely restored the district judge's order on *Cordle* principles and the district judge had not stated any particular principle in arriving at her figure of £250,000 per annum. Needs had been put at £128,000 and the eventual award was about one-third of the husband's net income. Bennett J was similarly imprecise when he reduced the figure to £180,000, merely saying that he thought this would do justice to both parties. The significance of the decision seemed to lie in the imposition of a term which, as will be seen, was an important issue before the House of Lords.

3 MILLER

The facts in *Miller*

3.1   The husband was English and 41 years of age. The wife was American and 36 years of age. The husband was an exceptionally successful fund manager.

3.2   The wife, who was American, arrived in England in February 1995, the parties met in the summer of 1995 and shortly thereafter commenced an intimate relationship. There was a considerable financial disparity between them, the wife having a salary of about £85,000 per annum and living in a rented flat and the husband's earnings inclusive of bonus possibly exceeding £1m per annum.

3.3   This intimate relationship, which did not include cohabitation, continued for 4 years before the couple became engaged in the summer of 1999 and married on 14 July 2000. In preparation, the husband bought the matrimonial home in February 2000 for £1.8m. The wife moved to London and to a London job at about that date. In March 2000 the husband received £20m, being the second tranche of sums due to him as a result of transactions completed some 5 years earlier.

3.4   The husband was closely allied in business to John Duffield, who in May 2000 had started to invest in a company called New Star and entered into a gentlemen's agreement with the husband to give him 20% of the venture if and when the husband could be extricated from his then employment. This objective was achieved on 29 January 2001 when the husband joined New Star as it commenced trading. The husband received 200,000 £1 shares in New Star issued at par. As a result of the move, the husband suffered a huge reduction in basic salary but acquired at par 200,000 shares which at the date of their issue were already being placed elsewhere at £80.00 per share. Furthermore, these shares had the obvious potential to rise significantly in value above even that high plane. Although the husband in August 2003 granted an option to Mr Duffield to purchase 75,000 of his shares at £80.00 a share in December 2006, the remaining 125,000 shares hold the potential for further gain.

3.5   In May 2001 the wife gave up her employment. She had developed a considerable interest in interior design, the London home was complete and attention turned to a villa in the south of France offered to the wife on her birthday in June and purchased in joint names in September 2001. Its refurbishment was completed by April 2002.

3.6   The parties had agreed deferring children at the outset of marriage. In August 2002 the wife miscarried and did not conceive again. On 23 April 2003 the husband left to pursue his relationship with another woman, whom he has since married. The parties were divorced and ancillary proceedings followed quite quickly.

The litigation

3.7   At the unsuccessful FDR hearing on 6 February 2004, the directions order contained the following recital:

> 'And upon the respondent declaring that she will not be relying upon Section 25 (2) (g) of the Matrimonial Causes Act 1973 in the prosecution of her claim for ancillary relief against the petitioner.'

3.8   There followed a pre-trial review before the President on 29 July 2004 at which nothing was said about the wife's promise not to rely upon conduct. However, on 6 August her solicitors wrote to say that counsel had 'come across the only recently reported case of *G v G* [2004] 1 FLR 1011'. They continued by saying that at the trial they intended to rely on *G v G* 'to establish the facts that led to the end of the marriage, and as a defensive shield to the reliance that no doubt will be made by your client on the duration of the marriage'.

3.9   At the outset of the trial before Singer J the husband applied to the judge to rule that the wife was bound by her declaration and was, therefore, precluded from asserting that it was the husband's conduct that had destroyed the marriage. The judge refused that application, emphasising his statutory duty to consider all the circumstances of the case and particularly the criteria in s 25(2). He noted that each of the parties had given a lengthy account of the marriage and its breakdown in their narrative affidavits and that the husband was not proposing to withdraw any of his criticisms of the wife.

3.10   The submissions of the parties were polarised. The husband submitted that the wife was only entitled to be returned to her former position as a professional woman living in a flat with a net income of about £50,000 per annum. That could be achieved by allowing her £500,000 to purchase a flat and £120,000 to cover 3 years of revenue shortfall whilst she worked her way back to her former level. The husband offered £1.3m, which he said was generous.

3.11   The wife asserted that as a consequence of the decision in *White v White* [2001] 1 AC 596, the proper approach was to calculate her award by reference to the marital acquest, ie the increase in the husband's fortune during the period of marriage. The extent of the acquest was much in dispute. Fundamentally, it was argued for the husband that the New Star shares were acquired before the marriage, since they were the subject of the gentlemen's agreement between the husband and Mr Duffield in May 2000. The wife's reply was that since they were not acquired by the husband until January 2001 they were the product of the years of marriage. There were differences between the wife's accountant's estimate of the husband's wealth (£20m) and that of the husband's accountant (£14m). The wife submitted that her award should be £7.2m, representing 37.5% of the marital acquest.

3.12 Singer J accepted the wife's evidence as to the circumstances of the marriage and its breakdown and declined either to rule on the difference of opinion between the forensic accountants or to put a value on the New Star shares.

3.13 He rejected the approach advocated by both counsel, ordering that:

(1) The wife's half-share of the French villa should go to the husband but that the wife should have the London home valued at £2.3m.

(2) The husband pay the wife a lump sum of £2.7m.

3.14 He concluded his judgment with the following sentence:

'A global award equivalent to £5m (plus the furniture and chattels which have agreed) seems to me a fair outcome irrespective of what ever value the husband in due course may achieve for the New Star shares.'

The appeal

3.15 The husband appealed. In his grounds of appeal and skeleton argument it was contended that the judge had erred in permitting the wife to adduce evidence as to the cause of the breakdown in the face of her FDR declaration, and in holding that the husband was to blame for the breakdown of the marriage and that this consideration shielded the wife from the husband's reliance on the short duration of the marriage. It was said that the judge was plainly wrong to justify his substantial award on the ground that the wife had a legitimate expectation that she would live at a higher standard of affluence than she had enjoyed prior to the marriage on a long-term basis and that he wrongly rejected a clear line of authority that established the principle on which claims were to be determined in short marriage cases. In particular he relied upon *S v S* [1976] FLR 640, *H v H* [1981] 2 FLR 392, *Robertson v Robertson* [1983] 4 FLR 387 and *Hedges v Hedges* [1991] 1 FLR 196.

3.16 Much of this was given short shrift and at the conclusion of the submissions on behalf of the husband, the wife's counsel was asked to address only two questions, namely:

(a)   Was the judge's conclusion sufficiently explained and reasoned?

(b)   Was the judge's overall award plainly excessive?

3.17 The wife argued that the judge was clearly impressed by her commitment to the marriage. Its short duration was neutralised by the combination of that commitment and the wife's comparable innocence in its breakdown. Furthermore, the judge had had proper regard to the wife's needs. As to the scale of the overall award it was emphasised that it represented something between one-sixth and one-seventh of the husband's fortune. The product of the marriage was something between £12m and £16m. Taking a middle figure, £5m represented 34% of the marital acquest.

3.18 Finally it was submitted that before the court could interfere it would not be enough to conclude that the judge's reasoning was too attenuated if it were satisfied that the overall award lay within the very wide ambit of his discretion. Only if the court concluded that the award was plainly excessive as well as inadequately reasoned could it interfere.

The decision of the Court of Appeal in *Miller*

3.19 The appeal was heard by a strong court consisting of Thorpe LJ, Wall LJ and Black J, the first two of whom gave detailed and considered judgments. The various elements of the judgments may be summarised as follows.

The procedural issue

3.20 Thorpe LJ held that while a retreat from a clear declaration is generally to be deprecated and may in many cases result in a heavy costs penalty, such a declaration cannot possibly override or circumscribe the trial judge's obligation to investigate whatever he conceives relevant and necessary to enable him to discharge his statutory duty. Ancillary relief proceedings are quasi-inquisitorial and the judge is never confined by what the parties elect to put in evidence or by whatever they may agree to exclude from evidence. Singer J had been indisputably right to rule as he did on 11 October, particularly given that the declaration had to be weighed in the context of the contentious affidavits filed by the parties both before and after the making of the declaration.

3.21 The husband had sought to meet that difficulty by asserting that as a matter of principle and construction, allegations of conduct in ancillary relief could only be advanced under s 25(2)(g) and if that paragraph was excluded by agreement or concession then conduct could not be introduced as an aspect of any other of the statutory criteria. Thus it was not open to a party to disavow s 25(2)(g) and then contend that the other spouse's contribution, which s 25(2)(f) requires the court to assess, was valueless or devalued because of attitude or conduct. It was further submitted that it was not open to an applicant to finesse the other party's reliance on the short duration of the marriage by asserting that the breakdown was the consequence of the other's conduct. That case could only be mounted under s 25(2)(g), as the wife had here correctly recognised by her response to the husband's questionnaire. Were the court to hold otherwise, it would be flouting the principle established in the seminal case of *Wachtel v Wachtel* [1973] Fam 72 and opening the floodgates to ancillary relief trials that would be akin to the bitter defended divorces that flourished prior to the Divorce Reform Act 1969.

3.22 Thorpe LJ said that those submissions could not be right. The statutory criteria were not to be rigidly characterised. The judge had an overriding obligation to regard and to reflect in his judgment 'all the circumstances of the case'. Conduct that would not merit advancing under s 25(2)(g) was not therefore irrelevant or inadmissible. Often the court's assessment of the worth of the comparable contributions would require consideration of motives, attitudes, commitments and responsibilities. Like the wife's solicitors in their letter raising the issue, and like Singer J, he relied on his own judgment in the case of *G v G (Financial Provision: Separation Agreement)* [2004] 1 FLR 1011, where he said (para [34]):

> 'A judge has to do fairness between the parties, having regard to all the circumstances. He must be free to include within that discretionary review the factors which compelled the wife to terminate the marriage as she did. The point was essentially taken as a defensive shield to the reliance upon the duration submission. There must surely be room for the exercise of a judicial discretion between the pole of a wife who is driven to petition by the husband's unfeeling misconduct and that of a wife who exits from a marriage capriciously and for her own advantage. It seems to me that the judge was doing no more than taking his bearings as to where he stood along that path.'

3.23 Singer J had directed himself by reference to *G v G* and Thorpe LJ said that he was clearly right so to do. Having seen and heard the parties extensively cross-examined, he was plainly entitled to conclude that the husband was to blame for the breakdown of the marriage.

3.24 Wall LJ agreed. Singer J had been plainly right to follow and apply paras [32]–[34] of Thorpe LJ's judgment in *G v G*, which his Lordship found to be an entirely accurate analysis of how a judge exercises a proper judicial discretion when dealing with s 25(2)(d) of the Matrimonial Causes Act 1973 (MCA 1973) in a short marriage case.

3.25   As to what the proper approach in a short marriage case should be, the husband had argued that cases decided about twenty-five years ago settled the principle to be applied. That principle was that the award should be enough to get the unhappy applicant back on her feet, deriving from the judgment of Balcombe J in *Robertson v Robertson*.

3.26   Thorpe LJ said that there were a number of very good reasons why that should no longer be the modern approach. First, it originated and developed during long years in which the yardstick for measuring the extent of the applicant's claim was an assessment of her reasonable requirements.

3.27   Second, a marriage was not to be equated to a purely financial venture where the court might redress breach of contract or the disintegration of a partnership by an award of damages or other financial relief. Section 25 required a more sophisticated evaluation of the extent of the wife's commitment to and investment in the marriage, emotionally and psychologically. In some cases it may be necessary for the court to assess emotional and psychological damage and the extent to which the applicant's future capacity and opportunity to enter into a fulfilling family life has been blighted. What a party has given to a marriage and what a party has lost on its failure cannot be measured by simply counting the days of its duration.

3.28   Third, the husband's reliance on the old cases was clearly precluded by the decision of the Court of Appeal in *Foster v Foster* [2003] 2 FLR 299 where Hale LJ, as she then was, had considered the impact of the decisions in *White v White*, *Cowan v Cowan* [2002] FAM 97 and *Lambert v Lambert* [2003] 1 FLR 139. Her Ladyship had emphatically rejected the submission that those authorities were solely concerned with the problem of evaluating the very different contributions of breadwinner and homemaker over a long marriage where there had been children to bring up and that they were of no relevance to a short, childless marriage where both parties had been working. Hale LJ had rejected that submission emphatically. She recorded counsel's eventual concession that where a substantial surplus had been generated by joint efforts it could not matter whether they had taken a short or long time to do so. Thorpe LJ said that even though the facts of that case were very different, it was clear that Hale LJ was signalling a fresh approach to measuring of awards in cases involving marriage of short duration.

3.29   Wall LJ agreed, adding 'the case [*Foster*], in my view, is a warning of the dangers which can flow if there is a disproportionate emphasis on the brevity of the marriage'. Furthermore, his Lordship had received no help on the difficult issue of quantum from comparisons with awards for libel or professional negligence or personal injuries. Not only were such comparisons irrelevant, but they seemed to Wall LJ both to demean the status of marriage, and to take no account of the serious social, financial and psychological effects which irretrievable breakdown frequently have on those who suffer it. He had no doubt at all that Singer J was right to reject the pre-*White* cases and right to 'hold on to the terms of section 25 and the discretionary exercise, and to follow the guidance of Thorpe LJ in *McFarlane v McFarlane; Parlour v Parlour* [2004] 2 FLR 893'.

3.30 Both Thorpe LJ and Wall LJ considered that the only ground of appeal which held substantial prospects of success was whether the judge was right to found his award on the wife's legitimate expectation. Was his award plainly excessive? As Wall LJ put it:

> 'In my judgment, Mr. Marks [for the husband] had two powerful arguments, both capable of very simple expression. The first was that the judge had simply not explained himself. The second was that the award was so large that, in the absence of a proper rationalisation, it was simply outside the band of reasonable decisions, and must, accordingly, be plainly wrong.'

Why did Singer J decide as he did?

3.31 Thorpe LJ was constrained to say that the judge's explanation for the end result was 'by no means straightforward or clear'. The case had been extremely hard fought by the best available professionals on both sides and at its conclusion the husband was surely entitled to a clear explanation as to why the judge had opted for an award much closer to the submission of the wife's counsel Mr Mostyn. His Lordship confessed that he had 'read and re-read the judgment in a search for its true ratio'. In the end, he thought he could discern the following rationale.

3.32 The relevant paragraph revealed that the decisive factor for the judge was that the marriage, taken in its full context, gave the wife a legitimate entitlement to a long-term future on a higher plane of affluence than she had enjoyed prior to marriage. Thorpe LJ accepted that in the context of this case the judge was entitled to regard as 'the key element' the wife's 'legitimate expectation' of living to a higher standard as the ex-wife of Mr Miller, while emphasising that this was a fact-dependent conclusion and was not to be elevated into a principle or yardstick filling a vacuum created by the rejection of the restitutionary objective sought in the old cases.

3.33 As to the length of the marriage, Singer J had found that there was no mutual commitment to make their lives together until their engagement in July 1999. Until then their ties were tentative and their separate expectations did not accord. There had been no pre-engagement honeymoon to blend seamlessly into marriage. Singer J had tended, therefore, to favour the husband's submissions and treat this as a marriage of relatively short duration.

3.34   As to the way the marriage ended, the judge had left the middle ground to accept the wife's case. His essential findings were that the husband may well have developed an irritation with aspects of the wife's personality and behaviour, but this reflected more his lack of adaptability than any shortcomings on her part. The sum of his complaints was 'not marriage-breaking stuff'. His burgeoning relationship with the woman with whom he now lived was not a consequence rather than a cause of the breakdown. Singer J had concluded:

> 'None of this, to state the obvious, is conduct which it would be inequitable to disregard in arriving at a resolution of the financial dispute. But it has the result that it would be unfair to W to concentrate solely on the bare chronology of this marriage without acknowledging that she did not seek to end it nor did she give H any remotely sufficient reason for him to do so.'

3.35   As to contributions, Singer J had concluded that while the wife's contributions to the family life were non-financial (save to the extent that she worked at the start of the marriage), she aspired to provide:

> '… the domestic and social fabric in which they could both enjoy the fruits of H's success and the opportunities for leisure, relaxation and enjoyment which were available. A major contribution in this context was the planning and oversight she brought to the refurbishment, equipping and furnishing of the French property to which H has become so attached. Neither the modest period during which she was able to make this contribution nor the very considerable scale of H's efforts and the rewards they brought him affect the proposition, which I accept, that incommensurable though these contributions are as chalk and cheese, nevertheless no discriminatory attitude should be allowed to treat them as other than equivalent'.

3.36   Looking at the award in the round, Thorpe LJ said that it would be easy and superficial to characterise it as a pay-off of £5m for a mere 2¾ years of marriage. In his judgment the reality was very different. Although the judge did not attach much weight to the 4 years preceding engagement, the fact was that at the age of 26 the applicant committed herself to this man. At the outset of the marriage, she worked to ensure the emergence of a primary home and a holiday home fit for his status as a leader in his chosen field. Once that was achieved, she tried for a family. The responsibility for the collapse of that endeavour must in part be ascribed to the husband's decision to end the marriage. Finally it must not be forgotten that the net value of the award was in reality £4.5m given the judge's decision that the wife's half-share in the French villa was to go to the husband.

3.37   On that analysis, Thorpe LJ's ultimate conclusion was that the judge's award was both sufficiently if obliquely explained and that it could not be labelled plainly excessive. It lay at the top end of the permissible bracket and, had Thorpe LJ been sitting at first instance, he did not think that he would have gone so high. However, he emphasised that the facts and circumstances of the case were highly unusual. The ambit of the judge's discretion in cases involving very large assets and a short childless marriage was particularly wide and the court had to bear in mind the limits of the appellate court in interfering with the trial judge's discretion (see the words of Lord Hoffmann in *Piglowska v Piglowska* [1999] 1 WLR 1360 HL).

3.38 The limited nature of the approach may be indicated by Thorpe LJ's final words:

> 'Although I have not found this an easy appeal, in the end I am firm in my conclusion that it must be dismissed. My judgment may well only serve to increase the husband's sense the courts have been hard on him but the limitations on the role of the appellate court are clearly spelt out.'

3.39 Wall LJ referred to the words with which Russell LJ had begun his judgment in *Gojkovic*s [1992] Fam 40 at 49 where he had responded to counsel's invitation to lay down guidelines which would be of assistance in deciding the appropriate level of lump sum payments in cases where very substantial capital assets are available. Russell LJ did not think that such an exercise was possible. The guidelines already existed in s 23 and s 25 MCA 1973 as amended. These required the court to have regard to all the circumstances of the case and subsection (2), under no less than eight subparagraphs, set out the matters to which the court in particular shall have regard.

3.40 Wall LJ concluded as follows:

> 'If those words have a familiar ring, it is because they have been spoken by every judicial generation since section 25 of the MCA 1973 had its first expression as section 5 of the Matrimonial Proceedings and Property Act 1970. I first heard them in the well-known judgment of Ormrod LJ in *Martin v Martin* [1978] Fam 12 at 19, which I will not repeat. The consistent message from this court has been that the judge must apply the factors identified in section 25(2) to the facts of the individual case. The House of Lords in *White* now tells us, and *Foster* in this court confirms, that the objective is a fair result that avoids discrimination. Proposed outcomes can be tested against the yardstick of equality. These are the guidelines which practitioners and the courts must strive to follow.'

Comment on *Miller*

3.41 It is fair to say that most practitioners and legal commentators were, to some extent, critical of this decision. Certain points could of course be made; every case is, to some extent, fact-dependent, and Wall LJ was clear (para [87]) in advocating caution about the use of this or any other decision as a template for others. The powers of an appellate court are limited, and even though the

Court of Appeal clearly thought this award verged on the excessive, it considered that it could not interfere. Essentially, the decision was more right than wrong. Any hope of clear guidelines other than those in s 25 and *White* was misplaced.

3.42   However, some clear lessons seemed to appear from this case, not all of them new but usefully highlighted in the judgments. They could be summarised as follows:

- There was no doubt now that the older cases as to short marriages were now of little value. The Court of Appeal's decision in this case, reaffirming *Foster v Foster*, made it clear that the older approach of putting the applicant (normally a wife) back on her feet was inappropriate. The court could not avoid considering all the factors set out in s 25, and it was still necessary to find some good reason for departing from equality.

- 'Conduct' which falls short of the level required by s 25(2)(g) might still be relevant as part of 'all the circumstances'.

- The fact that this was to be a clean break seemed to have helped persuade Wall LJ at least that the large capital award was justified (para [85]).

3.43   The criticisms of many commentators could be summarised as follows:

(1)   The law as to awards in short marriages was never easy, but there were at least some guidelines or rules of thumb which could be adopted. That seemed no longer to be the case; the only 'rule of thumb' left was that, following *Foster*, one might look at what each party had brought to the marriage, but even that could not be a substitute for considering all the circumstances and all the s 25 factors. Attempting to bring any short-cut into this was now clearly forbidden, but of course that did not make life any easier either for practitioners advising clients on the likely outcome, nor for the judge at FDR trying to do the same. In fact, some were tempted to ask how far the length of the marriage came into the calculations in *Miller* at all; what difference would it have made if this had been a 10-year marriage?

(2)   The issue of whether 'conduct' is conduct properly so-called or just part of the circumstances was even more problematic. Granted, *Miller* said nothing new; Thorpe LJ had said it before in *G v G* but, even so, this might have come as something of a surprise to some practitioners and it did not simplify the judge's task. In this case the court seemed to have taken account of the fact that the husband broke up the marriage by his adultery, the wife was 'innocent', and wanted the marriage to continue, and the husband should not therefore be entitled to rely on the shortness of the marriage. Given the delphic quality of Singer J's judgment, it was difficult to see exactly how far these matters were weighed in the balance,

but he certainly took them into account and the Court of Appeal said he was right to do so. Without wishing to exaggerate this aspect of the case, it seemed that the Court of Appeal had given some ammunition to those who wish to depart from the general principle of leaving conduct out of ancillary relief. Read in conjunction with Thorpe LJ's statement that these days there is required

'… a more sophisticated evaluation of the extent of the wife's commitment to and investment in the marriage emotionally and psychologically. In some cases it may be necessary for the court to assess emotional and psychological damage and the extent to which the applicant's future capacity and opportunity to enter into a fulfilling family life has been blighted',

the possibilities of rancorous litigation in the run of the mill case seemed to have been opened up.

(3) Singer J placed some reliance on the fact that the wife had a legitimate expectation that she would be the wife of a rich man and that she would share in his affluence. The Court of Appeal did not criticise this. Presumably this expectation was part of 'all the circumstances'. It seemed therefore that, whereas the court could not now decide a short marriage case by looking at what the applicant has lost by the marriage, it could legitimately look at what she had lost by the divorce and at what she hoped to gain by it.

3.44 The distinguished authority John Ekelaar described the decision as 'the descent into chaos' and concluded '[t]he House of Lords needs to take control. Our system may be discretionary but the discretion must be based on firm principle and policy' ([2005] Fam Law 871). Many agreed with this view, and it therefore came as somewhat of a relief when Mr Miller decided to appeal to the House of Lords. It was hoped that the result of the combined appeals of *Miller* and *McFarlane* would be to bring much-needed clarity to the law, and resolve some of the confusion which had existed since *White*. We must now consider whether those hopes have been fulfilled.

Part B – The House of Lords decision in *Miller* and *McFarlane*

4 INTRODUCTION

4.1   The combined appeals were heard between 30 January and 2 February 2006 and the Lords' Opinions were delivered on 24 May. The result in brief was that Mr Miller's appeal was dismissed and Mrs McFarlane's appeal allowed; in her case, the 5-year term imposed by the Court of Appeal was removed, leaving her with a joint lives order.

4.2   However, that bald statement does not do justice to the many important issues raised by this case, which will now be considered. The Law Lords sitting on this case were Lords Nicholls, Hope, Hoffmann and Mance and Baroness Hale. The two substantive speeches were those of Lord Nicholls and Lady Hale. Lord Hope said that he agreed with both speeches, and confined himself to reviewing the position in Scotland. Lord Hoffmann expressly endorsed the speech of Lady Hale, and Lord Mance, noting that there were some areas of difference between Lord Nicholls and Lady Hale, identified himself more with the approach of Lady Hale than with that of Lord Nicholls.

5 SOME GENERAL PRINCIPLES

5.1   Both Lord Nicholls and Lady Hale set out what they regarded as general principles at the beginning of their speeches, and achieved a high degree of consensus. First, it must be said that both built on the principles of *White v White*, which they took as their starting points. Unsurprisingly, therefore, the *White* principles remain good law. However, as Lord Nicholls said (at para [8]), with the rejection in *White* of the concept of 'reasonable requirements', there was a need for some further judicial enunciation of general principle.

Fairness

5.2   The first principle enunciated by Lord Nicholls was fairness. The courts must seek a fair outcome, in which discrimination plays no part. He accepted that fairness was an elusive concept, which is grounded in social and moral values (at para [4]). These are not susceptible to logical reasoning, and change from one generation to the next. He submitted that this starting point was surely not controversial, and that fairness generates obligations as well as rights. Financial provision for a party to a marriage was not largesse, nor a matter of taking from one to give to the other. Each party to the marriage was *entitled* to a *fair* share of the available property. The search was always for what were the *requirements* of fairness in the particular case (his italics throughout). Lord Nicholls then turned to what the requirements of fairness might be.

Welfare of children

5.3   Lord Nicholls recorded this first consideration, which he obviously regarded as so obvious as to require no further elucidation.

Financial needs

5.4   Every marriage gives rise to a relationship of interdependence. This generates mutual obligations of support. Lord Nicholls continued (at para [11]):

> 'When the marriage ends fairness requires that the assets of the parties should be divided primarily so as to make provision for the parties' housing and financial needs, taking into account a wide range of matters such as the parties' ages, their future earning capacity, the family's standard of living, and any disability of either party. Most of these needs will have been generated by the marriage, but not all of them. Needs arising from age or disability are instances of the latter.'

5.5   As Lord Nicholls remarked, most cases begin and end at this stage, the available assets being insufficient to provide further.

Compensation

5.6   The next strand was compensation, now recognised more than formerly. At para [13]:

> 'This is aimed at redressing any significant prospective economic disparity between the parties arising from the way they conducted their marriage. For instance, the parties may have arranged their affairs in a way which has greatly advantaged the husband in terms of his earning capacity but left the wife severely handicapped so far as her own earning capacity is concerned. Then the wife suffers a double loss: a diminution in her earning capacity and the loss of a share in her husband's enhanced income. This is often the case. Although less marked than in the past, women may still suffer a disproportionate financial loss on the breakdown of a marriage because of their traditional role as home-maker and childcarer.'

5.7   Lord Nicholls said that, while compensation and financial needs often overlapped, they were distinct concepts and 'far from co-terminous. A wife may be able to earn her own living but she may still be entitled to a measure of compensation' (at para [15]).

Sharing

5.8   Lord Nicholls recorded sharing as a further strand (at para [16]):

> 'This "equal sharing" principle derives from the basic concept of equality permeating a marriage as understood today. Marriage, it is often said, is a partnership of equals. In 1992 Lord Keith of Kinkel approved Lord Emslie's observation that "husband and wife are now for all practical purposes equal partners in marriage": *R v R* [1992] 1 AC 599, 617. This is now recognised widely, if not universally. The parties commit themselves to sharing their lives. They live and work together. When their partnership ends each is entitled to an equal share of the assets of the partnership, unless there is a good reason to the contrary. Fairness requires no less. But I emphasise the qualifying phrase: "unless there is good reason to the contrary". The yardstick of equality is to be applied as an aid, not a rule.'

5.9   Lord Nicholls went on to say (at para [17]) that this principle of sharing was as applicable as much to short marriages as to long marriages, and expressly approved *Foster v Foster*:

> 'A short marriage is no less a partnership of equals than a long marriage. The difference is that a short marriage has been less enduring. In the nature of things this will affect the quantum of the financial fruits of the partnership.'

5.10   He said that he was unable to agree with the 'different approach' of Mr Nicholas Mostyn QC, sitting as a deputy High Court Judge in *GW v RW (Financial Provision: Departure from Equality)*, where the learned judge had held that 'It would be "fundamentally unfair" that a party who has made domestic contributions during a marriage of 12 years should be awarded the same proportion of the assets as a party who has made the domestic contributions for more than 20 years'. Lord Nicholls observed that in *M v M (Financial Relief: Substantial Earning Capacity)* [2004] EWHC 688 (Fam) this point had been regarded as 'well made'. He continued (at para [19]):

> 'I am unable to agree with this approach. This approach would mean that on the breakdown of a short marriage the money-earner would have a head start over the home-maker and childcarer. To confine the *White* approach to the "fruits of a long marital partnership" would be to re-introduce precisely the sort of discrimination the *White* case [2001] 1 AC 596 was intended to negate.'

5.11   Lord Nicholls said at para [20] that the court should be 'exceedingly slow' to introduce a distinction between 'family' assets and 'business or investment' assets:

> 'In all cases the nature and source of the parties' property are matters to be taken into account when determining the requirements of fairness. The decision of Munby J in *P v P (Inherited Property)* [2005] 1 FLR 576 regarding a family farm is an instance. But "business and investment" assets can be the financial fruits of a marriage partnership as much as "family" assets. The equal sharing principle applies to the former as well as the latter. The rationale underlying the sharing principle is as much applicable to "business and investment" assets as to "family" assets.'

5.12   However, this gave rise to the following problem.

The distinction between matrimonial and non-matrimonial property

5.13   Lord Nicholls regarded this distinction as 'a complication'. He pointed out that the 1973 Act draws no distinction between matrimonial and other property, and expressly requires the court to have regard, quite generally, to the property and financial resources each of the parties has or is likely to have in the foreseeable future. However, he continued (at paras [22] and [23]):

> 'This does not mean that, when exercising his discretion, a judge in this country must treat all property in the same way. The statute requires the court to have regard to all the circumstances of the case. One of the circumstances is that there is a real difference, a difference of source, between (1) property acquired during the marriage otherwise than by inheritance or gift, sometimes called the marital acquest but more usually the matrimonial property, and (2) other property. The former is the financial product of the parties' common endeavour, the latter is not. The parties' matrimonial home, even if this was brought into the marriage at the outset by one of the parties, usually has a central place in any marriage. So it

should normally be treated as matrimonial property for this purpose. As already noted, in principle the entitlement of each party to a share of the matrimonial property is the same however long or short the marriage may have been.

The matter stands differently regarding property ("non-matrimonial property") the parties bring with them into the marriage or acquire by inheritance or gift during the marriage. Then the duration of the marriage will be highly relevant.'

5.14   Lord Nicholls went on to point out that the position as to non-matrimonial property had been summarised by himself in *White v White* at 610, and continued (at paras [24] and [25]):

'In the case of a short marriage fairness may well require that the claimant should not be entitled to a share of the other's non-matrimonial property. The source of the asset may be a good reason for departing from equality. This reflects the instinctive feeling that parties will generally have less call upon each other on the breakdown of a short marriage.

With longer marriages the position is not so straightforward. Non-matrimonial property represents a contribution made to the marriage by one of the parties. Sometimes, as the years pass, the weight fairly to be attributed to this contribution will diminish, sometimes it will not. After many years of marriage the continuing weight to be attributed to modest savings introduced by one party at the outset of the marriage may well be different from the weight attributable to a valuable heirloom intended to be retained in specie. Some of the matters to be taken into account in this regard were mentioned in the above citation from the *White* case. To this non-exhaustive list should be added, as a relevant matter, the way the parties organised their financial affairs.'

5.15   Lord Nicholls emphasised the need for flexibility, and said that in every case it might not be possible to draw a clear distinction between these two categories of property (at paras [26] and [27]):

'Fairness has a broad horizon. Sometimes, in the case of a business, it can be artificial to attempt to draw a sharp dividing line as at the parties' wedding day. Similarly the "equal sharing" principle might suggest that each of the party's assets should be separately and exactly valued. But valuations are often a matter of opinion on which experts differ. A thorough investigation into these differences can be extremely expensive and of doubtful utility. The costs involved can quickly become disproportionate. The case of Mr and Mrs Miller illustrates this only too well.

Accordingly, where it becomes necessary to distinguish matrimonial property from non-matrimonial property the court may do so with the degree of particularity or generality appropriate in the case. The judge will then give to the contribution made by one party's non-matrimonial property the weight he considers just. He will do so with such generality or particularity as he considers appropriate in the circumstances of the case.'

5.16   He went on mention a further matter where flexibility was important, namely big money cases where the capital assets were more than sufficient to meet the financial needs of the parties and the need for compensation, and asked whether needs and the requirements of compensation should be met first and the residue then shared, or whether needs and compensation should be simply subsumed into the equal division of assets. His answer was as follows (at para [29]):

> 'There can be no invariable rule on this. Much will depend upon the amounts involved. Generally a convenient course might be for the court to consider first the requirements of compensation and then to give effect to the sharing entitlement. If this course is followed provision for the parties' financial needs will be subsumed into the sharing entitlement. But there will be cases where this approach would not achieve a fair outcome overall. In some cases provision for the financial needs may be more fairly assessed first along with compensation and the sharing entitlement applied only to the residue of the assets. Needless to say, it all depends upon the circumstances.'

Periodical payments and the clean break principle

5.17   Having dealt at length with issues arising as to division of capital, Lord Nicholls turned to periodical payments, and recorded that the *McFarlane* appeal raised two issues in this respect, namely 'the reach' of periodical payments orders, that is to say, whether such orders might be made for the purpose of providing compensation as distinct from maintenance, and the impact of the clean break principle on a spouse awarded compensatory periodical payments.

5.18   On the first issue (compensation in periodical payments), Lord Nicholls could not have been more clear (at paras [31] and [32]):

> 'I see no difficulty on this point. There is nothing in the statutory ancillary relief provisions to suggest Parliament intended periodical payments orders to be limited to payments needed for maintenance. Section 23(1)(a) empowers the court, in quite general language, to order one party to the marriage to make to the other "such periodical payments, for such term, as may be specified in the order". In deciding whether, and how, to exercise this power the statute requires the court to have regard to all the circumstances of the case: s 25(1). The court is required to have particular regard to the familiar wide-ranging checklist set out in s 25(2). These provisions, far from suggesting an intention to restrict periodical payments to the one particular purpose of maintenance, suggest that the financial provision orders in s 23 were intended to be flexible in their application.
>
> In particular, I consider a periodical payments order may be made for the purpose of affording compensation to the other party as well as meeting financial needs. It would be extraordinary if this were not so. If one party's earning capacity has been advantaged at the expense of the other party during the

marriage it would be extraordinary if, where necessary, the court could not order the advantaged party to pay compensation to the other out of his enhanced earnings when he receives them. It would be most unfair if absence of capital assets were regarded as cancelling his obligation to pay compensation in respect of a continuing economic advantage he has obtained from the marriage.'

5.19 He later said (at para [34]) that the wife's financial needs or her 'reasonable requirements' were now no more a determinative or limiting factor on an application for periodical payments than they were on an application for a lump sum.

5.20 However, that being so, the second issue of the clean break arose. Lord Nicholls recorded the modern approach of regarding continuing financial ties between parties as undesirable, as expressed by Lord Scarman in *Minton v Minton* [1979] AC 593 at 608, and set out s 25A in full. He continued (at paras [37]–[39]):

> 'By s 25A(1) and (2) duties are imposed on the court but the court is left with a discretion. The court is required to "consider" whether it would be "appropriate" to exercise its powers in a particular way. But the section gives no express guidance on the type of circumstance which would render it inappropriate for the court to bring about a clean break.

> In one respect the object of s 25A(1) is abundantly clear. The subsection is expressed in general terms. It is apt to refer as much to a periodical payments order made to provide compensation as it is to an order made to meet financial needs. But, expressly, s 25A(1) is not intended to bring about an unfair result. Under s 25A(1) the goal the court is required to have in mind is that the parties' mutual financial obligations should end as soon as the court considers just and reasonable.

> Section 25A(2) is focused more specifically. It is concerned with the termination of one party's "financial dependence" on the other "without undue hardship". These references to financial dependence and hardship are apt when applied to a periodical payments order making provision for the payee's financial needs. They are hardly apt when applied to a periodical payments order whose object is to furnish compensation in respect of future economic disparity arising from the division of functions adopted by the parties during their marriage. If the claimant is owed compensation, and capital assets are not available, it is difficult to see why the social desirability of a clean break should be sufficient reason for depriving the claimant of that compensation.'

6   SPECIFIC ISSUES

6.1   Having dealt with these issues of general principle, Lord Nicholls turned to the instant cases, and some particular issues arising from them.

Short marriages

6.2   This issue arose in particular in *Miller*, where Mr Miller's counsel had urged the court to adopt the principles as to short marriages enunciated in earlier cases such as in *S v S* [1977] Fam 127, *H v H (Financial Provision: Short Marriage)* [1981] 2 FLR 392, *Robertson v Robertson* [1983] 4 FLR 387, *Attar v Attar (No 2)* [1985] FLR 653 and *Hedges v Hedges* [1991] 1 FLR 196.

6.3   Lord Nicholls said that the courts below had been right not to adopt that submission, and continued (at para [55]):

> 'In the 1980s cases attention was directed predominantly at the wife's needs. There may be cases of short marriages where the limited financial resources of the parties necessarily mean that attention will still have to be focused on the parties' needs. That is not so in big money cases. Then the court is concerned to decide what would be a fair division of the whole of the assets, taking into account the parties' respective financial needs and any need for compensation. The court will look at all the circumstances. The general approach in this type of case should be to consider whether, and to what extent, there is good reason for departing from equality. As already indicated, in short marriage cases there will often be a good reason for departing substantially from equality with regard to non-matrimonial property.'

Legitimate expectations

6.4   It will be remembered that the Court of Appeal had approved Singer J's ruling to the effect that the husband gave the wife a legitimate expectation that that in future she would be living on a higher economic plane. Lord Nicholls said that he doubted whether in fact the judge was doing more than taking into account the standard of living enjoyed by the parties during the marriage, as he was required to do. However, he continued (at para [58]):

> 'If the judge meant to go further than this I consider he went too far. No doubt both parties had high hopes for their future when they married. But hopes and expectations, as such, are not an appropriate basis on which to assess financial

needs. Claims for expectation losses do not fit altogether comfortably with the notion that each party is free to end the marriage. Indeed, to make an award by reference to the parties' future expectations would come close to restoring the "tailpiece" which was originally part of s 25. By that tailpiece the court was required to place the parties, so far as practical and, having regard to their conduct, just to do so, in the same financial position as they would have been had the marriage not broken down. It would be a mistake indirectly to re-introduce the effect of that discredited provision.'

Conduct

6.5   It will again be remembered that this was a controversial aspect of Singer J's decision in *Miller*. He was following Thorpe LJ's dicta in *G v G (Financial Provision: Separation Agreement)*, and, unsurprisingly, the Court of Appeal approved his decision. In this context, the words of Lord Nicholls are quite pointed. He recited the history of the issue of conduct, resulting in the statutory changes of 1984, and continued (at paras [64] and [65]):

> 'This history is well known. I have mentioned it only because there are signs that some highly experienced judges are beginning to depart from the criterion laid down by Parliament. In *G v G (Financial Provision: Separation Agreement)* [2004] 1 FLR 1011, 1017, para 34, Thorpe LJ said the judge "must be free to include within [his discretionary review of all the circumstances] the factors which compelled the wife to terminate the marriage as she did". This approach was followed by both courts below in the present case. Both the judge and the Court of Appeal had regard to the husband's conduct when, as the judge found, that conduct did not meet the statutory criterion. The husband's conduct did not rank as conduct it would be inequitable to disregard.

> This approach, I have to say, is erroneous. Parliament has drawn the line. It is not for the courts to re-draw the line elsewhere under the guise of having regard to all the circumstances of the case. It is not as though the statutory boundary line gives rise to injustice. In most cases fairness does not require consideration of the parties' conduct. This is because in most cases misconduct is not relevant to the bases on which financial ancillary relief is ordered today. Where, exceptionally, the position is otherwise, so that it would be inequitable to disregard one party's conduct, the statute permits that conduct to be taken into account.'

Contributions

6.6   Readers will be familiar with the controversies raised by some post-*White* cases such as *Cowan v Cowan* and *Parlour v Parlour* as to evaluation of 'special' or even 'stellar' contributions. Lord Nicholls' view was as follows (at paras [67] and [68]):

'On this I echo the powerful observations of Coleridge J in *G v G (Financial Provision: Equal Division)* [2002] EWHC 1339 (Fam); [2002] 2 FLR 1143, 1154–1155, paras 33–34. Parties should not seek to promote a case of "special contribution" unless the contribution is so marked that to disregard it would be inequitable. A good reason for departing from equality is not to be found in the minutiae of married life.

This approach provides the principled answer in those cases where the earnings of one party, usually the husband, have been altogether exceptional. The question is whether earnings of this character can be regarded as a "special contribution", and thus as a good reason for departing from equality of division. The answer is that exceptional earnings are to be regarded as a factor pointing away from equality of division when, but only when, it would be inequitable to proceed otherwise. The wholly exceptional nature of the earnings must be, to borrow a phrase more familiar in a different context, obvious and gross.'

7   LORD NICHOLLS' CONCLUSIONS

7.1   In the *Miller* case, as suggested above, Lord Nicholls accepted that the courts below had misdirected themselves as to conduct and legitimate expectations. However, he dismissed Mr Miller's appeal for two reasons. First, he found that although Mr Miller had been extremely wealthy at the beginning of the relationship,

> '... the accretion to [his] wealth during the marriage, as a result of work he did during the marriage, was very substantial indeed. Although the marriage was short, the matrimonial property was of great value. The gain in the husband's earned wealth during the marriage was huge' (at para [71]).

7.2   Second, the judge was entitled to regard the high standard of living during the marriage as a key feature: 'This was not a standard of living the wife would be likely to achieve for herself' (at [72]).

7.3   Lord Nicholls estimated that the husband's wealth was approximately £32m. An award of £5m represented less than one-third of the increase in the value of shares accrued during the marriage, and less than one-sixth of the husband's total worth. This seemed appropriate, and Mr Miller's appeal was dismissed.

7.4   As to *McFarlane*, Lord Nicholls thought the Court of Appeal was correct to restore the district judge's order of £250,000 per annum, and proceeded to consider in detail the imposition of the 5-year term. He drew attention to the unusual combination of circumstances in this case, which may be summarised as follows:

(1)   The capital assets were insufficient to make an immediate clean break possible, but there was a substantial excess of income.

(2)   The husband's earnings after the breakdown of marriage were the result of the parties' joint endeavours at an earlier stage when the wife had given up her career to devote herself to homemaking and child-rearing. This was a contribution which would continue.

(3)   The career foregone by the wife had been as successful and highly paid as that of the husband.

(4)   As primary carer for the children, the wife continued to be at an economic disadvantage.

7.5   Lord Nicholls regarded this as 'a paradigm case for an award of compensation in respect of the significant future economic disparity, sustained by the wife, arising from the way the parties conducted their marriage' (at para [93]). He had difficulty with the approach of the Court of Appeal, and said (at para [95]):

> 'The Court of Appeal, however, seems not to have had the distinction between needs and compensation clearly in mind when considering the way ahead. The court appears to have treated the surplus of income over expenditure as simply a means whereby the wife could accumulate a capital reserve. But that would be to mistake the purpose of this part of the district judge's award.'

7.6   He continued (at paras [96] and [97]):

> 'This leads me to the point where I fundamentally disagree with the Court of Appeal: the replacement of a joint lives order with a five-year order. I agree with the Court of Appeal that when the husband has repaid the mortgage on his new home, and the wife's earning capacity has revived, the time may be ripe for a reassessment of the parties' position to see if a deferred clean break is practicable. A clean break might then be achievable by the court exercising its power to order the husband to make a lump sum payment to the wife as consideration for discharging his liability to make further periodical payments. The court has this power under s 31(7A) and (7B) inserted into the 1973 Act by s 66 of the Family Law Act 1996.
>
> That is something which will merit careful consideration at a suitably early date. But I do not see how this leads to the conclusion that the district judge's joint lives order should be set aside in favour of an extendable five years' order. The practice in the family courts seems to be that on an application for extension of a periodical payments order made for a finite period the applicant must surmount a high threshold: *Fleming v Fleming* [2003] EWCA Civ 1841; [2004] 1 FLR 667, 670, paras 12–14. In the present case it would be altogether inappropriate, indeed unjust, to make a five-year order and place the wife in that position when five years has elapsed. In the present case a five-year order is most unlikely to be sufficient to achieve a fair outcome. Further financial provision of some sort will be needed. So, far from compelling the wife to apply for an extension of a five-year order, and requiring her to shoulder the heavy burden accompanying such an application, it is more appropriate for the husband to have to take the initiative in applying for a variation of a joint lives order when he considers circumstances make that appropriate. Certainly the district judge cannot be said to have erred in principle in making a joint lives order, especially when this was common ground between the parties. I would allow this appeal and restore the order of District Judge Redgrave.'

8 BARONESS HALE'S SPEECH

8.1   We can now turn to Baroness Hale's speech. She began by recording the fact of interdependence (at para [123]):

'English law starts from the principle of separate property during marriage. Each spouse is legally in control of his or her own property while the marriage lasts. But in real life most couples' finances become ever-more inter-linked and inter-dependent. Most couples now choose to share the ownership of much of their most significant property, in particular their matrimonial home and its contents. They also owe one another duties of support, so that what starts as individual income is used for the benefit of the whole family. There are many different ways of doing this, from pooling their whole incomes, to pooling a proportion for household purposes, to one making an allowance to the other, to one handing over the whole wage packet to the other (see Jan Pahl, *Money and Marriage*, 1989). Some couples adopt one or other of these systems and retain it throughout their marriage. But as the gender roles also become more flexible within the marriage, with bread-winning and home-making responsibilities being shared and changing over time, so too their financial arrangements may also become more flexible and change over time. It also becomes less and less relevant to ask who technically is the owner of what.'

General principles

8.2   Under the heading 'the search for principle' she recorded 'three pointers in the 1973 Act', as follows:

(1)   The priority of the welfare of the children.

(2)   Despite the repeal of the statutory objective (to put the parties in the position they would have been in had the marriage not broken down), the court is still concerned with the foreseeable (and on occasions more distant) future as well as with the past and the present. The court has to consider, not only the parties' present resources, but also those that they will have in the foreseeable future: s 25(2)(a).

(3)   The statutory encouragement of a clean break settlement. Baroness Hale pointed out the 'clear steer in the direction of lump sum and property adjustment orders with no continuing periodical payments', but added that this did not tell us much about what an appropriate result would be.

8.3   Enlarging on point 3 above, Baroness Hale said (at para [133]):

'Section 25A is a powerful encouragement towards securing the court's objective by way of lump sum and capital adjustment (which now includes pension sharing) rather than by continuing periodical payments. This is good practical sense. Periodical payments are a continuing source of stress for both parties. They are also insecure. With the best will in the world, the paying party may fall on hard times and be unable to keep them up. Nor is the best will in the world always evident between formerly married people. It is also the logical consequence of the retreat from the principle of the lifelong obligation. Independent finances and self-sufficiency are the aims. Nevertheless, s 25A does not tell us what the outcome of the exercise required by s 25 should be. It is mainly directed at how that outcome should be put into effect.'

8.4   She then turned to *White v White*, and referred to the principles of fairness and non-discrimination and the 'yardstick of equality' which had been established. But, she continued (at para [136]):

'... the House was careful to point out (see p 605f) that the yardstick of equality did not inevitably mean equality of result. It was a standard against which the outcome of the s 25 exercise was to be checked. In any event, except in those cases where the present assets can be divided and each can live independently at roughly the same standard of living, equality of outcome is difficult both to define and to achieve. Giving half the present assets to the breadwinner achieves a very different outcome from giving half the assets to the homemaker with children'.

8.5   Baroness Hale therefore came to the central issue of how the court is to operate the principles of fairness, equality and non-discrimination in the less straightforward cases. She thought that there were three elements of any rationale for this exercise, which will now be considered.

Needs

8.6   Baroness Hale summarised the position as follows (at paras [138] and [139]):

'The most common rationale is that the relationship has generated needs which it is right that the other party should meet. In the great majority of cases, the court is trying to ensure that each party and their children have enough to supply their needs, set at a level as close as possible to the standard of living which they enjoyed during the marriage (note that the House did not adopt a restrictive view of needs in *White*: see pp 608g to 609a). This is a perfectly sound rationale where the needs are the consequence of the parties' relationship, as they usually are. The most common source of need is the presence of children, whose welfare is always the first consideration, or of other dependent relatives, such as elderly parents. But another source of need is having had to look after children or other family members in the past. Many parents have seriously compromised their ability to attain self-sufficiency as a result of past family responsibilities. Even if they do their best to re-enter the employment market, it will often be at a lesser level than before, and they will hardly ever be able to make up what they have lost in pension entitlements. A further source of need may be the way in which the parties chose to run their life together. Even dual career families are difficult to manage with completely equal opportunity for both. Compromises often have to be made by one so that the other can get ahead. All couples throughout their lives together have to make choices about who will do what, sometimes forced upon them by circumstances such as redundancy or low pay, sometimes freely made in the interests of them both. The needs generated by such choices are a perfectly sound rationale for adjusting the parties' respective resources in compensation.

But while need is often a sound rationale, it should not be seen as a limiting principle if other rationales apply. This was the error into which the law had fallen before *White*. Need had become "reasonable requirements" and thus more generous to the recipient, but it was still a limiting factor even where there was a substantial surplus of resources over needs: see *Page v Page* [1981] 2 FLR 198. Counsel would talk of the "discipline of the budget" and suggestions that a wife's budget might properly contain a margin for savings and contingencies, or to pass on to her grandchildren, were greeted with disbelief.'

Compensation

8.7 Baroness Hale said that the second rationale was compensation for relationship-generated disadvantage (at para [140]):

'Indeed, some consider that provision for need is compensation for relationship-generated disadvantage. But the economic disadvantage generated by the relationship may go beyond need, however generously interpreted. The best example is a wife, like Mrs McFarlane, who has given up what would very probably have been a lucrative and successful career. If the other party, who has been the beneficiary of the choices made during the marriage, is a high earner with a substantial surplus over what is required to meet both parties' needs, then a premium above needs can reflect that relationship-generated disadvantage.'

Sharing the fruits of the matrimonial partnership

8.8 Baroness Hale said (at para [141]) that there was now a widespread perception that marriage is a partnership of equals. She continued (at paras [142] and [143]):

'Of course, an equal partnership does not necessarily dictate an equal sharing of the assets. In particular, it may have to give way to the needs of one party or the children. Too strict an adherence to equal sharing and the clean break can lead to a rapid decrease in the primary carer's standard of living and a rapid increase in the breadwinner's. The breadwinner's unimpaired and unimpeded earning capacity is a powerful resource which can frequently repair any loss of capital after an unequal distribution: see, eg, the observations of Munby J in *B v B (Mesher Order)* [2002] EWHC 3106 (Fam); [2003] 2 FLR 285. Recognising this is one reason why English law has been so successful in retaining a home for the children.

But there are many cases in which the approach of roughly equal sharing of partnership assets with no continuing claims one against the other is nowadays entirely feasible and fair. One example is *Foster v Foster* [2003] EWCA Civ 565; [2003] 2 FLR 299, a comparatively short childless marriage, where each could earn their own living after divorce, but where capital assets had been built up by their joint efforts during the marriage. Although one party had earned more and thus contributed more in purely financial terms to the acquisition of those assets, both contributed what they could, and the fair result was to divide the product of their joint endeavours equally. Another example is *Burgess v Burgess* [1996] 2 FLR 34, a long marriage between a solicitor and a doctor, which had produced three children. Each party could earn their own living after divorce, but the home, contents and collections which they had accumulated during the marriage could be equally shared. Although one party might have better prospects than the other in future, once the marriage was at an end there was no reason for one to make further claims upon the other.'

8.9   Summarising the position so far, and agreeing with the basic principles enunciated by Lord Nicholls, Baroness Hale said that 'the ultimate objective is to give each party an equal start on the road to independent living' (at para [144]).

8.10   She then turned to consider some issues in the instant cases.

Specific issues

Conduct

8.11   Baroness Hale agreed with Lord Nicholls in firmly rejecting conduct as a relevant factor. The older cases had attempted to apply a discount for a wife's conduct. This was no longer applicable. At para [145]:

'But once the assets are seen as a pool, and the couple as equal partners, then it is only equitable to take their conduct into account if one has been very much more to blame than the other: in the famous words of Ormrod J in *Wachtel v Wachtel* [1973] Fam 72, at 80, the conduct had been "both obvious and gross". This approach is not only just, it is also the only practicable one. It is simply not possible for any outsider to pick over the events of a marriage and decide who was the more to blame for what went wrong, save in the most obvious and gross cases. Yet in *Miller v Miller*, both Singer J and the Court of Appeal took into account the parties' conduct, even though it fell far short of this. In my view they were wrong to do so.'

Contributions

8.12   Baroness Hale's view was that contributions should be approached in much the same way as conduct. She disapproved the references in some judgments to exceptional or 'stellar' contributions, and, like Lord Nicholls, approved the words of Coleridge J in *G v G (Financial Provision: Equal Division)*. She continued (at para [146]):

> 'It had already been made clear in *White v White* [2001] 1 AC 596 that domestic and financial contributions should be treated equally. Section 25(2)(f) of the 1973 Act does not refer to the contributions which each has made to the parties' accumulated wealth, but to the contributions they have made (and will continue to make) to the welfare of the family. Each should be seen as doing their best in their own sphere. Only if there is such a disparity in their respective contributions to the welfare of the family that it would be inequitable to disregard it should this be taken into account in determining their shares.'

The area of disagreement

8.13   As indicated above, there is one important area where, at the very least, Baroness Hale suggests that the law should move in a different direction from that explained by Lord Nicholls. This is the fairness, or otherwise, of dividing great wealth which has either been brought into the marriage or generated by the business efforts and acumen of one party. She said that it was principally in this context that there was a perception that the size of the non-business partner's share should be linked to the length of the marriage.

8.14   She continued (at para [148]):

> 'The strength of these perceptions is such that it could be unwise for the law to ignore them completely. In *White v White* [2001] 1 AC 596, it was recognised that the source of the assets might be a reason for departing from the yardstick of equality (see p 610c–g). There, the reason was that property had been acquired from or with the help of the husband's father during the marriage, but the same would apply to property acquired before the marriage. In *White*, it was also recognised that the importance of the source of the assets will diminish over time (see p 611b). As the family's personal and financial inter-dependence grows, it becomes harder and harder to disentangle what came from where. But the fact that the family's wealth consists largely of a family business, such as a farm, may still be taken into account as a reason for departing from full equality: see *P v P (Inherited Property)* [2004] EWHC 1364 (Fam); [2005] 1 FLR 576. So too may be the nature of the assets, where these are businesses which will be crippled or lose much of their value, if disposed of prematurely in order to fund an equal division: see *N v N (Financial Provision: Sale of Company)* [2001] 2 FLR 69.'

8.15   She posed the question for the court as follows:

'Whether in the very big money cases, it is fair to take some account of the source and nature of the assets, in the same way that some account is taken of the source of those assets in inherited or family wealth. Is the "matrimonial property" to consist of everything acquired during the marriage (which should probably include periods of pre-marital cohabitation and engagement) or might a distinction be drawn between "family" and other assets?'

8.16   Baroness Hale set out the competing arguments (at paras [150] and [151]):

'More difficult are business or investment assets which have been generated solely or mainly by the efforts of one party. The other party has often made some contribution to the business, at least in its early days, and has continued with her agreed contribution to the welfare of the family (as did Mrs Cowan). But in these non-business-partnership, non-family asset cases, the bulk of the property has been generated by one party. Does this provide a reason for departing from the yardstick of equality? On the one hand is the view, already expressed, that commercial and domestic contributions are intrinsically incommensurable. It is easy to count the money or property which one has acquired. It is impossible to count the value which the other has added to their lives together. One is counted in money or money's worth. The other is counted in domestic comfort and happiness. If the law is to avoid discrimination between the gender roles, it should regard all the assets generated in either way during the marriage as family assets to be divided equally between them unless some other good reason is shown to do otherwise.

On the other hand is the view that this is unrealistic. We do not yet have a system of community of property, whether full or deferred. Even modest legislative steps towards this have been strenuously resisted. Ownership and contributions still feature in divorcing couples' own perceptions of a fair result, some drawing a distinction between the home and joint savings accounts, on the one hand, and pensions, individual savings and debts, on the other (*Settling Up*, para 128 earlier, chapter 5). Some of these are not family assets in the way that the home, its contents and the family savings are family assets. Their value may well be speculative or their possession risky. It is not suggested that the domestic partner should share in the risks or potential liabilities, a problem which bedevils many community of property regimes and can give domestic contributions a negative value. It simply cannot be demonstrated that the domestic contribution, important though it has been to the welfare and happiness of the family as a whole, has contributed to their acquisition. If the money maker had not had a wife to look after him, no doubt he would have found others to do it for him. Further, great wealth can be generated in a very short time, as the Miller case shows; but domestic contributions by their very nature take time to mature into contributions to the welfare of the family.'

8.17   Baroness Hale considered that these arguments were irrelevant in the great majority of cases. As to the cases where they might be relevant, of which *Miller* was one, her conclusions were as follows (at paras [152] and [153]):

'... the answer is the same as that given in *White v White* [2001] 1 AC 596 in connection with pre-marital property, inheritance and gifts. The source of the assets may be taken into account but its importance will diminish over time. Put the other way round, the court is expressly required to take into account the duration of the marriage: s 25(2)(d). If the assets are not "family assets", or not generated by the joint efforts of the parties, then the duration of the marriage may justify a departure from the yardstick of equality of division. As we are talking here of a departure from that yardstick, I would prefer to put this in terms of a reduction to reflect the period of time over which the domestic contribution has or will continue (see Bailey-Harris, *Comment on GW v RW (Financial Provision: Departure from Equality)* [2003] Fam Law 386, at 388) rather than in terms of accrual over time (see Eekelaar, *Asset Distribution on Divorce – Time and Property* [2003] Fam Law 828). This avoids the complexities of devising a formula for such accruals.

This is simply to recognise that in a matrimonial property regime which still starts with the premise of separate property, there is still some scope for one party to acquire and retain separate property which is not automatically to be shared equally between them. The nature and the source of the property and the way the couple have run their lives may be taken into account in deciding how it should be shared. There may be other examples. Take, for example, a genuine dual career family where each party has worked throughout the marriage and certain assets have been pooled for the benefit of the family but others have not. There may be no relationship-generated needs or other disadvantages for which compensation is warranted. We can assume that the family assets, in the sense discussed earlier, should be divided equally. But it might well be fair to leave undisturbed whatever additional surplus each has accumulated during his or her working life. However, one should be careful not to take this approach too far. What seems fair and sensible at the outset of a relationship may seem much less fair and sensible when it ends. And there could well be a sense of injustice if a dual career spouse who had worked outside as well as inside the home throughout the marriage ended up less well off than one who had only or mainly worked inside the home.'

8.18 Applying all this to the instant cases, Baroness Hale agreed with the final decision of Lord Nicholls.

Part C – Comment

9   COMMENT

9.1   There is no doubt that the House of Lords has given clear and helpful guidance in this case, which will be of assistance to practitioners. Some of this is the result of a consensus between Lord Nicholls and Baroness Hale, while further interest in the case arises out of the possible divergence between them. These issues will now be considered in more detail.

White v White re-affirmed

9.2   Both judges tried to set out a clear list of principles to be followed. However, they began with some fairly obvious but nonetheless important points: the court must be fair, and the statutory first consideration of the welfare of the children must be observed. The principles of *White v White*, such as fairness, non-discrimination and the yardstick of equality, were repeated and remain of the first importance.

Three principles

9.3   Both judges underlined the fact that financial relief is not a matter of taking from one party to give to the other, but is rather a matter of a proper and fair sharing of assets which both of them, in their interdependent and joint lives, have acquired.

9.4   The three principles which this case establishes and/or confirms as being the rationale for financial provision contained in the 1973 Act may be summarised as follows:

(1)   **Meeting the needs of the parties.** Lord Nicholls said that mutual dependence begets mutual obligations of support. Fairness requires that the assets of the parties should be divided so as to meet their housing and financial needs.

Baroness Hale said that the most common rationale for redistribution is that the relationship has generated needs which it is right that the other party should meet. Needs may arise as a result of one party having been a homemaker and child-carer, and needs generated by such a choice are 'a perfectly sound rationale for adjusting the parties respective resources in compensation'.

(2)   **Compensation.** Lord Nicholls said that compensation is aimed at redressing any significant prospective disparity between the parties arising from the way they conducted their marriage. Baroness Hale described this as compensation for relationship-generated disadvantage, which goes beyond need.

(3)   **Sharing.** Lord Nicholls sees sharing as derived from the basic concept of equality permeating a marriage. Husband and wife are equal partners in marriage.

Baroness Hale described this as the sharing of the fruits of the matrimonial partnership.

9.5   These three principles may be taken as the foundation for any intellectual approach to the task of awarding financial provision. However, both judges made it clear that these are general principles and that they must be adapted to suit the requirements of a particular case. In particular, Lord Nicholls emphasised that equality applies 'unless there is good reason to the contrary. The yardstick of equality is to be applied as an aid, not a rule'.

Short marriages

9.6   If it were not clear before *Foster v Foster*, it must now be clear that the old law relating to short marriages was swept away by *White v White*. The old principle of trying to restore one party, normally the wife, to her position before the marriage, is no longer applicable.

9.7   The principles of *White*, particularly the yardstick of equality and the concept of sharing, apply as much to short as to long marriages. *Foster v Foster* had made clear that all the s 25 guidelines must be applied in such a case. Having said that, Lord Nicholls also makes clear that the application of these principles will not necessarily result in equal division. When he says that the length of the marriage 'will affect the quantum of the financial fruits of the partnership' he can only mean that the court must look at what the partnership produced during the term of the relationship, and that will be one of the factors to be considered.

9.8   Lord Nicholls applied this test to the *Miller* case. One of the principal features leading him to uphold Singer J's award seems to have been the quantum of the financial fruits acquired during the married life. This is emphatically not the same as Mr Mostyn QC's test in *GW v RW*; the amount of capital accrued during the period is relevant, but not who accrued it, since marriage is a partnership and to identify and reward the party who was responsible for the accrual would offend *White v White* principles.

9.9 Unsurprisingly, Baroness Hale agreed with the approval of the *Foster* principles. Referring to *Foster*, she said that '[a]lthough one party had earned more and thus contributed more in purely financial terms to the acquisition of those assets, both contributed what they could, and the fair result was to divide the product of their joint endeavours equally'.

Legitimate expectations and standard of living

9.10 Most practitioners will be immensely relieved that the House strongly disapproved the concept of legitimate expectations. Had it remained, life would have been much more difficult.

9.11 However, the importance of the standard of living of the parties during the marriage has been affirmed, and this was one of the statutory factors prayed in aid by Lord Nicholls to justify the *Miller* award. For obvious reasons, it will only be important in cases where assets exceed needs, but this is an important reminder of the need to consider all the s 25 factors.

Conduct

9.12 Similarly, practitioners will be delighted that the principles of *G v G*, as applied in *Miller*, have been disapproved. To take into account conduct which fell short of the statutory standard was always fraught with difficulty, and the importance of the statute and the earlier cases relating to conduct has been re-affirmed.

Contributions

9.13 *White v White* had already established that the contributions of the breadwinner are not to be favoured over those of the homemaker and childcarer. Both Lord Nicholls and Baroness Hale sought to deal with the vexed issue of the evaluation of special or exceptional contributions – such as, for example, those of an exceptionally gifted sportsman, musician or entrepreneur (these are the author's examples, not those of the court).

9.14 Lord Nicholls deprecated any lengthy and costly inquiry into such matters. Adopting the approach of Coleridge J, he set out the principle to be followed:

'The question is whether earnings of this character can be regarded as a "special contribution", and thus as a good reason for departing from equality of division. The answer is that exceptional earnings are to be regarded as a factor pointing away from equality of division when, but only when, it would be inequitable to proceed otherwise. The wholly exceptional nature of the earnings must be, to borrow a phrase more familiar in a different context, obvious and gross.'

9.15   Baroness Hale agreed, equating contributions with conduct. The words she added are important and worth repeating:

'Section 25(2)(f) of the 1973 Act does not refer to the contributions which each has made to the parties' accumulated wealth, but to the contributions they have made (and will continue to make) to the welfare of the family. Each should be seen as doing their best in their own sphere. Only if there is such a disparity in their respective contributions to the welfare of the family that it would be inequitable to disregard it should this be taken into account in determining their shares.'

Periodical payments and the clean break

9.16   Both Lord Nicholls and Baroness Hale stress the importance of self-sufficiency and the clean break as one of the key features of the statute which must always be in the court's mind. Baroness Hale referred to the statutory provisions as a clear steer towards capital orders with no continuing periodical payments, to bring mutual obligations to an end. However, it is also made clear that this can only be achieved where it is fair to do so. In particular, the practice of imposing a term order on the basis that the recipient can always apply for extension is disapproved. Where there is any doubt as to self-sufficiency, there should be no term order and it can be left to the paying party to apply for variation and dismissal where appropriate.

9.17   Perhaps the most interesting aspect of the speeches as to periodical payments is the clear statement that periodical payments are not confined to maintenance nor the meeting of needs. They can be designed to enable one spouse to share in the future financial good fortune of the other and as a means of redressing capital imbalance. This is not the same as a lump sum by instalments, since the capital is not available at the time of the order. Rather, it recognises the kind of case where the fortunes of one party are likely to improve disproportionately to those of the other, and it would be unjust to the disadvantaged party not to allow her to share them.

9.18   In case this seems to be contrary to the spirit of the clean break, it is worth repeating Baroness Hale's definition of the 'ultimate objective':

'In general, it can be assumed that the marital partnership does not stay alive for the purpose of sharing future resources unless this is justified by need or compensation. The ultimate objective is to give each party an equal start on the road to independent living.'

9.19 Clearly there were reasons of compensation which led to this result in *McFarlane*, but they are not universally applicable.

Application to smaller money cases

9.20 One of the problems with discussing decisions of the higher courts is that they normally involve very large amounts of money and rich parties. Practitioners will be more interested in whether or not they apply to the normal run of cases.

9.21 It must first be said that the *White v White* principles of fairness, non-discrimination and the yardstick of equality apply to all cases, big or small and regardless of the length of the marriage. However, Lord Nicholls makes it clear that while the approach has to be the same, the result will be different in cases where the needs exceed the assets because the funds are not available to take the matter further. It is worth repeating his words:

'When the marriage ends fairness requires that the assets of the parties should be divided primarily so as to make provision for the parties' housing and financial needs, taking into account a wide range of matters such as the parties' ages, their future earning capacity, the family's standard of living, and any disability of either party. Most of these needs will have been generated by the marriage, but not all of them. Needs arising from age or disability are instances of the latter.

In most cases the search for fairness largely begins and ends at this stage. In most cases the available assets are insufficient to provide adequately for the needs of two homes. The court seeks to stretch modest finite resources so far as possible to meet the parties' needs. Especially where children are involved it may be necessary to augment the available assets by having recourse to the future earnings of the money-earner, by way of an order for periodical payments.'

9.22 Baroness Hale expressed similar views. An equal partnership does not always dictate equal sharing of the assets. One could interject there the view that, in lower value cases, it almost never does. As Baroness Hale said, equal division may have to give way to the needs of one party or the children.

'Too strict an adherence to equal sharing and the clean break can lead to a rapid decrease in the primary carer's standard of living and a rapid increase in the breadwinner's. The breadwinner's unimpaired and unimpeded earning capacity is a powerful resource which can frequently repair any loss of capital after an unequal distribution.'

9.23   Baroness Hale adds that recognising this is one reason why English law has been successful in retaining a home for the children.

The area of dispute

9.24   The difference between Lord Nicholls and Baroness Hale relates to the relevance of 'non-matrimonial property'. The position is well summarised by Lord Mance (at paras [167] and [168]):

> 'On the one hand, on Lord Nicholls' approach, non-matrimonial property is viewed as all property which the parties bring with them into the marriage or acquire by inheritance or gift during the marriage (plus perhaps the income or fruits of that property), while matrimonial property is viewed as all other property. The yardstick of equality applies generally to matrimonial property (although the shorter the marriage, the smaller the matrimonial property is in the nature of things likely to be). But the yardstick is not so readily applicable to non-matrimonial property, especially after a short marriage, but in some circumstances even after a long marriage.

> On the other hand, Baroness Hale's approach takes a more limited conception of matrimonial property, as embracing "family assets" (cf *Wachtel v Wachtel* [1973] Fam 72, 90 per Lord Denning MR) and family businesses or joint ventures in which both parties work (cf *Foster v Foster* [2003] EWCA Civ 56; [2003] 2 FLR 299, 305, para 19, per Hale LJ). In relation to such property she agrees that the yardstick of equality may readily be applied. In contrast, she identifies other "non-business-partnership, non-family assets", to which that yardstick may not apply with the same force particularly in the case of short marriages; these include on her approach not merely (a) property which the parties bring with them with into the marriage or acquire by inheritance or gift during the marriage (plus perhaps its income or fruits), but also (b) business or investment assets generated solely or mainly by the efforts of one party during the marriage.'

9.25   Baroness Hale's view was that the source of assets may be taken into account but that this would become less important with the passage of time; she points out that the court is directed to take account of the length of the marriage. She continues:

> 'If the assets are not "family assets", or not generated by the joint efforts of the parties, then the duration of the marriage may justify a departure from the yardstick of equality of division. As we are talking here of a departure from that yardstick, I would prefer to put this in terms of a reduction to reflect the period of time over which the domestic contribution has or will continue rather than in terms of accrual over time.'

9.26   Baroness Hale refers, apparently with approval, to the comments of Professor Bailey Harris at [2003] Fam Law 386, at p 388. There, the learned author, in her comment on *GW v RW (Financial Provision: Departure from Equality)*, records that in that case an inherited asset was treated as a resource of, and a contribution by, the spouse to whom it was bequeathed. It is a factor in the s 25 exercise and the weight to be accorded to it will depend entirely on the facts of the individual case. The same approach was adopted in relation to the husband's already developed career, capital assets and earning potential, which were collectively treated as a non-matrimonial asset.

9.27 Professor Eekelaar, at [2003] Fam Law 828, suggests a more formulaic approach, but Baroness Hale makes clear that she prefers the Bailey Harris approach, which avoids the complexities of devising a formula. She concludes, on this issue:

'This is simply to recognise that in a matrimonial property regime which still starts with the premise of separate property, there is still some scope for one party to acquire and retain separate property which is not automatically to be shared equally between them. The nature and the source of the property and the way the couple have run their lives may be taken into account in deciding how it should be shared.'

9.28 Lord Mance approves this approach.

'To take into account the shortness of a marriage could enable a court to cut through some of these more intricate arguments in a manner consistent with s 25(2)(d) of the 1973 Act. More fundamentally, to allow the duration of a marriage as a relevant factor would cater for the considerations that, while some people may make a large amount of money in a short time, the nature of their work or other factors may mean that they do not do so at a consistent rate over their lives as a whole or for more than a short period of their lives, and furthermore, as Baroness Hale has pointed out, that there may be long-term risks in relation to non-business-partnership, non-family assets which remain with those directly involved in generating them. The longer the marriage, the less likely these are to be significant considerations. In a short marriage, the timing of which may or may not coincide with a period of significant increase in the value of non-business-partnership, non-family assets, such considerations argue in favour of some further flexibility in the application of the yardstick of equality of division. I see force in and would agree with the views expressed by Baroness Hale in paras 152–153 of her judgment to the effect that the duration of a marriage, mentioned expressly in s 25(2)(d) of the Act, cannot be discounted as a relevant factor.'

9.29 Given this approval, and the fact that Lord Hoffmann expressly identified himself with Baroness Hale's speech and not with that of Lord Nicholls (Lord Hope favouring both equally), it can fairly be said that the true ratio of this case on this issue is that expressed by Baroness Hale.

Conclusion

9.30 In conclusion, therefore, it may be said that the House has given important guidance on a number of key issues. It remains the case that each case must be decided on its own merits, with no magic formula to be applied, and that, as before and unsurprisingly, the statute remains the first source of law in these difficult cases.

APPENDIX

McFARLANE v McFARLANE;
PARLOUR v PARLOUR
[2004] EWCA CIV 872

Court of Appeal

Thorpe, Latham and Wall LJJ

7 July 2004

Financial provision – Periodical payments – Capital element – Clean break – Substantial future surplus of income over expenditure – Whether periodical payments could include an element of capital

In two cases, the issue arose whether the court was entitled to order a division of future income by way of a periodical payments order which exceeded current needs. In both cases the division of the family capital had been agreed, but both wives were seeking periodical payments in excess of needs, on the basis that fairness required that they have a share of future earnings which had been made possible by their past contribution to their husbands' careers. Both husbands earned very large sums of money, substantially in excess of the combined household expenditure of husband and wife. In the first case, the income of the husband, who was a chartered accountant, had increased considerably year on year, and seemed likely to continue to do so for a number of years. In the second case, the income of the husband, a professional footballer, was very large, but was likely to reduce dramatically once his present contract expired.

Held –

(1)   There could be no doubt of the court's power to order periodical payments to reflect more than the recipient's mere aliment, provided that all the criteria in s 25(2) of the Matrimonial Causes Act 1973, all the circumstances of the case and overall fairness so required. Clearly, in assessing periodical payments, as in assessing capital provision, the overriding objective was fairness. Over the years, the hallowed distinction between capital and income had been eroded, if not eliminated, and was not now very relevant. In exceptional cases, and on the basis of term rather than joint lives orders, periodical payments could be used by the recipient to accumulate capital (see paras [99], [106], [107], [109], [136]).

(2)   The original once-for-all capital division that resulted in the dismissal of capital claims might now be supplemented by a later transfer of capital, agreed or judged to be the fair consideration for the dismissal of the surviving claim to periodical payments. In any case in which, despite a substantial capital base available for division, clean break was not presently practicable, a court had a statutory duty to consider the future possibility of a clean break. That duty assumed particular prominence in cases where there was a certain and substantial surplus of future income over future needs, which surplus could provide the consideration for the dismissal of the wife's outstanding claims. Quantification of those outstanding claims would depend on the size of the surplus in each of the future years (see paras [53], [56], [66]).

(3)   Neither case should have been argued primarily as a claim for indefinite and continuing periodical payments. In both cases the past surplus which had been

converted into capital assets had been divided by agreement, and it was the scale of the contemplated future surplus that prevented the clean break dismissing all claims. In both cases the agreement as to capital was seen, or should have been seen, as but the first stage in the progress to clean break. If, as in one of the cases, the surplus would be predictably short-lived, the first option for consideration should have been the planned progress to clean break by means of a substantial term order open to a later application for extension (see paras [53], [54], [56], [66]).

(4)   The obligation on the parties to achieve financial independence was mutual. The earner must give the proper priority to making payments on account out of the surplus income. The payee must invest the surplus sensibly, or risk that her failure to do so might count against her on an application for discharge under s 31(7A) and (7B) of the Matrimonial Causes Act 1973. Given the mutuality of the obligation, the opportunity and responsibility to invest should be shared. It was discriminatory and, therefore, wrong in principle, for the earner to have sole control of the surplus through the years of accumulation. The preferred mechanism by which the surplus was to be divided annually must be periodical payments, which were, unlike lump sum orders, variable. The practicality of such an order would depend upon many factors. Essentially the completion of the process must be foreseen within a relatively short span; a term of 5 years might be towards the limit of the foreseeable (see para [66]).

(5)   The focus in the first of the two cases, in which the husband's income was likely to increase year on year, should have been on termination and not on post-retirement provision. The husband could borrow, using his home as security, to finance a clean break years before either party approached retirement. The district judge had recognised the wife's entitlement to a fair share of the husband's surplus income, although she failed to identify the overriding purpose to which it had to be put, wrongly identifying pension provision and insurance, rather than the greater priority to achieve financial independence. The district judge should not have provided for a joint lives order (see paras [70], [73], [74]).

(6)   In the second case, in which the husband's very large income was likely to plummet within 4 or 5 years, a substantial periodical payments order should have been made over a 4-year extendable term, at which time a clean break might then be achievable on the basis of an assessment of the husband's earning capacity thereafter, and of the wife's independent fortune derived from the original capital settlement and augmented by the substantial annual surplus built into her periodical payments order in the interim (see para [77]).

(7)   In cases such as the present, the calculation of the amount of surplus income could not be achieved without first establishing what both the payer and the payee needed in order to meet their projected expenditure. In preparation for the trials below, both wives advanced budgets which were generously cast and which at trial were subjected to rigorous cross-examination. In both cases the husbands failed to complete the relevant section of the Form E, and one refused subsequent requests for information. The practice had apparently grown for substantial earners to decline any statement of their needs on the grounds that they could afford any order that the court was likely to make. An end must be put to that practice (see paras [78], [79], [83]).

Per curiam: these were exceptional cases. In the majority of cases the income of the earner was insufficient to cover the outgoings of the two households. In many others the single income was sufficient only to provide for both households at a standard below that which the family enjoyed before separation. In many others the income would provide for both amply. In many more it would provide for both and a measure of luxury which each contended was not disproportionate to the standard enjoyed before separation. In all such instances, the court's discretionary judgment would be dominated by an assessment of needs or, for the more affluent, reasonable requirements (see para [86]).

Statutory provisions considered

Matrimonial Causes Act 1866, s 1
Married Women's Property Act 1882
Matrimonial Causes Act 1965
Matrimonial Proceedings and Property Act 1970, ss 1, 6
Matrimonial Causes Act 1973, Part II, ss 22, 23, 25(2), 25A, 27, 31(7A)–(7F)
Matrimonial and Family Proceedings Act 1984
Family Law Act 1996
Access to Justice Act 1999, s 55
Family Proceedings Rules 1991 (SI 1991/1247), r 8.1(3)

Cases referred to in judgment

A v A (Maintenance Pending Suit: Provision for Legal Fees) [2001] 1 WLR 605, [2001] 1 FLR 377, FD
Boylan v Boylan [1988] 1 FLR 282, FD
Campbell v Campbell [1998] 1 FLR 828, CA
Cordle v Cordle [2001] EWCA Civ 1791, [2002] 1 WLR 1441, [2002] 1 FLR 207, CA
Cornick v Cornick (No 2) [1995] 2 FLR 490, CA
Cornick v Cornick (No 3) [2001] 2 FLR 1240, FD
de Lasala (Ernest Ferdinand Perez) v de Lasala (Hannelore) [1980] AC 546, [1979] 3 WLR 390, (1979) FLR Rep 223, [1979] 3 All ER 1146, PC
Doherty v Doherty [1976] Fam 71, [1975] 3 WLR 1, [1975] 2 All ER 635, CA
G v G (Financial Provision: Equal Division) [2002] EWHC 1339 (Fam), [2002] 2 FLR 1143, FD
G v G (Maintenance Pending Suit: Costs) [2002] EWHC 306 (Fam), [2003] 2 FLR 71, FD
Martin (BH) v Martin (D) [1978] Fam 12, [1977] 3 WLR 101, (1977) FLR Rep 444, [1977] 3 All ER 762, CA
Minton v Minton [1979] AC 593, [1979] 2 WLR 31, (1978) FLR Rep 461, [1979] 1 All ER 79, HL
N v N (Financial Provision: Sale of Company) [2001] 2 FLR 69, CA
O'Brien v O'Brien (1985) 66 NY 2d 576
Pearce v Pearce [2003] EWCA Civ 1054, [2004] 1 WLR 68, [2003] 2 FLR 1144, CA
Trippas v Trippas [1973] Fam 134, [1973] 2 WLR 585, [1973] 2 All ER 1, CA
Wachtel v Wachtel [1973] Fam 72, [1973] 2 WLR 366, [1973] 1 All ER 829, CA
White v White [2001] 1 AC 596, [2000] 3 WLR 1571, [2000] 2 FLR 981, [2001] 1 All ER 1, HL

Barry Singleton QC and Deepak Nagpal for Mrs McFarlane
Jeremy Posnansky QC and Stephen Trowell for Mr McFarlane
Nicholas Mostyn QC and Deborah Bangay for Mrs Parlour
Nicholas Francis QC and Brent Molyneux for Mr Parlour

Cur adv vult

THORPE LJ:

Introduction

[1]   On 3 October 2003 Bennett J gave judgment on an appeal brought by Mr McFarlane, the husband, against a periodical payments order at the rate of £250,000 pa made by District Judge Redgrave in the Principal Registry on 19 December 2002. For reasons which I will subsequently examine critically, Bennett J

allowed the husband's appeal and, in the exercise of his own discretion, substituted the lesser order of £180,000.

[2]   On 23 January 2004 Bennett J gave judgment on a contested periodical payments claim brought by Mrs Parlour.[1] He awarded her periodical payments at the rate of £212,500 pa.

[3]   In each case there were three children of the marriage and orders for periodical payments to the children augmented the liability of the husband. There were further orders in each case dealing with ancillary issues that had been contested. However, in each case the only fundamental and difficult issue was the quantification of the wife's periodical payments.

[4]   The outcome of these two cases has been much debated by specialist practitioners. It has been said that the cases raise a novel point of principle which may be formulated thus: if the decision in *White v White* [2001] 1 AC 596, [2000] 2 FLR 981 introduces the yardstick of equality for measuring a fair division of capital why should the same yardstick not be applied as the measure for the division of income?

[5]   Mr Singleton QC's skeleton argument supporting his permission application of 16 October on behalf of Mrs McFarlane resulted in the grant of permission on 4 December 2003. The order was an acknowledgement that the case raised important issues that this court needed to consider, since the permission application fell to be judged by the stricter standards that s 55 of the Access to Justice Act 1999 imposes.

[6]   The application for permission on behalf of Mrs Parlour was filed on 6 February 2004. Permission was granted and arrangements made for the two appeals to be heard together. At a later stage Mr Francis QC, for Mr Parlour, sought permission to cross-appeal. That application was adjourned to be heard together with the two appeals.

[7]   Subsequently at an informal directions hearing it was agreed that Mr Singleton would present Mrs McFarlane's appeal followed by Mr Mostyn QC for Mrs Parlour. Thereafter Mr Posnansky QC would respond for Mr McFarlane and Mr Francis would then advance his permission application and respond for Mr Parlour. Further agreement was reached for the division of territory between the advocates, particularly foreign authority, to make the best use of the 2 days allocated to the appeals.

McFarlane v McFarlane

The facts

[8]   The parties are 44 years of age. They married in September 1984 after 2 years of cohabitation. Their three children are aged respectively 15, 13 and 8 and are educated at fee-paying schools.

[9]   At the outset of their cohabitation in 1982, the husband was a trainee chartered accountant working for a leading international firm; and the wife was a trainee solicitor with a leading city firm. By the date of their marriage they had both qualified in their respective professions. The husband has throughout remained with the firm with which he trained. In advancing her career the wife moved to work for a large venture capital company and then in due course moved to another leading city firm. She returned to work soon after the birth of her first child but the couple agreed that she should not return to work after the birth of her second child in 1991. The

---

1   Editor's note: see *J v J* [2004] EWHC 53 (Fam); [2004] Fam Law 408.

husband had become a partner in 1990 and the understandable agreement was that the wife should abandon her legal career in order to devote all her time and energy to their two babies and the developing family. The husband's prospects would amply provide for the family's financial needs. In one sense this was a substantial sacrifice on the wife's part, since in the years prior to the husband achieving partnership she had earned as much or more than he.

[10]   In 1994 the couple bought in the wife's name a house in Barnes which remains the home for the wife and the children to this day. It was purchased with a substantial mortgage which they planned to discharge over 5 years. Shortly after that was achieved in 1999 the couple purchased in their joint names a holiday home in Salcombe. At the date of the trial before the district judge the house in Barnes was valued at £1.5m and the Salcombe home at about £250,000. In January 2001 the parties separated, the husband having purchased in June 2000 a flat in Clerkenwell for £415,000, financed by a tax-efficient partnership loan paid off over approximately 18 months.

[11]   The husband formed a relationship with one of his partners and in August 2002 they purchased in the ratio of their respective financial contributions a house in Barnes for £2.94m inclusive of costs. The husband sold his flat in Clerkenwell and his new partner sold her flat. Again the purchase was largely financed by a substantial mortgage and by tax-efficient partnership loans. Their anticipation is that the mortgage will be paid off over 5 years. The husband planned to spend nearly £350,000 from his net income in payment of interest and repayment of capital. This was plainly an achievable target given that the husband's net earned income as a partner had increased over the 5 years between 31 May 1999 and 31 May 2003 along the following route expressed in thousands: 272–427–579–633–753.

The case before the district judge

[12]   Equal division of the family capital of about £3m was agreed. The wife retained the former matrimonial home which represented her half-share. Nor was there any disagreement as to the available income. The only question was how the husband's net income of £753,000 pa should be divided. It was common ground that the husband would pay the school fees and periodical payments fixed at £20,000 pa per child by the district judge. What should be the wife's share was the question for the court.

[13]   The wife in her Form E quantified her spending needs at about £128,000 a year. The husband failed to complete this section of his Form E and declined subsequent requests to do so.

[14]   In her Form E the wife sought the payment of instalment lump sums to enable her to accumulate capital in order to fund a clean break. However this approach was soon abandoned.

[15]   It was common ground that neither the husband nor the wife had any significant pension provision and that provision had to be made from future income for the years of retirement. It was not disputed that the wife was entitled to a conventional joint lives order.

[16]   As to standard of living it was agreed that the family had enjoyed a comparatively modest standard of living, certainly until the mortgage on the matrimonial home had been discharged. In the circumstances the husband was able to contend that the budget sought by the wife was considerably greater than the family's

spending during the marriage. Questions directed to the wife's budget were to dominate her cross-examination.

[17]   None of the other criteria in s 25(2) of the Matrimonial Causes Act 1973 was of particular application. On those battle lines the wife sought an order of £275,000 pa and the husband an order of £100,000 pa.

The judgment of the district judge

[18]   Having heard the oral evidence the district judge made some important findings on the disputed areas. These were her findings on contributions:

(a)   'In terms of contributions, from 1991 to date the husband has been the breadwinner for this family. He has worked extremely hard and has been and continues to be very successful. In 1991 the parties made a joint decision that their children would be brought up by the mother on a day-to-day basis and she would abandon her career. It has been suggested on behalf of the husband that the wife did not enjoy her work and found it stressful; that she willingly gave up her career; implying thereby that it diminished the value of her contribution in running the home and protecting the husband from the day-to-day stresses of the child rearing. I reject this argument. The value of the wife's contribution is derived from what she did and how well she did it, rather than her motivation for doing it and, in any event, she disputes that she did not enjoy her job. There has not been a scintilla of criticism of the wife, either as a partner or as a mother. The parties' contribution to this long marriage has been different but of equal value.'

(b)   'Part of the overall circumstances of this case is that the joint decision of the parties to concentrate on the husband's career in order to provide the funding of the family's lifestyle has resulted in the greatest fruits of his endeavours being available towards the end of the marriage and after its breakdown. In effect, the spadework for these rewards was carried out over a long period and it would be unfair to take the view that recent increases in the husband's earnings since the breakdown of the marriage have not been contributed to by the wife. The wife's contributions enabled the husband to create a working environment which has produced greater rewards, in respect of which she should have her fair share. She also continues to make a contribution to the family in her nurturing of the children in a single-parent household. That contribution did not come to an end when the parties separated.'

[19]   Of the husband's proposed future expenditure the district judge had this to say:

(a)   'The husband has estimated his own financial needs, exclusive of housing costs, at £60,000–£80,000 pa, giving no particulars. He plans to pay off his share of the borrowings incurred in the purchase of [his new home] over a 5-year period, which will require payments of approximately £347,500 pa. This is an entirely voluntary responsibility which he is perfectly entitled to take on, but it is not a reasonable one … Doing the best that I can I therefore conclude that he has paid almost half a million pounds more for his housing than, in my judgment, is reasonable.'

(b)   'This would have resulted in the husband having to service less debt than he has actually incurred and I do not consider that the wife and children should be penalised because of the husband's decision with his partner to buy [his new home] which was beyond his reasonable requirements.'

[20]   In relation to the wife's earning capacity this was the finding:

'In the context of this case, the joint decisions made by the parties about how these children should be brought up and financially supported and the husband's earning capacity, it is, in my judgment, unreasonable to expect this wife to take steps to acquire or improve her earning capacity in the foreseeable future, and that is, at the very least, until [the youngest child] reaches secondary school age, when the matter might be very different.'

[21]   This is how the district judge dealt with pension provision:

'The taxation concessions available to the husband in obtaining partnership loans to finance the purchase of property are very generous. Tax relief is available to him on all interest repayments on these loans at higher rates and this is how he has financed part of purchase of [his new home]. I take the view that, after determining what is a fair outcome in respect of the wife's claim for maintenance, taking into account the eight factors specified in s 25(2) of the Matrimonial Causes Act 1973, none of which predominates over the others, and against the background of all these circumstances of the case, that how the parties choose to spend their available income is a matter for them. I am far from satisfied that either of them intends to provide for their later years by way of conventional pension fund investments.'

[22]   Finally I record the district judge's direction and conclusion:

(a)   'The court's fundamental duty is to apply s 25 of the Matrimonial Causes Act 1973 as amended to all the circumstances of the case in order to arrive at a fair outcome, and I remind myself that fairness does not necessarily mean equality, even where the parties have agreed in principle to an equal division or thereabouts of capital assets.'

(b)   'In my view, the appropriate maintenance award for this wife is £250,000 pa which equates to 33.18% of the husband's present net income. This reflects her needs, obligations and the contribution that she has made over the years of the marriage. It may well need to be revised in later years for a variety of reasons. It is a matter for her whether she chooses to make pension provision, but she will not be able to avail herself of tax-relief on pension contributions while she is not an income tax payer and it is a matter for her whether she takes out insurance to protect her and the children's position in the event that the husband dies or is ill and unable to work.'

[23]   Implicit within the district judge's reasoning is first, the conclusion that the wife should have the same opportunity as the husband to make provision for the years of retirement, and secondly, the conclusion that she should have the means with which to insure herself and the children against the risk of premature cessation of the husband's high professional earnings.

The judgment of Bennett J

[24]   Mr Posnansky advanced his appeal to Bennett J on six grounds:

(1)   The order was manifestly excessive given that the wife had not put her annual requirements at more than £128,000 pa.

(2)   The district judge had wrongly allowed for the wife to build up a retirement fund and/or to insure herself against the husband's incapacity or premature death.

(3)   The district judge had taken insufficient account of the standard of living during the marriage.

(4)   The district judge had taken insufficient account of the husband's need to make provision for his retirement out of present income.

(5)   Fresh evidence as to the husband's income for the year ending 31 May 2004 invalidated the rate of £250,000 a year.

(6)   The district judge's finding that the husband had unreasonably overspent in housing himself was wrong and miscalculated.

[25]   Miss Lucy Stone QC countered all these criticisms to the judge's satisfaction save one, namely Mr Posnansky's second ground, which, during the course of argument, emerged as a submission that the judge had impermissibly subverted a periodical payments order as a mechanism to provide the wife with additional capital.

[26]   Furthermore it is important to emphasise that Bennett J adopted all the district judge's findings of fact and did not otherwise criticise her approach or her conclusions. That is plain from the paragraph of his judgment in which he explained his decision not to remit to the district judge but to exercise his discretion afresh. In that paragraph he said:

> 'In doing so I shall give the same weight to the s 25 factors as did the district judge. She saw and heard the wife and the husband. She has made important findings to which I propose to be completely loyal. It is clear to me, as I have endeavoured to set out in this judgment, that she placed considerable weight on the wife's contribution both past, present and future.'

[27]   The judge's reasons for concluding that the district judge had fallen into error of principle are explained succinctly in the following three paragraphs of the judgment:

> '[53]   The effect of the order of £250,000 pa by way of periodical payments for the wife is to give her a sum of money which is arithmetically way, way above her needs. I repeat: her budget of £128,000 pa is not a historical one, but is designed, and has been carefully thought out, for current and future needs. Her needs, of course, are not the be all and end all of her application, for, if they were, that would fly in the face of s 25. The court must apply all the criteria, giving such weight to each factor as the court determines is appropriate in the particular circumstances of the case. However, the fact is that the wife has been awarded a sum so much over her needs that there are only two possible results. Either she spends the difference or she saves the difference. If she saves it, as the thrust of her case suggests she will and she wants to, she is thereby in fact accumulating capital.
>
> [54]   Miss Stone, in her excellent submissions to me, specifically conceded that the size of the award gives the wife the opportunity to save if she so wishes. Thus the reality, in my judgment, is that the husband will be paying over to the wife from his resources monies which are likely to be directed into financial vehicles for the accumulation of capital. In my judgment, Mr Posnansky has made good his submission that the effect of the order is to subvert the principle set out in many cases that an award of capital is made once and once only, and that the purpose of periodical payments is maintenance.
>
> [55]   It is my judgment, with all due respects to the district judge, that, having given the wife an award from which she is likely to be able to save large sums of money and thereby accumulate capital, it is no answer to say, as she did, that it is a matter for the wife whether she chooses to make provision for pension and other matters.'

[28]   In exercising his discretion afresh Bennett J substituted the figure of £180,000 pa for the district judge's figure of £250,000 pa. His reasons are set out in the following five paragraphs of his judgment which I must cite in full:

> '[58]   I wholly reject Mr Posnansky's submission that the fair award for the wife is £100,000 pa. To suggest that the wife in all the circumstances of this case should walk away with £100,000 pa when set against the husband's net income of £753,000 pa is, in

my judgment, thoroughly mean and would be unfair. It goes nowhere near reflecting the s 25 factors as, I repeat, evaluated by the district judge.

[59]   At the end of the marriage the husband's income was rising and rising pretty rapidly. The standard of living was increasing. The husband's income and his standard of living has resulted from what the district judge described at p 20 in her judgment as a result of the "spadework". The wife's contribution is continuing and will continue in the future vis-à-vis the children, something which, following a divorce, is a contribution that is sometimes overlooked or even played down. The district judge did neither and properly, in my judgment, gave it appropriate weight.

[60]   What figure should then be substituted for £250,000? The quantification of periodical payments is more an art that a science. The parameters of s 25 are so wide that it might be said that it is almost impossible to be "scientific". In my judgment, I would be doing justice to both parties if I award the wife £180,000 pa by way of periodical payments.

[61]   The husband may say that still exceeds her budget by a significant amount and thereby I am falling into the same error as did the district judge. I agree that the figure I propose to order does exceed her budget and significantly. But if I am right to reject the husband's case, then I ask the rhetorical question: how else are all the s 25 factors, as evaluated by the district judge, to be given full weight other than by making the kind of award that I propose? The more that an award is refined down closer and closer to £100,000, the greater would be the criticism that I would be devaluing the s 25 criteria (other than the wife's needs) as evaluated by the district judge.

[62]   I am sure the parties will understand that no family judge in exercising this jurisdiction can achieve perfection given the width of s 25. He or she can only do his best to get as near to it as possible in the circumstances of any particular case.'

[29]   Bennett J also removed the order for the index linking of the periodical payments for the wife and the children imposed by the district judge. That point of detail has not been challenged on this appeal.

[30]   It is important to bear in mind that the judge exercised powers confined by the decision of this court in *Cordle v Cordle* [2001] EWCA Civ 1791, [2002] 1 WLR 1441, [2002] 1 FLR 207. That subsequently found expression in an amendment to r 8.1(3) of the Family Proceedings Rules 1991 which now provides that on an appeal from a district judge of an order made on an application for ancillary relief:

'The appeal should be limited to a review of the decision or order of the district judge.'

[31]   Accordingly once Bennett J concluded that the award was not manifestly excessive and that the judge's findings of fact were not open to criticism, only if he was satisfied that the district judge had erred in law was he entitled to substitute his figure for hers.

[32]   The error identified by Bennett J is defined in para [54] of his judgment, cited above. The district judge had subverted 'the principle set out in many cases that an award of capital is made once and once only, and that the purpose of periodical payments is maintenance'. Mr Singleton, in arguing the appeal, essentially submits that there is no such principle. Mr Posnansky submits that the principle is elementary and recognised by all ancillary relief lawyers. I will return to this essential question in due course.

Parlour v Parlour

The facts

[33]   The issue in this appeal can be relatively briefly stated. Again the division of capital between the parties had been agreed at the financial dispute resolution (FDR) appointment. The only issue that went to trial was the quantum of the wife's periodical payments order. That issue was directed to be tried by a judge of the Division and accordingly, in giving judgment on 23 January 2004, Bennett J was exercising his own discretion rather than reviewing the prior discretion of a district judge. The case had much in common with the case of *McFarlane v McFarlane* and by the date of the hearing on 12 January both Mr Mostyn, for the wife, and Mr Francis, for the husband, were armed with Bennett J's previous judgment. Since the point at issue could not be distinguished, Mr Mostyn had the difficult task of attempting to persuade Bennett J to reconsider and reject his previous statement of principle. Of course he failed, and he then applied to this court for permission to appeal and for the appeal to be heard together with the pending appeal in *McFarlane v McFarlane*.

[34]   The case before Bennett J took 4 days and a number of factual issues were contested. However the judge's findings on those issues (such as whether the husband was a gambler and whether he had conspired to conceal one of his streams of income) are of no relevance to the issue of principle raised by this appeal. In the circumstances the relevant facts can be briefly summarised.

[35]   The parties met in February 1990 when the wife was a 20-year-old employed by a local optician. The husband, 3 years her junior, was an apprentice footballer, having signed a contract with Arsenal Football Club in July 1989. Their relationship developed swiftly and, although they did not cohabit, the wife generally slept with the husband at his parents' home several nights a week. The husband progressed with Arsenal to become a full-time professional in March 1991 and to reach the first team in January 1992. At the end of 1994 the wife gave up her employment with the husband's encouragement and thereafter became financially dependent upon him. They had announced their engagement earlier in the year. However they did not cohabit until May 1995 when they moved into their first home. Their first child was born in October 1995. In October 1997 their second child was born and they upgraded into their final matrimonial home. The marriage was not in fact celebrated until June 1998. In May 1999 their third child was born. In November 2001 the husband left the home. He has since found another partner with whom he has a one-year-old child.

[36]   Under the agreement reached at the FDR hearing the wife took the matrimonial home, a property of modest value in Norfolk, and a lump sum of £250,000. Her share represented about 37% of the available capital assets. The affluence all results from the husband's success at Arsenal. On 16 August 2001 he signed his current contract which expires on 30 June 2005. His gross earnings at Arsenal for the season 2001/2002 amounted to just over £1.5m. The forensic accountant called by Mr Mostyn estimated the husband to have earned an average of almost £1.2m net for the 3 years ending 2004/2005. The judge accepted Mr Mostyn's submission that the husband will continue to receive a net income of the order of £1.2m pa until the expiry of his current contract. The scale of the husband's net income is explained by the fact that such bonuses as he receives in addition to his salary are made available to him through sophisticated and tax-efficient channels.

The findings of Bennett J

[37]   I turn now to the judge's findings on the s 25(2) criteria. In para [26] Bennett J dealt with the age of each party and duration of marriage. His finding comes in the last sentence of para [26]:

'Accordingly although the marriage only lasted some 3½ years it would not be just, in my judgment, to ignore the fact that their relationship endured for 7 or slightly more years.'

[38]   Bennett J's assessment of the standard of living during the relationship was as follows:

'I am satisfied that compared to the lifestyles of other footballers in the same bracket as the husband, the wife and husband in this case did lead a comfortable but not an extravagant way of life.'

[39]   Of the wife's contribution he said at para [15]:

'She is a full-time mother of three children aged 8, 6 and 4. I am satisfied that she bore the brunt of bringing the children up whilst the parties cohabited. Furthermore it is obvious that she will have to bear the burden of bringing them up during their childhood. Thus by the time the youngest child is 16 the wife will have had a further 12 years of caring for the children. If the youngest remains at home until she is 18 then the period would be 14 years. That I recognise at once is, together with her past caring for the children, an enormous contribution. I am satisfied too that she has no earning capacity. She told me in evidence that she made no sacrifices in giving up her work with the opticians in 1994 nor has she been disadvantaged in staying at home. She accepted that she had not given up any career. There is no dispute, as I understand it, that the wife was a marvellous mother and ran the household efficiently and looked after the children and the husband to the very best of her considerable ability.'

[40]   In his assessment of the husband's contribution Bennett J gave further credit to the wife, as appears from the following paragraphs:

'As to the husband's contribution he was and is a very talented footballer. That sprang from his natural talent, being a member of the Arsenal Football Club, and having the good fortune to be coached by Arsène Wenger, a top-class coach. So, strictly speaking, the financial wealth of the family was created by the husband. However, in my judgment, there is a very significant factor in the success of the husband in which the wife played a vital role. The wife has suggested in her evidence that the husband was and is a drinker. From what I have read in the papers and been told by the husband and wife in evidence, I am satisfied that the husband was in an environment where, before the advent of Arsène Wenger in 1996, there was very considerable drinking amongst certain players in the Arsenal Football Club. In the early days I am satisfied that the husband did participate in some of those drinking sessions. However the wife realised that that was the way to ruin and unhappiness and I am satisfied that in about the mid-1990s or slightly later she took a grip on the situation and encouraged and persuaded her husband to move away from that style of living. That rather bland description of what she did probably understates her contribution in this respect. In the mid-1990s the husband gave interviews to the press in which he publicly praised the wife for all that she did to bring him back from the brink.

    Thus the wife did make a contribution to the husband's success as a footballer for Arsenal and also for England (in the late 1990s and in 2000 the husband played for England and was capped 10 times).'

[41]   Bennett J's assessment of the income, earning capacity, property and other financial resources which each of the parties has or is likely to have in the foreseeable future is crucial. I, therefore, set out para [32] of his judgment in full:

'The wife has no income or if she can invest what she has not spent of the lump sum, such income would, in the circumstances of this case, be insignificant. I am satisfied, as I have already said, that she has no earning capacity now or in the foreseeable future. Her life is bound up with her children and will be for some considerable time in the future.

I have already set out [the husband's] income and other financial resources. He is secure in a very large income until June 2005. What will happen thereafter is unknown. The husband told me in evidence, which I accept, that after a player reaches the age of 31 and his contract expires, he will not be given a contract which lasts for more than a year but it may be renewed for a year at a time. In June 2005 the husband will be 32 years old. So, if Arsenal retain his services, he will be given a year's contract, renewable thereafter. The husband has no plans for his future thereafter. However, it may be that any new contract might not contain such high remunerations, and/or discretionary payments under EBTs [employee benefit trusts] may decline or possibly cease. After he has ceased to be a professional footballer – at least with Arsenal – it is likely that his income will decline very considerably.'

[42]   Of financial needs, obligations and responsibilities which each of the parties has or is likely to have in the foreseeable future, the judge recorded that the wife's major responsibility now and in the foreseeable future was to look after her children and herself. Having considered the rival submissions as to her requisite budget he concluded:

'However, I am satisfied, looking at needs alone, generously construed, the figure of £180,000 pa for the wife and the three children is substantially too high. If I were to allow £30,000 for all of the three children and £120,000 for the wife, in my judgment that would be fair and just.'

[43]   Bennett J's corresponding finding in relation to the husband is to be found in para [37] of his judgment:

'So far as the obligations and responsibilities of the husband are concerned he now has two families to maintain. However, in fairness to him, he has not suggested that the wife and the children should be in any way disadvantaged by the fact that he has to maintain his partner and their child. In any event I am satisfied that now and for the foreseeable future there will be more than adequate income to properly maintain his partner and child without in any way affecting his primary obligation and responsibility to the wife and the children.'

[44]   For completion Bennett J recorded that none of the other s 25(2) criteria was relevant to his decision.

Bennett J's conclusions

[45]   Bennett J then carefully reviewed Mr Mostyn's extensive submissions, designed to persuade him that his judgment in *McFarlane v McFarlane* was erroneous, and Mr Francis's submissions in response. He succinctly stated his conclusions on counsel's submissions in eight numbered paragraphs:

'(1)   In exercising the powers under s 23(1)(a) and (d) of the 1973 Act the court must have regard to all the circumstances of the case, first consideration given to the welfare of the children.

(2)   The court must, in particular, have regard to the matters set out in s 25(2).

(3)   In carrying out that exercise, the court is entitled to place such importance and weight on each matter in s 25(2)(a) as it thinks appropriate in the circumstances of the case (see *White v White* [2001] 1 AC 596, [2000] 2 FLR 981).

(4)	However, "needs" or "reasonable requirements" is not a determinative or limiting factor in cases where the payor has an ability to pay more than the payee's needs (see *Cornick v Cornick (No 2)* [1995] 2 FLR 490, *White v White*, and *Cornick v Cornick (No 3)* [2001] 2 FLR 1240).

(5)	Thus the objective implicit in the exercise of the court's discretion under s 25 is to achieve a fair outcome in the financial arrangements between the parties (see *White v White*).

(6)	In seeking to achieve a fair outcome there is no place for discrimination between the spouses and their respective roles. There should be no bias in favour of the money-earner and against the home-maker and child-carer (see *White v White*).

(7)	The English statutory code allows of only one allocation of capital between spouses. Where, as in this case, capital claims are compromised and receive the court's approval by way of order, they cannot be revisited or reissued (see *Pearce v Pearce* [2003] EWCA Civ 1054, [2003] 2 FLR 1144 and the House of Lords and Privy Council cases referred to therein at para [17]).

(8)	Where there has been or is to be capital provision made in favour of a spouse then, generally speaking, a subsequent or concurrent award of periodical payments ought to be for that spouse's maintenance, and ought not to be used to further distribute monies to the payee so as to give her (or him) savings, ie capital. But such a factor must yield to a greater or lesser extent to the particular circumstances of the case if fairness so dictates. Thus, with that qualification, I broadly accept the thrust of Mr Francis's submissions.'

[46]	Applying those principles to his earlier findings these then were his reasons for awarding the wife and children periodical payments in the global sum of £250,000, to be split between the wife and the children by the court in default of agreement between the parties:

'In my judgment, to confine in this instant case an award of periodical payments for the wife to a ceiling of "needs" or "reasonable requirements" where the husband has the ability to pay more, indeed far more, than the wife's needs would be a faulty exercise of the court's discretion. For that could be to determine her application by reference to one only of the matters in s 25(2) and ignore the other matters. I accept that the wife's contribution (as I have found it to be) made a significant difference to the success of the husband. She was part of the circumstances that persuaded the husband to drop the laddish culture and, as she put it, "grow up". Her contributions to the home, and the children, both now and in the future must not be underestimated, overlooked, or played down.

[107] The husband's open offer of periodical payments is equivalent to about 10% of his net income. To suggest that in the circumstances of this case the wife should walk away with £120,000 (for her and the children) when set against the husband's net income of about £1.2m is thoroughly mean and would be unfair. However, to award her £444,000 because that represents 37.5% of his net income which is the same percentage of the capital she received, would be an unprincipled and unfair award on the facts of this case. She would in one year receive sufficient monies, which, after making provision for her and the children's needs, would leave her with a sum equivalent to her present lump sum or more. If the award were backdated to March 2003 and were to run to June 2005, a period of 2 years and 3 months, she would effectively have acquired further capital to the tune of £500,000 and more. That, in my judgment, could be seen to be blowing a large hole through the middle of *Pearce v Pearce* [2003] EWCA Civ 1054, [2003] 2 FLR 1144 and in the instant case would be quite unwarranted.

[108] Thus, in my judgment, the court must seek a way that does justice to the parties and which does not, so far as is possible, impose a glass ceiling on the one hand but which does not hand out capital on the other. It surely must be implicit in the concept of

periodical payments when placed next to the concepts of lump sum and property adjustments that where there has been a capital adjustment between spouses in accordance with *White v White* [2001] 1 AC 596, [2000] 2 FLR 981, as it was in the instant case, the function of periodical payments should not then or at some later date be seen to further the claimant spouse's ability to mine the paying spouse's income for further capital. I see the force in Mr Mostyn's submissions that my decision in *M v M* contains irreconcilable tensions and contradictions. Indeed the decision that I will make in the instant case may be subject to the same criticism. But as I endeavoured to explain in *M v M*, the quantification of periodical payments is more of an art than a science, given the width of the discretion expressly given to the court by Parliament.'

Counsel's submissions on the appeals

[47]   The skeleton arguments prepared for the appeals demonstrate a great deal of industry, erudition and originality. They address the very general question: what should be the principles governing an award of periodical payments during joint lives or until remarriage in any case where the net income of the payer significantly exceeds what both parties need in order to meet their outgoings at the standard of living which the court has found to be appropriate? Mr Singleton has advanced the arguments unsuccessfully advanced by Miss Stone in the court below. He has reviewed the development of the statute law over the past 150 years and he has analysed the manner in which the judges have interpreted and applied those provisions, particularly in recent years. He submits that academic commentators and judgments in the USA support his conclusions.

[48]   Mr Mostyn has repeated the submissions that he advanced unsuccessfully in the court below. He advances this cogent criticism of Bennett J's judgment: in *McFarlane v McFarlane* were the principle asserted by Bennett J sound, then, as he himself partially recognised, his order breached it, albeit to a lesser extent than that of the district judge. What was the rationalisation for the uplift of over £50,000 that Bennett J allowed the wife above her annual need for expenditure? If there were no need that could be categorised as 'income' then the surplusage has to be categorised as capital or as income available for the acquisition of capital. He also relies upon the trend of the authorities in Canada, Australia and New Zealand, which he submits demonstrate a global shift which Bennett J dismissed out of hand. Mr Mostyn and Mr Singleton each adopted the submissions of the other in areas which, by sensible agreement, only one had tackled.

[49]   Mr Singleton and Mr Mostyn contend for models that emphasise entitlement based on past contribution or continuing compensation for a sacrificed career or for the loss of benefits which the payee would have enjoyed but for the breakdown of the marriage. That last consideration they submit has statutory recognition in s 25(2)(h).

[50]   Mr Posnansky repeated the submissions which succeeded before Bennett J. Although criticising Bennett J's award to Mrs McFarlane above Bennett J's generous assessment of her needs, he did not at any stage seek to cross-appeal.

[51]   Equally Mr Francis repeated the submissions accepted by Bennett J at the trial. In advocating his application for permission to cross-appeal he made it plain that he was no longer contending for orders totalling £120,000 pa and would accept the judge's quantification of the needs of the wife and children at £150,000 pa.

[52]   Mr Posnansky and Mr Francis assert that the court's simple task is to order such proportion of the income as will enable the carer to discharge the outgoings on the single-parent family home and the other anticipated family expenses.

Conclusions

The principle that governed the judgments of Bennett J

[53]   In a narrow sense Bennett J's principle that an award of capital can be made once and once only is undoubtedly correct. Capital orders were described as 'once-for-all orders' by Lord Diplock in the case of *de Lasala (Ernest Ferdinand Perez) v de Lasala (Hannelore)* [1980] AC 546, (1979) FLR Rep 223. Bennett J quite rightly pointed out that I had emphasised the principle in my judgment in the recent case of *Pearce v Pearce* [2003] EWCA Civ 1054, [2004] 1 WLR 68, [2003] 2 FLR 1144. However since the decision in *de Lasala (Ernest Ferdinand Perez) v de Lasala (Hannelore)* we have seen the amendments to the Matrimonial Causes Act 1973 that introduced s 25A and ss 31(7)(A)–(F). The effect of those amendments, in cases where capital claims have already been dismissed, is first to impose upon the court a duty to terminate the only continuing financial relationship as soon as that can be achieved without undue financial hardship; and secondly to empower the court to compensate the payee for the discharge of the periodical payments order with additional capital. So the old principle has to be qualified thus: the original once-for-all capital division that resulted in the dismissal of capital claims may be supplemented by a later transfer of capital, agreed or judged to be the fair consideration for the dismissal of the surviving claim to periodical payments. So much is implicit in the decision in *Pearce v Pearce* and would no doubt have been acknowledged by Bennett J if the cases had not been argued before him primarily as claims for indefinite and continuing periodical payments.

[54]   For reasons which I will develop, in my judgment neither case should have been approached on that basis. In both cases a clean break had been partially achieved and a proper concentration on s 25A both by the parties and by the court would have provided a short answer to the issue of principle so extensively debated.

[55]   The present appeals are far removed from any norm. In one case the single net income probably exceeds the expenditure of the two households (at a very high standard but excluding housing costs for the husband) by about £550,000 pa. In the other, the single net income probably exceeds the expenditure of the two households by about £900,000 pa. It is only the huge excess over need that creates the debate as what are the principles governing the quantification of the payee's award. Only that excess allows the advancement of the appellants' ambitious models. Only that excess renders the respondents' contrary propositions unconvincing.

[56]   There is another feature of the present appeals that must be emphasised. In both cases the past surplus which had been converted into capital assets was divided by agreement. In the one case the division was equal, in the other the earner took about 60%. It was the scale of the contemplated future surplus that prevented the complete agreement, namely the clean break dismissing all claims. In both cases the agreement was seen, or should have been seen, as but the first stage in the progress to clean break. The future surplus could provide the consideration for the dismissal of the wife's outstanding claims. How many years of garnering of surplus would be necessary could not be calculated but only estimated. All depended on the surplus in each of the future years.

Section 25A of the Matrimonial Causes Act 1973

[57]   Of the amendments achieved by the Matrimonial and Family Proceedings Act 1984 the insertion of s 25A far outweighs in importance the deletion of the cosmetic minimal loss objective. Section 25A provides:

'Exercise of court's powers in favour of party to marriage on decree of divorce or nullity of marriage

(1)   Where on or after the grant of a decree of divorce or nullity of marriage the court decides to exercise its powers under section 23(1)(a), (b) or (c), 24, 24A or 24B above in favour of a party to the marriage, it shall be the duty of the court to consider whether it would be appropriate so to exercise those powers that the financial obligations of each party towards the other will be terminated as soon after the grant of the decree as the court considers just and reasonable.

(2)   Where the court decides in such a case to make a periodical payments or secured periodical payments order in favour of a party to the marriage, the court shall in particular consider whether it would be appropriate to require those payments to be made or secured only for such term as would in the opinion of the court be sufficient to enable the party in whose favour the order is made to adjust without undue hardship to the termination of his or her financial dependence on the other party.

(3)   Where on or after the grant of a decree of divorce or nullity of marriage an application is made by a party to the marriage for a periodical payments or secured periodical payments order in his or her favour, then, if the court considers that no continuing obligation should be imposed on either party to make or secure periodical payments in favour of the other, the court may dismiss the application with a direction that the applicant shall not be entitled to make any future application in relation to that marriage for an order under section 23(1)(a) or (b) above.'

[58]   Its origins can be traced to the case of *Minton v Minton* [1979] AC 593, (1978) FLR Rep 461 where Lord Scarman said in his speech at 608F and 471 respectively:

'There are two principles which inform the modern legislation. One is the public interest that spouses, to the extent that their means permit, should provide for themselves and their children. But the other – of equal importance – is the principle of "the clean break". The law now encourages spouses to avoid bitterness after family breakdown and to settle their money and property problems. An object of the modern law is to encourage each to put the past behind them and to begin a new life which is not overshadowed by the relationship which has broken down.'

[59]   The Law Commission in its 1981 report (Law Com No 112) advocated three policy objectives for the reform of the Matrimonial Causes Act 1973 as follows:

–   priority for the needs of the children;

–   greater weight to be given to the divorced wife's earning capacity and to the desirability of both parties becoming self-sufficient; and

–   imposing a 'clean break' where practicable and appropriate.

[60]   In relation to the second objective there are in paras 26 and 27 the following passages:

'There was, however, a wide-spread feeling amongst those who commented on the Discussion Paper that greater weight should be given to the importance of each party doing everything possible to become self-sufficient, so far as this is consistent with the interests of the children; and we believe that the statutory provisions should contain a positive assertion of this principle.

The court has, under the existing law, power to make orders for a limited term, and this power is sometimes exercised when it is felt that a spouse (usually the wife) needs some time to readjust to her new situation but could not or should not expect to rely on continuing support from her husband. We think that it would be desirable to require the courts specifically to consider whether an order for a limited term would not be appropriate in all the circumstances of the case, given the increased weight which we believe should be attached to the desirability of the parties becoming self-sufficient.'

[61]   In relation to imposing a clean break the report recommended in para 28:

'Nevertheless, the response to the Discussion Paper showed strong support for the view (with which we agree) that such finality should be achieved wherever possible, as for example where there is a childless marriage of comparatively short duration between a husband and a wife who has income, or an earning capacity, or in cases of a longer marriage, where there is an adequate measure of capital available for division.'

[62]   Then there is this conclusion in para 30:

'The response to the Discussion Paper indicated wide support for the view that the court should be more clearly directed to the desirability of promoting a severance of financial obligations between the parties at the time of divorce; and to give greater weight to the view that in the appropriate case any periodical financial provision ordered in favour of one spouse (usually the wife) for her own benefit – as distinct from periodical payments made to her to enable her to care for the children – should be primarily directed to secure wherever possible a smooth transition from marriage to the status of independence. We believe that this general objective should be embodied in the legislation.'

[63]   In my judgment the underlying policy of the legislature in inserting s 25A into the statutory scheme is not open to doubt.

[64]   The court's duty to seek a clean break was replicated in s 31 of the Matrimonial Causes Act 1973 to make plain that it applied not only at the stage of making the financial provision orders but equally at any later stage when the court considered its variation.

[65]   The court's powers to bring about the clean break objective that had not appeared practicable at the first stage were significantly strengthened by the addition to s 31 of subss (7A)–(7F) by the Family Law Act 1996 with effect from 1 November 1998. The additional powers were set out and considered in the case of *Pearce v Pearce* [2003] EWCA Civ 1054, [2004] 1 WLR 68, [2003] 2 FLR 1144 and it is unnecessary to repeat that review here.

[66]   In any case in which, despite a substantial capital base available for division, clean break is not presently practicable, the court has a statutory duty to consider the future possibility. That duty assumes particular prominence in cases where there is a certain and substantial surplus of future income over future needs. If, as in one of the present appeals, the surplus will be predictably short-lived, the first option for consideration should be the planned progress to clean break by means of a substantial term order open to a later application for extension. The obligation on the parties to achieve financial independence is mutual. The earner must give proper priority to making payments on account out of the surplus income. The payee must invest the surplus sensibly, or risk that her failure so to do might count against her on an application for discharge under s 31(7A) and (7B). Given the mutuality of the obligation, the opportunity and responsibility to invest should, in my judgment, be shared. It strikes me as discriminatory, and, therefore, wrong in principle, for the earner to have sole control of the surplus through the years of accumulation. The preferred mechanism by which the surplus is to be divided annually must be periodical payments. They are variable, which lump sum orders are not. They can, therefore, reflect fluctuations in the payer's income. They are determined by the court in the event of dispute. They terminate on the remarriage of the recipient. The practicality of such an order will depend upon many factors. Essentially the

completion of the process must be foreseen within a relatively short span. A term of 5 years which these cases illustrate may be towards the limit of the foreseeable.

[67]   I recognise the validity of Mr Posnansky's argument that because orders for periodical payments terminate on the death or remarriage of the payee the payer's future liability is to that extent contingent. Thus it can be said to be unjust to the payer to order the immediate sharing of surplus on account of a liability which may never materialise. That argument, however, is of little force where the sharing of the surplus is effected by a periodical payments order and where the duration of the scheme for sharing surplus income on account of the capitalisation of a periodical payment claims is relatively short term. Furthermore there is an element of speculation involved in any scheme for the capitalisation of periodical payments whether undertaken at the time of divorce or on a subsequent application for variation by discharge.

Outcome in McFarlane v McFarlane

[68]   How then do these generalisations apply to the facts of these appeals? In my judgment the resolution of the contest in *McFarlane v McFarlane* was flawed by a failure to give sufficient weight to the duties created by s 25A. That is perhaps the result of the way the wife's case was advanced. In her Form E the wife sought 'to achieve a clean break in retirement' and to that end applied for annual instalment lump sums of £64,000 pa until the year 2017 (a span of 15 years).

[69]   Three months later that part of her case was abandoned in correspondence on the ground that the scheme presented too many potential complications to be viable. At the hearing before the district judge, 5 months later, what was sought in Miss Stone's skeleton was 'as part of her periodical payments a sum which she too can invest towards her old age'.

[70]   It is of course easy to criticise with the advantage of hindsight, but the focus should have been on termination and not on post-retirement provision. The key was the husband's capacity to borrow in a tax-efficient way on the security of his home. Although he had borrowed very substantially to acquire an excessively expensive home, his proposal was to discharge the mortgage over 5 years by annual instalments of £347,500. Plainly on completion of that exercise he could remortgage his interest to finance the clean break. Over the intervening years he could make what would effectively be payments on account. The alternative presentation of a joint lives order adopted by both husband and wife diverted the court's attention from the opportunity to achieve a clean break years before either party approached retirement. Were this an appeal from a first exercise of judicial discretion I would set aside the judgment below and in the exercise of this court's discretion substitute an order for periodical payments at an increased annual rate for an extendable term of 5 years. Within the life of the order either side would be free to apply for variation dependent on the fluctuation of the husband's earnings. After 5 years the court could reassess the prospects of clean break in the light of:

(i)   The husband's capacity to remortgage.

(ii)   The extent to which the wife had built up a capital reserve from the surplus of income over expenditure in the intervening years.

(iii) The revival of the wife's earning capacity, the youngest child having reached secondary school age.

[71]   However this is a second appeal in which we must review the error of principle in the district judge's judgment identified by Bennett J. Accordingly there

may be no basis for a fresh exercise of discretion. The discretion exercised by the district judge, if held to be without error of principle, must be restored.

[72]   Additionally I would emphasise that the focus on achieving independence without financial hardship at the earliest practicable date is inconsistent with the liberty which the district judge attached to the wife's joint lives order. At p 12 of her judgment she said:

'... How the parties choose to spend their available income is a matter for them.'

Later she said:

'It is a matter for her whether she chooses to make pension provision ... and it is a matter for her whether she takes out insurance to protect her and the children's position in the event that the husband dies or is ill and unable to work.'

[73]   In my judgment the wife's responsibility to contribute to the financing of the clean break requires her to put the surplus periodical payments above needs (on the district judge's figures £122,000 pa) to achieving financial self-sufficiency. The evidence advanced was that the premium on a policy to secure her against the husband's death or disability would be £40,000 pa. Given the reduction of the years of risk, it would not seem to me reasonable for the wife to spend surplus on insurance. The greater priority is to achieve financial independence.

[74]   It follows from the conclusions which I have already expressed that I am not persuaded that the district judge did fall into error of principle in making the order that she did. I acknowledge that her reasoning created the opportunity for the argument successfully advanced by Mr Posnansky before Bennett J but it is implicit in her reasoning that she recognised the wife's entitlement to a fair share of the husband's surplus income, albeit that she did not correctly identify the overriding purpose to which it had to be put.

Outcome in Parlour v Parlour

[75]   In the case of *Parlour v Parlour* the imperative to achieve finality is even stronger. The husband's income is substantially greater but the graph is likely to plummet within 4 or 5 years, in contrast to Mr McFarlane's prospect of steady ascent until retirement.

[76]   Unfortunately the argument at the trial was directed as to the quantum of the joint lives order. The judge was not urged to focus on terminating the wife's financial dependency and it is, therefore, entirely understandable that he approached the case as he did. However in fairness to Mr Mostyn, in his final written submissions he concluded with these paragraphs:

'32   The court should have little difficulty in concluding that in about 4 years' time H will enter his twilight years and that there is a real risk that he will not have husbanded his income responsibly so as to make proper long-term support for his family.

33   The court should also conclude that the prognosis of net income set out by JW in her second report is reasonable (about £1.2m net pa until June 2003).

34   Thus the court should conclude that to award W £444,000 from March 2003 to June 2004 from this income, which derives in large measure from a contract signed during the marriage, is wholly fair. It is a reasonable sharing of income. If it enables W to make savings then that is right and proper, on the facts of this case.

35   W will accept in any future capitalisation that she should bring into account such sum of periodical payments that she is awarded in excess of her aliment. The judgment can make this explicit.'

[77]   Mr Francis in his submissions was at pains to say that his client was approaching the end of his career at its present exalted height; he was prone to injury; his contract might not be renewed at its conclusion when he will be 32 years of age. These considerations only underline the obvious need for a substantial proportion of the income in the present fat years to be stored up against the future famine. Again I conclude that it would be wrong in principle to leave the responsibility and opportunity to the husband alone. The wife's and the children's needs were put at £150,000 by the judge. To award her the global figure of £444,000 pa sought by Mr Mostyn allows her and obliges her to lay-up £294,000 pa as a reserve against the discharge of her periodical payments order. I would in this case order a 4-year extendable term. Hopefully a clean break will be achievable then on an assessment of the husband's earning capacity at 35 years of age and the wife's independent fortune derived from the original capital settlement augmented by the substantial annual surplus built into her periodical payments order in the interim.

Reciprocal assessment of needs

[78]   It is obvious that in cases such as the present the calculation of the amount of surplus income cannot be achieved without first establishing what both the payer and the payee need in order to meet their projected expenditure. In preparation for the trials below both applicants advanced budgets which were generously cast and which at trial were subjected to rigorous cross-examination. In both cases the trial judge then assessed the applicant's needs, endorsing the majority of the total sought.

[79]   In both cases the husbands failed to complete the relevant section of the Form E and in one case the husband refused subsequent requests for information.

[80]   Mr Posnansky submits that *Campbell v Campbell* [1998] 1 FLR 828 justified that refusal. That is certainly not the effect of the decision. The relevant observation provoked by the facts of the case appears at 833G where I said:

'It has never been the custom in ancillary relief litigation to look with scrupulous care at the budget items of the prospective payer. Of course, it is incumbent on the judge to cross-check to ensure that the adjudication that meets the applicant's needs is an adjudication which the respondent can afford. But that essential task the judge specifically performed, as is plain from the passage which I have already cited.'

[81]   I do not resile from that. It is the converse of passages in other authorities that deplore excessive investigation of the payee's budget.

[82]   The cavalier disregard of the obligation to complete that section implies precisely the discriminatory vice identified by the House of Lords in *White v White* [2001] 1 AC 596, [2000] 2 FLR 981 in condemning the quantification of a wife's capital share in a big-money case solely by reference to her reasonable requirements. More fundamental is the implicit rejection of the application of s 25(2)(b):

'... The financial needs ... which each of the parties to the marriage has or is likely to have in the foreseeable future.'

[83]   We were told by the Bar that a practice has grown up for substantial earners to decline any statement of their needs on the grounds that they can afford any order that the court is likely to make. These appeals must put an end to that practice.

The wider issues

[84]　　The disposal of the present appeals which I propose is achieved by giving what I believe to be the proper emphasis to s 25A and the amendments to s 31(7) introduced by the Family Law Act 1996. That route circumvents the arguments developed both before Bennett J and in the written skeletons submitted on these appeals. That wider presentation examines:

(a)　the evolution of the statutory powers between 1857 and 1970;

(b)　the definition of periodical payments;

(c)　the principles governing the assessment of periodical payments;

(d)　the guidance to be derived from judgments and academic analysis in other jurisdictions.

[85]　　I recognise that these areas are of some relevance to the present appeals and are likely to be of greater relevance to a number of other cases, either pending or certain to arise, in which s 25A is, for one reason or another, not prospectively engaged. A relatively benign tax regime has now been in force for many years and there is ample evidence of an increasing band of very high earners who may not possess a matching capital base. Accordingly I will express my opinion on each of the above topics briefly, in the context of cases in which the income of the party who earns is significantly greater than the combined outgoings of himself and the payee.

[86]　　It is worth re-emphasising that these are exceptional cases. In the majority of cases the income of the earner is insufficient to cover the outgoings of two households. In many others the single income is sufficient only to provide for both households at a standard below that which the family enjoyed before separation. In many others the income will provide for both amply. In many more it will provide for both and a measure of luxury which each contends is not disproportionate to the standard enjoyed before separation. In all the above instances the respondents are correct in their submission that the court's discretionary judgment will be dominated by an assessment of needs or, for the more affluent families, reasonable requirements.

The evolution of the statutory powers and the definition of periodical payments

[87]　　The statutory power to order periodic sums by way of maintenance first appeared in the Matrimonial Causes Act 1866. At that date a wife was incapable of property ownership, the corollary being that her husband was ordinarily liable for her debts, since she contracted as his agent of necessity. Section 1 of the Matrimonial Causes Act 1866 reads:

'In every such case it shall be lawful for the court to make an order on the husband for payment to the wife during their joint lives of such monthly or weekly sums for her maintenance and support as the court may think reasonable.'

[88]　　There can be no doubt that such payments were for the wife's maintenance, that is to say for her necessities, her needs, her aliment. The Married Women's Property Act 1882, which allowed the wife the power to own property independently, did not alter this construction. Nor did the statutory language vary greatly through succeeding reforms. The relevant section of the Matrimonial Causes Act 1965 still provided:

'An order requiring the husband to pay to the wife during their joint lives such monthly or weekly sum for her maintenance as the court thinks reasonable.'

[89]   There is no doubt, in my judgment, that to that date the court's power did not extend beyond ordering maintenance payments to meet the wife's needs.

[90]   The Matrimonial Proceedings and Property Act 1970 was a major reforming statute heralded by the 1969 Law Commission Report. The following paragraphs are of some relevance:

  (i)   Paragraph 17(a) makes plain that the Law Commission advocated new terminology rather than new powers. Financial provision was the generic term for periodical and lump sum payments.

  (ii)   Financial provision was contrasted with provision by property adjustments.

  (iii) Whilst the primary objective of financial provision orders was 'to provide income for the maintenance of spouses' the introduction of the lump sum order had 'blurred the line between provision from income and provision by way of adjustments to capital': see para 49 of the report.

[91]   Thus I find nothing in the report that suggests the limited role for periodical payments for which the respondents have contended.

[92]   Furthermore the statutory language itself clearly demonstrates the limitations of the respondents' submissions. The power to order periodical payments is to be found in s 23 of the Matrimonial Causes Act 1973. In awarding periodical payments the court has to have regard to the s 25(2) criteria in that Act, amongst which the recipient's needs are only one of a multi-factored checklist.

[93]   Furthermore the abolition of the agency of necessity by the Matrimonial Proceedings and Property Act 1970 supports the view that 'maintenance' was not being used by Parliament in the sense given to it when a wife could take advantage of the agency of necessity.

[94]   The term 'maintenance' survives only in s 22 and s 27 of the Matrimonial Causes Act 1973. In those contexts the term might be thought to have the traditional meaning. However, the judges have rejected that approach.

[95]   The argument that the court's power under s 22 to order maintenance pending suit was confined to sums necessary for the recipient's daily support was considered by Charles J in the case of *G v G (Maintenance Pending Suit: Costs)* [2002] EWHC 306 (Fam), [2003] 2 FLR 71. In para [48] of his judgment Charles J said that:

  'I do not accept that argument for the following reasons:

   (1)   The purpose of the 1970 Act was to change statutory provisions that were outdated and inadequate and to make a new start.

   (2)   Although the word "maintenance" was used in both ss 1 and 6 of the 1970 Act (now ss 22 and 27 of the MCA 1973) there are changes between s 6 of the 1970 Act (s 27 of the MCA 1973) and its predecessors and the word "maintenance" is not used in the predecessors to s 1 of the 1970 Act (s 22 of the MCA 1973).

   (3)   The subsequent amendments to s 27 of the MCA 1973 confirm or clarify that "maintenance" was not used by Parliament to refer to the old common law duty of a husband to maintain his wife.

   (4)   The report (read alone and together with the Working Paper) supports the conclusion that "maintenance" was not used by Parliament to refer to the old common law duty of a husband to maintain his wife.'

[96]   Furthermore Charles J in *G v G (Maintenance Pending Suit: Costs)* [2002] EWHC 306 (Fam), [2003] 2 FLR 71 followed the earlier decision of Holman J in *A v A (Maintenance Pending Suit: Provision for Legal Fees)* [2001] 1 WLR 605, [2001] 1 FLR 377 establishing that the court had power to provide funds for the wife's contemplated litigation costs by adding substantial monthly instalments to what she needed for her aliment.

[97]   The cases that have considered the boundary of the court's power in ordering periodical payments are to the same effect. In *Cornick v Cornick (No 2)* [1995] 2 FLR 490 Sir Stephen Brown P in upholding the decision of Hale J (as she then was) stated:

'I do not believe that Hale J erred in her approach in principle to this case, and I reject the submission which Mr Mostyn has made that there was a delimiting factor (as he termed it) which should have had the effect of restricting a judge hearing an application for variation to what he termed the budgetary or marital standard.'

[98]   In so deciding the court endorsed and followed the earlier decision in *Boylan v Boylan* [1988] 1 FLR 282. In *Cornick v Cornick (No 3)* [2001] 2 FLR 1240 Charles J stated in para [106] of his judgment:

'In my judgment, just as it is on the first application for orders for financial provision, *White v White* [2000] 2 FLR 981 is clear authority on an application for variation (and for an order for a lump sum on a discharge or variation of a periodical payment) for the following points, namely that (a) the court should not rely on the judicial concept of "reasonable requirements" as a determinative or limiting factor in cases when a payor has, or acquires, an ability to pay more than the payee's financial needs even when they are interpreted generously and called "reasonable requirements", and (b) the court should exercise its discretion by applying the words of the statute.'

[99]   Thus there can be no doubt of the court's power to order periodical payments to reflect more than the recipient's mere aliment, provided that all the s 25(2) criteria, all the circumstances of the case and overall fairness so require.

The principles upon which periodical payments are to be assessed

[100]   This question I have partially addressed in considering the definition of periodical payments. The respondents' submissions take us back to the 1969 Law Commission report. They cite the following passage from para 83:

'Of the criteria mentioned in para 82(a), (i) [the respective means, needs, earning capacity and financial responsibilities of each spouse] and (ii) [the standard of living of the parties] will be especially relevant to periodic cash provisions; the others to property adjustments and lump sum awards.'

[101]   The appellants' submissions point out that the force of that citation is diluted by adding the next following sentence:

'But, as already emphasised, the two types of financial provision cannot and should not be kept wholly distinct, and all criteria are, or may be, relevant.'

[102]   Thus I do not derive help on this issue from that source. It is almost trite to emphasise that the assessment of periodical payments must be governed by the language of s 25. No one factor in the s 25(2) checklist predominates. The submissions of the respondents seek to elevate the applicants' needs to a dominant priority. However, in deference to authority they accept that it cannot be aliment or bare needs but some form of enhanced needs. That acceptance leads them into a position that is difficult to defend. How is the surplus above needs to be defined or assessed? Bennett J recognised the difficulty in his judgment and met it by saying that the assessment of periodical payments was an art and not a science. However, practitioners rightly

complain that art depends greatly upon the individual judge and consequently art imports unpredictability of outcome.

[103]   The same difficulty confronted Mr Posnansky. He was fluent in negative statements. He said that there must be no reference to entitlement based on some contribution during marriage without which the payer would not be able to achieve his elevated future earnings graph. Equally proscribed, he submitted, was any reference to compensation for an earning capacity either sacrificed or irretrievably abandoned by agreement during the marriage. The only positive consideration that Mr Posnansky was able to advance as the basis for the assessment of surplus over needs was the planned progress to clean break in implementation of the s 25(A) duty. Mr Posnansky's inability to suggest any other positive consideration leads me to understand his concept of 'needs plus' as the old concept of reasonable requirements, which was the measure for an applicant's capital award for about 20 years.

[104]   But why should Lord Nicholls of Birkenhead's demonstration of the discriminatory nature of the reasonable requirements measure in capital awards not apply equally to income awards? To cite again the familiar paragraph:

> 'But I can see nothing, either in the statutory provisions or in the underlying objective of securing fair financial arrangements, to lead me to suppose that the available assets of the respondent become immaterial once the claimant wife's financial needs are satisfied. Why ever should they? If a husband and wife by their joint efforts over many years, his directly in his business and hers indirectly at home, have built up a valuable business from scratch, why should the claimant wife be confined to the court's assessment of her reasonable requirements, and the husband left with a much larger share? Or, to put the question differently, in such a case, where the assets exceed the financial needs of both parties, why should the surplus belong solely to the husband? On the facts of a particular case there may be a good reason why the wife should be confined to her needs and the husband left with the much larger balance. But the mere absence of financial need cannot, by itself, be a sufficient reason. If it were, discrimination would be creeping in by the back door. In these cases, it should be remembered, the claimant is usually the wife. Hence the importance of the check against the yardstick of equal division.'

[105]   Although this paragraph was not written with periodical payment assessment in mind, why should the principle defined not be of equal application?

[106]   My present view is that in this jurisdiction we should not flirt with, still less embrace, any of the categorisations of the defining purposes of periodical payments advanced by academic authors. The judges must remain focused on the statutory language, albeit recognising the need for evolutionary construction to reflect social and economic change. The statutory checklist and the overall circumstances of the case allow the judge to reflect factors which are said to be inherent in either the entitlement model or the compensation model. But to adopt one model or another or a combination of more than one is to don a straitjacket and to deflect concentration from the statutory language. Clearly in the assessment of periodical payments, as of capital provision, the overriding objective is fairness. Discrimination between the sexes must be avoided. The cross-check of equality is not appropriate for a number of reasons. First, in many cases the division of income is not just between the parties, since there will be children with a priority claim for the costs of education and upbringing. Secondly, Lord Nicholls of Birkenhead suggested the use of the cross-check in dividing the accumulated fruits of past shared endeavours. In assessing periodical payments the court considers the division of the fruits of the breadwinner's future work in a context where he may have left the child-carer in the former matrimonial home, where he may have to meet alternative housing costs and where he may have in fact or in contemplation a second wife and a further child.

[107]   Returning to the specific question considered by Bennett J, I doubt the modern relevance of the distinction sought to be drawn between income and capital.

[108]   In the twentieth century social and economic shifts broke down the hallowed distinction which our Victorian forbears drew between capital and income. In days of zero inflation, or even deflation, and before the introduction of income tax, capital assets were invested for the steady yield which produced the income from which family expenditure was met. The spending or the reduction of capital signalled the road to ruin.

[109]   In the aftermath of the Second World War rates of tax upon unearned income approached 100%. The avoidance of such penal rates became for some a paramount objective. In an age when the annual rate of inflation spiralled, the acquisition of capital by substantial borrowing, which could often be set-off against earned income otherwise liable to tax, became the ordinary means of acquiring substance, particularly as the rise in property values frequently outstripped the rise in inflation. The consequence has been the erosion, if not the elimination, of the hallowed distinction between capital and income. What people spend is money which is likely to be derived from a variety of sources. Spending needs may well be met from the sale of capital assets or the realisation of capital appreciation. Provision for the future may be by investment in an income fund or by the acquisition of capital assets held for subsequent realisation. All these realities are well illustrated by the financial arrangements and choices that the McFarlane family have made.

The guidance to be derived from judgments and academic analysis in other jurisdictions

[110]   In my judgment these sources were of only passing relevance to the two appeals presently before us. The respondents stressed that in any event the Australian, New Zealand and Canadian decisions are founded on statutory criteria that differ from the provisions of the Matrimonial Causes Act 1973. Nevertheless there can be no doubt that the trend in these common law jurisdictions is towards the recognition of wider purposes, objectives and factors in the quantification of spousal support orders. Nowhere are the needs of the applicant the dominant consideration. I would, therefore, mark these common law decisions and guard against any approach that would put this jurisdiction out of step where the application of our statutory provisions is open to more than one interpretation. It seems inevitable that a future appeal will require a closer analysis of Commonwealth authority.

[111]   The New York case-law is, in my judgment, plainly of lesser relevance. Mr Mostyn sought to persuade us to follow the approach reflected in what he described as the leading and landmark case of *O'Brien v O'Brien* (1985) 66 NY 2d 576. There the court assessed the likely excess over average earnings of the husband's future earnings as a medical practitioner. It then capitalised that anticipated achievement and awarded the applicant 40% of the capital sum payable by 11 equal annual installments. That approach seems to me to be open to obvious criticism in any jurisdiction in which the recipient's entitlement terminates on death or remarriage. I share the misgivings expressed by Coleridge J in recent decisions. In *N v N (Financial Provision: Sale of Company)* [2001] 2 FLR 69 he said:

> 'In the current climate now, where the court is engaged more in dividing up assets than in calculating a party's reasonable needs, there would be logic in trying to calculate and include a figure for any asset which generates a secure income. At its most extreme that might include the valuation of a party's earning capacity. However, in my judgment, the evaluation of such an ephemeral item would be pregnant with problems and lead to

endless debate incapable of fair resolution. It would be even more problematic where there was ongoing provision for children.'

[112]   In *G v G (Financial Provision: Equal Division)* [2002] EWHC 1339 (Fam), [2002] 2 FLR 1143 Coleridge J said in para [27] of his judgment:

'The valuation of a person's earning capacity by its reduction to a fixed figure is not an exercise that can usefully be embarked upon. There are too many imponderables. However, it seems to me perfectly proper to pray in aid, by way of makeweight to an argument in relation to any particular capital division, an earning capacity available to one party or another over and above income generated from the capital being divided.'

Orders

[113]   Given the views which I have expressed on the two appeals, Mr Francis's application for permission to appeal is manifestly hopeless. I would dismiss it. In *McFarlane v McFarlane* I would set aside the order of Bennett J and restore the order of the district judge without the provision for index linking but for a term of only 5 years from the date of her order. In the case of *Parlour v Parlour* I would allow the appeal and substitute the order sought by Mr Mostyn for the term of only 4 years from the date of the trial. Obviously during that term the value of the wife's percentage share will fluctuate, and probably reduce, as the husband's earnings vary from their present level.

LATHAM LJ:

[114]   The vast majority of the problems which the courts have to resolve in relation to matrimonial finance involves a difficult exercise in ensuring that limited resources are distributed in such a way as to reduce the financial hardship of divorce as much as possible. But we are dealing in the present appeals with cases where the position is very different. In neither case, however, is there sufficient capital for there to be an immediate solution by way of a clean break. But in both there is, in *Parlour v Parlour* at least at present, annual income far in excess of the needs or reasonable requirements of the parties. As Thorpe LJ has pointed out, that excess amounts in one case to approximately £550,000 pa and in the other approximately £900,000 pa.

[115]   Counsel for the husbands both accepted that the wives' entitlement was not restricted to their reasonable requirements, accepting as they did that that would be an unwarranted restriction on the court's discretionary powers bearing in mind the matters set out in s 25(2) of the Matrimonial Causes Act 1973. Their submissions, however, came perilously close to submitting that there is little room for other considerations. That applies in particular to Mr Posnansky's argument that a periodical payments order cannot be used as a means to enable a wife to build up capital, as this would cut across the principle established in *de Lasala (Ernest Ferdinand Perez) v de Lasala (Hannelore)* [1980] AC 546, (1979) FLR Rep 223.

[116]   I have considerable sympathy, in one sense, for the view that the 'reasonable requirements' approach has the merit of being both flexible, in that the word 'reasonable' can take into account a number of the matters set out in s 25(2) and also being capable of pragmatic evaluation. The problem quite simply is that it does not give proper effect to the words of s 25(2). In particular, in the context of Mr Posnansky's argument, it does not give effect in any way to the provisions of s 25(2)(b) and (f) which require the court to look to the future. This not only permits, but in an appropriate case, may also require the use of income to generate capital for future eventualities. It is clear that there will be cases where the assessment of the parties' reasonable requirements will be the only sensible route to a fair division of limited resources. But where, as here, there is an excess of income, that can only be part of the inquiry.

[117]   It is, however, a necessary part of the inquiry. For it is only by examining the reasonable requirements of both parties that the quantum of the excess can be identified so as to enable sensible decisions as to its disposal to be made. That necessarily involves the husband providing the relevant information to the court. The practice which has developed of not providing that information in cases such as these is, in my view, not only discriminatory but also demeaning to the wife. It concentrates the forensic battle on an examination of the wife's claim in a way which is, in my view, inappropriate. The exercise required by statute is one which is intended to produce a fair result. I consider that *White v White* [2001] 1 AC 596, [2000] 2 FLR 981 applies as much to claims for periodical payments as to capital provision. And an examination of the husbands' reasonable requirements will be part of that exercise.

[118]   The problem is that the concept of fairness is elastic and often subjective. Attempts to identify what society would consider to be an appropriate yardstick to use to determine fairness have found the answer elusive and the material with which we have been provided from other jurisdictions has merely underlined how difficult the search for the answer has proved to be. In the absence of a consensus, decisions will have to continue to be made on a pragmatic and individual basis, which is inevitably unsettling for litigants and their advisors.

[119]   But in the present cases, I agree with Thorpe and Wall LJJ, both of whose judgments I have read in draft, that the solution is to be found in s 25A. The duty imposed on the court by that section requires us to consider the extent to which it is possible within the family resources to achieve a clean break. In the present cases, this can only be done by use of periodical payment orders enabling the respective wives to accumulate capital. For the reasons that I have already given, that seems to me to be a perfectly proper use of such an order. Like both Thorpe and Wall LJJ, I recognise that this is an approach which was not argued either before Bennett J, or us. I am satisfied, however, that it is the right route to take in order to resolve these appeals. For the reasons that they give, I would allow these appeals in the terms proposed by Thorpe LJ, and dismiss the application for permission to appeal in *Parlour v Parlour*.

WALL LJ

[120]   I agree that these two appeals should be allowed for the reasons given by Thorpe LJ, whose judgment I have had the advantage of reading in draft. I also agree with the orders he proposes. I add a short judgment of my own partly to reflect the interest which the two cases have generated within the profession, but primarily because we are disagreeing with an experienced judge of the Family Division, who conscientiously applied himself to the arguments addressed to him, and decided both cases on the basis of those arguments.

[121]   It is a frequent (albeit informally expressed) complaint of judges at first instance that cases argued before them bear little resemblance to the decisions which emerge after the self-same cases have been argued in the Court of Appeal. Bennett J would, I think, be entitled to voice that complaint in relation to these two appeals.

[122]   Both decisions, one arising by way of appeal from the district judge and the other by way of the exercise of a first instance discretion, were, it seems to me, dictated by what appears to have been an analysis agreed at the Bar and then put to the judge. That analysis appears to have been that because there had been in each case (1) a

consensual capital distribution by way of lump sum and property adjustment orders and (2) an agreement that the capital distribution was insufficient to bring about a clean break, it therefore followed (3) that there should be indefinite orders for periodical payments expressed to last during joint lives or until the remarriage of the payee or further order of the court.

[123] For ease of reference, although it is not strictly accurate, I will refer to such orders as 'joint lives' orders. In my judgment, proposition (3) in para [122] above is both a non sequitur and contrary to the statutory objective contained in s 25A of the Matrimonial Causes Act 1973.

[124] With the exception of the concluding paragraphs of Mr Mostyn's closing submissions on behalf of Mrs Parlour (set out by Thorpe LJ in para [76] of his judgment, and which go to future capitalisation rather than to s 25A), no consideration appears in either case to have been given to, and no substantive argument addressed to the judge on, s 25A(1) and (2) of the Matrimonial Causes Act 1973, which Thorpe LJ has set out in para [57] of his judgment, but which bears repetition:

> 'Exercise of court's powers in favour of party to marriage on decree of divorce or nullity of marriage
>
> (1) Where on or after the grant of a decree of divorce or nullity of marriage the court decides to exercise its powers under s 23(1)(a), (b) or (c), 24, 24A or 24B above in favour of a party to the marriage, it shall be the duty of the court to consider whether it would be appropriate so to exercise those powers that the financial obligations of each party towards the other will be terminated as soon after the grant of the decree as the court considers just and reasonable.
>
> (2) Where the court decides in such a case to make a periodical payments or secured periodical payments order in favour of a party to the marriage, the court shall in particular consider whether it would be appropriate to require those payments to be made or secured only for such term as would in the opinion of the court be sufficient to enable the party in whose favour the order is made to adjust without undue hardship to the termination of his or her financial dependence on the other party.'

[125] In *McFarlane v McFarlane*, the district judge recorded the parties' agreement that there was insufficient capital to achieve a clean break, and dealt summarily with s 25A(2) simply stating her satisfaction that this was not a case where the wife could adjust, without undue hardship, to the termination of periodical payments in her favour. Although Mrs McFarlane had at one point posited a clean break by lump sum instalments of £65,000 pa indexed linked until 2017, she abandoned that approach before the hearing, and her case was put to the district judge on the basis that there was no reason why she should not receive income at the level of £275,000 pa net index linked on an indefinite basis to enable her to make provision for the future for herself, for as long as such a level of periodical payments was within Mr McFarlane's means. Accepting the district judge's award of £250,000 pa, her case was advanced both to the judge and to this court on the same basis. Section 25A receives only a passing mention in two and a half lines of Mr Singleton's erudite and exhaustive 131-paragraph skeleton argument prepared for this court. It was only in his written submissions in reply that Mr Singleton addressed s 25A directly.

[126] As Mr Posnansky points out, both his skeleton arguments before the judge in the court below and in this court make reference to s 25A and to the statutory aim of the clean break. But the former does so in the context of it being common ground that *McFarlane v McFarlane* was not a clean break case, and in the context of a submission that joint lives maintenance fixed at a high level was both inimical to the achievement of a clean break and wrong in principle because it included an element for future long-term provision by way of capital accretion or pension fund. The same argument, in a slightly more sophisticated form, appears in his skeleton argument prepared for this court.

[127]   The absence of any reference to s 25A of the Matrimonial Causes Act 1973 in *Parlour v Parlour* is, in my judgment, even more surprising because it was manifest that a substantial question mark hangs over Mr Parlour's future earning capacity. The judge, being invited to make a joint lives order at a fixed percentage of the husband's net income (a global sum of £444,000 pa for the wife and the three children) declined to do so, as it seems to me, on two bases. First, on the facts, he held that the husband was likely to put aside significant sums from his income and other interests in the next year and a half, and there would, accordingly, be a 'greater capital pot of the husband for the support of the wife and children if his income thereafter declines significantly'. Secondly, the judge expressed the view that 'the time for (Mrs Parlour) to seek the court's assistance in mitigating as far as possible risks to her economic livelihood, both present and future, was at any final hearing as to capital. She was not obliged to settle her capital (or any other) claims at the FDR but she did so'. Why then, the judge asked rhetorically, should it be possible for her to seek an award for periodical payments way, way beyond her needs (generously interpreted) the effect of which, on her own evidence, would give her substantial savings and thus capital? He therefore concluded:

> '... It surely must be implicit in the concept of periodical payments when placed next to the concepts of lump sum and property adjustments that where there has been a capital adjustment between spouses in accordance with *White v White*, as it was in the instant case, the function of periodical payments should not then or at some later date be seen to further the claimant spouse's ability to mine the paying spouse's income for further capital.'

[128]   At the same time, of course, the judge recognised the tension between that statement, and the actual order he made which – almost exclusively because of the size of Mr Parlour's income – substantially exceeded Mrs Parlour's needs.

[129]   In my judgment, Bennett J's approach is a reflection of the manner in which the cases were presented to him. It is an approach which, in the vast majority of modest income cases, is likely to be correct. However, in my judgment, the conventional joint lives order approach to periodical payments does not fit easily with the highly unusual facts of these two cases, and in particular the two critical factors common to each, namely (1) the absence of sufficient capital to produce an immediate clean break; and (2) the fact that in each case the payer's income is easily able to accommodate periodical payments to the payee, in the judge's words 'way, way beyond her needs (generously interpreted)'. In this context, it seems to me that s 25A was of direct application, and it is unfortunate that its proper application did not form part of the argument.

[130]   In his written submissions in reply, Mr Singleton, it seemed to me, was dismissive of s 25(A). Although a clean break is a 'desirable objective', s 25A does not, he argued, justify reducing a wife's entitlement in order to effect a clean break. Thus, he submitted, the obligation on the court is only a duty to 'consider' effecting a clean break where 'appropriate' and there is not a presumption that there will be a clean break. The correct approach, therefore, is to establish the wife's entitlement by reference to s 25 and then consider whether or not a clean break is possible.

[131]   I cannot accept this analysis of the role of s 25A of the Matrimonial Causes Act 1973. Of course, any order predicated on s 25A must be fair, and by reference to the terms of the section itself will be an exercise of the court's powers which involves the application of the criteria contained in s 25(2) of the Matrimonial Causes Act 1973. In

my judgment, however, the philosophy of the clean break contained within s 25A, clearly identified by Lord Scarman in his speech in *Minton v Minton* [1979] AC 593, (1978) FLR Rep 461, at 608 and 471 respectively (well before the repeal of the s 25 tailpiece) as one of the two principles which inform the modern legislation, is at the heart of the amended statute.

[132]   Section 25A of the Matrimonial Causes Act 1973 was enacted at the same time as the tailpiece to the old s 25 was repealed. It is, of course, the case, as Lord Nicholls of Birkenhead points out in *White v White* [2001] 1 AC 596, [2000] 2 FLR 981, at 604G and 989 respectively, that when the tailpiece to s 25 was repealed, nothing was inserted in its place as a mandatory overarching statutory imperative as to the manner in which the court was to exercise its powers under s 25. This does not, however, in my judgment, detract either from the fact that s 25A is a statutory embodiment of the principle enunciated in *Minton v Minton* or from the fact that the clean break, in Lord Scarman's phrase, represents one of the two principles informing the modern legislation.

[133]   It is, of course, the case that s 25A of the Matrimonial Causes Act 1973 uses the word 'consider'. The omission of the words 'to consider whether it would be appropriate' in s 25A(1) would be to cause manifest injustice in those many cases where a clean break is not possible. But the statutory obligation, in my judgment, is clear. The court has a duty, in every case in which it makes orders for ancillary relief, to consider the appropriateness of exercising its powers in order to bring about a clean break within a reasonable time. This includes in s 25A(2) the particular duty to consider fixed-term orders for periodical payments. It seems to me, with respect, that this exercise was simply not undertaken in these two cases.

[134]   Mr Singleton and Mr Mostyn are, however, I think, right when they submit that a payee's right to periodical payments is to a share of the payer's income which the payee (in each of the current cases the wife) has, through her domestic contribution, helped the payer develop. I, therefore, agree that where the payer's income is sufficiently large (as here) a cut-off point for periodical payments based on generously interpreted needs, thereby leaving a large surplus of income for the payer to do with as he pleases, has no foundation in the statute and is discriminatory. But the danger of this approach seems to me to be that it runs the risk to reintroducing the repealed tailpiece of s 25 of the Matrimonial Causes Act 1973 by the back door. If the payee has, in effect, a vested, life-long interest in such an income, is she not being placed in the position in which she would have been if the marriage had not irretrievably broken down? And is the principle contained in s 25A not being simply by-passed?

[135]   I am the first to acknowledge that periodical payments based on a proportion of joint incomes (for example, the old 'one-third' rule) was discriminatory and may well have caused injustice to women payees. The balance which, it seems to me, needs to be struck in a case such as the present, is the need to achieve fairness to both wives whilst fulfilling the obligation imposed by s 25A. In my judgment, that is not achieved by open-ended orders of the type sought by both Mrs McFarlane and Mrs Parlour. It is achieved by orders which exceed need in amount, and which divide equitably the very large income enjoyed by both husbands. But with that division, in my judgment, comes a responsibility on the payee to use the surplus over needs towards financial independence and self-sufficiency.

[136]   Thus, in exceptional cases such as the present, and on the basis of term orders, I have no difficulty in contemplating periodical payments being used by the payee as a means of accumulating capital. That is because I perceive Part II of the Matrimonial Causes Act 1973 (as indeed it has been perceived from its inception as the

Matrimonial Proceedings and Property Act 1970) as a flexible code designed to ensure that its various components are used imaginatively to produce a fair result. In *Wachtel v Wachtel* [1973] Fam 72, at 91, this court described the Matrimonial Proceedings and Property Act 1970 as:

> '... a reforming statute designed to facilitate the granting of ancillary relief in cases where marriages have been dissolved ... We regard the provisions of ss 2,3, 4 and 5 of the Act of 1970 as designed to accord to the courts the widest possible powers in readjusting the financial position of the parties and to afford the courts the necessary machinery to that end ...'

[137]   The theme of flexibility was mirrored in *Trippas v Trippas* [1973] Fam 134 (see, in particular, the judgment of Scarman LJ (as he then was) at 144) and in many of the cases in this court dating from the early days of the statute. Thus in *Doherty v Doherty* [1976] Fam 71, this court eschewed technicality when considering the distinction between lump sum and property adjustment orders. Ormrod LJ (whose judgments, as Lord Nicholls of Birkenhead commented in *White v White* [2001] 1 AC 596, [2000] 2 FLR 981, at 607 and 991 respectively, are a valuable source of the jurisprudence of the period) said at 79:

> 'Whether it is right, or not, to accept counsel for the husband's submission that a clear distinction should be drawn between notices of application for financial provision under s 23 and notices of application for property adjustment orders under s 24, may be doubted. These two sections are, in effect, a statement by Parliament of the code to be adopted by the court in dealing with ancillary relief after divorce generally. The fact that they are two separate sections seems to me to be much more a matter of convenience and drafting than anything else. There is no reason that I can see why any distinction should be drawn between those two classes of relief which the court is now empowered to grant. In my view, these two sections should be, as far as possible, regarded as part and parcel of a single code. It may be very important in many cases when the matter comes to be investigated by the court that the court should be free to make either a property adjustment order or a lump sum order, whichever turns out to be the more convenient in the circumstances. It would be unfortunate, I think, if that degree of elasticity were lost for some technical reason. It is quite plain that the same principles apply in the assessment of claims under each of these two sections. That appears from s 25, and it is equally plain from the judgments in *Trippas v Trippas* of Lord Denning MR and Scarman LJ. Lump sum orders are alternatives to property adjustment orders, and in many cases one order may prove more convenient than another. I do not think there is any greater difference than that. So, in my judgment, the court should keep technical points of the kind with which we are dealing in this case to an absolute minimum.'

[138]   Of course it is the case that the statutory imperative which both *Wachtel v Wachtel* [1973] Fam 72 and *Doherty v Doherty* [1976] Fam 71 were serving was the now repealed tailpiece to s 25. But, in my judgment, the incremental changes to the statute over the years since 1970 which have changed its direction and remedied a number of injustices (notably in the field of pensions) have not altered the fundamental approach. The statute is a flexible code designed to enable the court to achieve a fair outcome. Periodical payments are one part of that code. The principle of the clean break is now, in my judgment, contained in s 25A. If, in exceptional cases such as the present, periodical payments can be used to enable a payee to accumulate capital and thus facilitate a termination of financial obligations within a reasonable time, such a use seems to me fair and square within the statutory objective. What do not, however, seem to me to be within the statutory objective in the present two cases are indeterminate and unfocused joint lives orders very substantially in excess of needs.

[139]   Speaking for myself, I do not see this approach as inconsistent with the decision of this court in *Pearce v Pearce* [2003] EWCA Civ 1054, [2004] 1 WLR 68, [2003]

2 FLR 1144. In that case the court was considering capitalisation of periodical payments under s 31(7B) of the Matrimonial Causes Act 1973. The judge had construed that section as giving him the power to make an additional capital award over and above that required to capitalise the wife's order for periodical payments. Such an additional award was in conflict with the principle that the capital distribution ordered or agreed on dissolution was once and for all. The present cases seem to me quite different. An award of periodical payments designed to enable the payee to accumulate capital which can then be taken into account when consideration is being given to the sum required to achieve the termination of the order for periodical payments, seems to me wholly consistent with the terms of both s 25A of the Matrimonial Causes Act 1973 (and for that matter, s 31(7B)) and does not conflict with the principle that capital awards are once and for all.

[140]   For all these reasons, therefore, I am in agreement with Thorpe LJ that neither order made by the judge can stand. I have found more difficult the question as to what orders this court should put in their place. In *McFarlane v McFarlane*, however, it seems to me that the outcome is effectively dictated by the fact that the case reaches us as at second appeal, and that the appeal from the district judge to Bennett J was governed by *Cordle v Cordle* [2001] EWCA Civ 1791, [2002] 1 WLR 1441, [2002] 1 FLR 207. Since I agree with Thorpe LJ that the judge was wrong to interfere with the order of the district judge on two bases: (a) that her order wrongly required the husband to pay over to the wife 'monies which were likely to be directed into financial vehicles for the accumulation of capital'; and (b) that the effect of her order was to 'subvert the principle set out in many cases that an award of capital is made once and once only, and that the purpose of periodical payments is maintenance', it follows that the only course properly open to this court is to restore the order of the district judge.

[141]   Despite the affluence of the parties, I am very conscious of the high cost of this litigation to them, and in any event, in practical terms I have doubts about the utility of a further hearing designed to identify a proper level of payments designed to fulfil the objectives of s 25A. In the event, therefore, I am persuaded by paras [68]–[74] of Thorpe LJ's judgment that whilst the district judge did not address her mind to s 25A(1) and left to Mrs McFarlane the use to which she put the surplus over needs in the order for periodical payments, that is not an error of principle, and thus the proper course is not to remit the matter but to restore the district judge's figure for periodical payments and to substitute for the joint lives order an extendable term of 5 years. At the conclusion of that period, which should coincide with the elimination of the husband's commitment to repay the mortgage on his property, it will be for the parties to negotiate, or for the courts to determine, whether a clean break can then be achieved, and if so on what terms, or whether the term of the order should be extended.

[142]   I have found the outcome in *Parlour v Parlour* more difficult. Whilst Mr Mostyn's global percentage has the attractive neatness of matching the level of capital distribution, I am less sure that an arbitrary figure calculated without reference to s 25A will necessarily produce a fair result in 4 years. At the same time, a further inquiry into the figures is likely to be both expensive and time-consuming, and may well encounter many of the unknown factors which currently confront us. Once again, therefore, I am in the event persuaded that the course proposed by Thorpe LJ in para [77] of his judgment is the correct one.

[143]   I end by reiterating a theme of this judgment, namely that these two cases are, in my view, exceptional. It may well be that the specialist profession has a number of cases in which a spouse has a high six-figure or even seven-figure net income which is not matched by sufficient capital to achieve an immediate clean break at the point when the wealth of the family falls to be distributed at the end of the marriage. No doubt, in certain professions (including sport), incomes of the magnitude

demonstrated by these appeals are more common than heretofore. However, such incomes remain exceptional. As Thorpe LJ has pointed out, in the overwhelming majority of cases, the income (whether generated by one spouse or jointly by both) on which the husband, wife and children have lived together is stretched to meet the needs of two households, and is frequently inadequate to do so. In such cases, the approach of the judge would be unimpeachable. I, therefore, repeat my agreement with Thorpe LJ that these two appeals arise on exceptional facts.

[144]   That said, however, such cases have to be fitted into the statutory framework. In my judgment, the profession, in attempting this exercise, asked itself the wrong question in these two cases. The question was not: what are the principles governing an award of periodical payments during joint lives or until remarriage in any case where the net income of the payer significantly exceeds what both parties need in order to meet their outgoings at the standard of living which the court has found to be appropriate? This question ignores the clear statutory language of s 25A.

[145]   The profession inevitably craves certainty so that it can advise its clients appropriately. That, of course, is not a new aspiration. In *Martin (BH) v Martin (D)* [1978] Fam 12, (1977) FLR Rep 444 in which this court upheld the right of a wife to remain indefinitely in a very modest matrimonial home against the claim of her former husband that it should be sold and the proceeds equally divided, Ormrod LJ said, at 20 and 449 respectively:

> 'I appreciate the point he (Mr Aglionby, counsel for the husband) has made, namely that it is difficult for practitioners to advise clients in these cases because the rules are not very firm. That is inevitable when the courts are working out the exercise of the wide powers given by a statute like the Matrimonial Causes Act 1973. It is the essence of such a discretionary situation that the court should preserve, so far as it can, the utmost elasticity to deal with each case on its own facts. Therefore, it is a matter of trial and error and imagination on the part of those advising clients. It equally means that decisions of this court can never be better than guidelines. They are not precedents in the strict sense of the word. There is bound to be an element of uncertainty in the use of the wide discretionary powers given to the court under the 1973 Act, and no doubt there always will be, because as social circumstances change so the court will have to adapt the ways in which it exercises discretion. If property suddenly became available all over the country many of the rationes decidendi of the past would be quite inappropriate.'

[146]   No doubt ancillary relief has become more sophisticated since 1977, but the speech of Lord Nicholls of Birkenhead in *White v White* [2001] 1 AC 596, [2000] 2 FLR 981 is a timely reminder that the only principled approach is the application of the words of the statute to the pursuit of fairness. For the reasons given by Thorpe LJ, I agree that this approach applies to both capital and income. In my judgment these two cases went awry because the terms of s 25A of the Matrimonial Causes Act 1973 were not properly considered, with the consequence that an attempt was made to impose joint lives orders in exceptional circumstances to which they were not fitted.

[147]   For these reasons, in addition to those given by Thorpe LJ, I would, accordingly, allow these appeals.

Appeal allowed; a minute of order be lodged with court.

Solicitors: *The Family Law in Partnership* for Mrs McFarlane
          Levison Meltzer Pigott for Mr McFarlane
          Clintons for Mrs Parlour
          Alexiou Fisher Philipps for Mr Parlour

PHILIPPA JOHNSON
Law Reporter

MILLER v MILLER
[2005] EWCA CIV 984

Court of Appeal

Thorpe, Wall LJJ and Black J

29 July 2005

Financial provision – Divorce – Short childless marriage – Principles to apply – Evidence as to causes of breakdown of marriage – 'Legitimate expectation' of wife as to standard of living post marriage

The husband, now 41, and wife, now 36, had been married for 2¾ years. There were no children of the marriage. The couple had conducted a relationship for 4 years before marrying, but had not cohabited at any stage before the marriage. At the time of the marriage, the husband was already an exceptionally successful fund manager, earning in the region of £1m a year; the wife had a salary of £85,000 a year. The husband purchased a home for £1.8m in preparation for the marriage, and shortly before the marriage received £20m in respect of an earlier business deal. Not long after the marriage, the husband moved firms, taking a huge reduction in basic salary, but acquiring a significant number of shares in the new firm with potential for substantial gains. At about the same time the wife gave up her job, and concentrated on furnishing the matrimonial home and a property in the south of France which had been purchased in their joint names. In the third year of the marriage, the husband left the wife for another woman, whom he subsequently married. At the hearing the judge permitted the wife to adduce evidence as to the cause of the breakdown of the marriage, notwithstanding that she had made a declaration at the conclusion of the financial dispute resolution (FDR) hearing that she would not be relying upon the husband's conduct. The judge awarded the wife £5m, accepting her evidence as to the circumstances of the marriage and its breakdown. The judge took the view that the husband could not rely on the short duration of the marriage because he was to blame for the breakdown, and that the wife had a legitimate expectation that she would live at a higher standard of affluence on marriage.

Held – dismissing the appeal –

(1)   The judge had been right to permit the wife to adduce evidence as to the cause of the breakdown, notwithstanding her declaration at the FDR that she would not be relying upon conduct in the prosecution of her claim for ancillary relief. A retreat from a clear declaration was generally to be deprecated and might in many cases result in a heavy costs penalty, but such a declaration could not possibly override or circumscribe the trial judge's obligation to investigate whatever he conceived was relevant and necessary to enable him to discharge his statutory duty (see paras [24], [25]).

(2)   The language of s 25(2)(g) of the Matrimonial Causes Act 1973 was intended to discourage allegations of conduct unless the conduct was such that it would be inequitable to disregard. However, it was not the case that allegations of conduct in ancillary relief could only be advanced under s 25(2)(g). It was pointless and risky in terms of costs to assert misconduct that did not measure high on the scale of gravity, but conduct that would not merit advancing under s 25(2)(g) was not, therefore, irrelevant or inadmissible. Often the court's assessment of the worth of the comparable

contributions would require consideration of motive, attitudes, commitments and responsibilities (see para [29]).

(3)   The judge was entitled to conclude that the husband was responsible for the breakdown of the marriage and that finding entitled him to give much less weight to the duration of the marriage than he would have done had he found that the wife was to blame, or that the parties had separated consensually (see para [31]).

(4)   The old principle that the award in a brief marriage should be enough to get the applicant back on her feet did not apply post-*White*.[1] A marriage was not to be equated to a purely financial venture; s 25 required a sophisticated evaluation of the extent of the wife's commitment to, and investment in, the marriage emotionally and psychologically (see para [33]).

(5)   The judge's explanation for the end result had been by no means straightforward or clear. However, he had been entitled to regard as 'the key element' the wife's 'legitimate expectation' of living to a higher standard, as a fact-dependent conclusion and had sufficiently explained the award, which was not outside the permissible bracket (see paras [38], [40], [42], [55]).

Statutory provisions considered
Divorce Reform Act 1969
Matrimonial Proceedings and Property Act 1970, s 5
Matrimonial Causes Act 1973, ss 23, 25
Access to Justice Act 1998, s 55

Cases referred to in judgment
Attar v Attar (No 2) [1985] FLR 653, FD
Cowan v Cowan [2001] EWCA Civ 679, [2002] Fam 97, [2001] 3 WLR 684, [2001] 2 FLR 192, CA
Foster v Foster [2003] EWCA Civ 565, [2003] 2 FLR 299, CA
G v G (Financial Provision: Separation Agreement) [2000] 2 FLR 18, FD
G v G (Financial Provision: Separation Agreement) [2004] 1 FLR 1011, CA
Gojkovic v Gojkovic and Another [1992] Fam 40, [1991] 3 WLR 621, [1991] 2 FLR 233, [1992] 1 All ER 267, CA
H v H (Financial Provision: Short Marriage) (1981) 2 FLR 392, FD
Hedges v Hedges [1991] 1 FLR 196, CA
Lambert v Lambert [2002] EWCA Civ 1685, [2003] Fam 103, [2003] 2 WLR 631, [2003] 1 FLR 139, [2003] 4 All ER 342, CA
Martin (BH) v Martin (D) [1978] Fam 12, [1977] 3 WLR 101, (1977) FLR Rep 444, [1977] 3 All ER 762, CA
McFarlane v McFarlane; Parlour v Parlour [2004] EWCA (Civ) 872, [2005] Fam 171, [2004] 3 WLR 1481, [2004] 2 FLR 893, [2004] 2 All ER 921, CA
Piglowska v Piglowski [1999] 1 WLR 1360, [1999] 2 FLR 763, [1999] 3 All ER 632, HL
Robertson v Robertson (1983) 4 FLR 387, FD
S v S [1977] Fam 127, [1976] 3 WLR 775, [1977] 1 All ER 56, CA
Wachtel v Wachtel [1973] Fam 72, [1973] 2 WLR 366, [1973] 1 All ER 829, CA
Wells v Wells [2001] Fam Law 656, FD
White v White [2001] 1 AC 596, [2000] 3 WLR 1571, [2000] 2 FLR 981, [2001] 1 All ER 1, HL

---

[1]   See *White v White* [2001] 1 AC 596, [2000] 2 FLR 981.

Lewis Marks QC and Alexander Thorpe for the petitioner
Nicholas Mostyn QC and Rebecca Bailey-Harris for the respondent

Cur adv vult

THORPE LJ

Introduction

[1]　　On 5 April 2005 Singer J handed down judgment in the present case.[2] For the parties it had been a long wait since the trial had commenced on the 11th and concluded on 15 October 2004. Singer J himself granted permission to appeal on 14 April 2005 saying:

> 'I agree that the Court of Appeal should review my decision in this case. The grounds advanced in oral argument ... were, in summary:
>
> (a)　the public and professional interest in this, the first post-*White* big money short marriage case;
>
> (b)　the quantum of the overall award;
>
> (c)　the manner in which I dealt with factual issues concerning the breakdown of the marriage.'

[2]　　The appeal has certainly generated a good deal of professional interest. Indeed Mr Marks QC, for the appellant husband, suggested that there was a string of cases awaiting the outcome of the appeal. However, in the end, the outcome depends not so much on the resolution of novel points but the familiar assessment of whether the judge's award falls within the generous ambit of discretion and whether its foundations are sound. The foundations in a number of instances are either not expressed or not expressed in much detail. That enabled Mr Marks to suggest that imprecisions were the result of the exceptional lapse of time between hearing and judgment. Mr Mostyn QC, for the respondent wife, however characterised the judgment as commendably succinct, a virtue that has allowed the judge to express some of his views by nuances. Mr Mostyn's characterisation is apt and Mr Marks was unable to demonstrate that the judgment's long gestation accounted for any obvious errors or omissions. However, undoubtedly the appeal has been difficult to decide and most of the difficulties can be ascribed to two shortcomings in the judgment. The first is the failure to make a fuller record and finding of all the facts and circumstances relevant to the exercise of the discretion conferred upon the judge by s 25 of the Matrimonial Causes Act 1973. The second is the judge's failure to explain his ultimate award more fully. His overall award of £5m is achieved by a transfer to the wife of the matrimonial home free of mortgage (agreed value £2.3m) and a capital fund of £2.7m to ensure her relative affluence. Mr Marks suggested, and Mr Mostyn did not demur, that the judge had first decided that the award should be £5m and then that it was reasonable for her to retain the home. The mathematical consequence was that the lump sum should be £2.7m. With that brief overview of what has emerged as the heart of this appeal, I will now record the basic facts.

2　　Editor's note: see *M v M (Short Marriage: Clean Break)* [2005] EWHC 528 (Fam), [2005] 2 FLR 533.

The history

[3] The husband is English and 41 years of age. The wife is American and 36 years of age. The husband first married in 1987, a marriage that was dissolved in 1992. He is an exceptionally successful fund manager. In turn he has worked for Gartmore, Jupiter and New Star.

[4] The wife arrived in this jurisdiction in February 1995 to take up a 2-year contract with a pharmaceutical company in Cambridge. The parties met in the summer of 1995 and shortly thereafter commenced an intimate relationship. Between their respective positions there was a considerable financial disparity. The wife had a salary of about £85,000 pa and lived in a rented flat in Cambridge. The husband was a high earner. With Jupiter his annual earnings, inclusive of bonus, might exceed £1m pa.

[5] Perhaps curiously, this intimate relationship, described by Mr Marks as courtship, continued for no less than 4 years before the couple committed to marriage by their engagement in the summer of 1999. Seemingly to avoid the disapproval of her parents, the wife was not prepared to cohabit in advance of marriage. It took place on 14 July 2000. In preparation, the husband bought the home at 16 Elm Park Road in February 2000 for £1.8m. The wife moved to London and to a London job at about that date. In March 2000 the husband received the enormous sum of £20m. This was the second tranche of sums due to him as a result of the sale of Jupiter to Commerzbank completed some 5 years earlier. The husband has always been closely allied in business to John Duffield. He was the founder of Jupiter and he had recruited the husband from Gartmore. In May 2000 Mr Duffield started to invest in New Star and entered into a gentlemen's agreement with the husband to give him a 20% of the venture if and when the husband could be extricated from Commerzbank.

[6] This objective was achieved on 29 January 2001 when the husband left Jupiter to join New Star as it commenced to trade. The husband brought with him from Jupiter three substantial hedge-funds and duly received 200,000 £1 shares in New Star issued at par. As a result of the move, the husband suffered a huge reduction in basic salary but acquired at par 200,000 shares which at the date of their issue were already being placed elsewhere at £80 per share. Furthermore, these shares had the obvious potential to rise significantly in value above even that high plane. Although the husband in August 2003 granted an option to Mr Duffield to purchase 75,000 of his shares at £80 a share in December 2006, the remaining 125,000 shares hold the potential for further gain.

[7] In May 2001 the wife gave up her employment. She had developed a considerable interest in interior design; the London home was complete and attention turned to a villa in the south of France offered to the wife on her birthday in June and purchased in joint names in September 2001. Its refurbishment was completed by April 2002.

[8] The parties had agreed deferring children at the outset of marriage. After all, at that date the wife was only just 31. The husband suggested that she should abandon the contraceptive pill first in autumn 2001 and again at Christmas. The wife wanted to wait until the work on the villa had been completed. Thus it was that in May she came off the pill and quickly conceived. Sadly, in late August she miscarried. Despite every effort, the wife did not conceive again and on 23 April 2003 the husband left to pursue his relationship with another woman, whom he has since married.

The proceedings

[9] Divorce proceedings swiftly followed and within the proceedings the real issue has been money. On 17 October 2003 District Judge Bowman made a substantial order for maintenance pending suit. Amongst other directions she provided for the simultaneous exchange of narrative affidavits dealing with all relevant s 25 factors not later than 6 weeks before the date fixed for the financial dispute resolution (FDR) hearing. She also provided that each should answer the other's questionnaire raised on their respective Forms E. I will refer later to the wife's answer to questionnaire and also to the contents of the narrative affidavits.

[10] Sumner J conducted the FDR hearing on 6 February 2004. The FDR failed its primary purpose and an order was drawn to prepare the case for trial. The order was preceded by the following recital:

> 'And upon the respondent declaring that she will not be relying upon s 25(2)(g) of the Matrimonial Causes Act 1973 in the prosecution of her claim for ancillary relief against the petitioner.'

[11] However, para 9 of the order provided for the simultaneous exchange of affidavits in reply to the narrative affidavits filed pursuant to the order of District Judge Bowman. These reply affidavits were duly filed in mid-April.

[12] The next relevant development was a pre-trial review before the President on the 29 July 2004. Nothing was then said concerning the wife's promise not to rely upon conduct. However, on 6 August her solicitors wrote to say that counsel had 'come across the only recently reported case of *G v G (Financial Provision: Separation Agreement)* [2004] 1 FLR 1011'. They continued by saying that at the trial they intended to rely on *G v G* 'to establish the facts that led to end of the marriage, and as a defensive shield to the reliance that no doubt will be made by your client on the duration of the marriage'.

The trial

[13] The husband's advisers inevitably regarded this as unprincipled and at the outset of the trial applied to the judge to rule that the wife was bound by her declaration and was, therefore, precluded from asserting that it was the husband's conduct that had destroyed the marriage. The judge refused that application for reasons which he explained in a brief extempore judgment. He emphasised his statutory duty to consider all the circumstances of the case and particularly the criteria in s 25(2). He noted that each of the parties had given a lengthy account of the marriage and its breakdown in their narrative affidavits and that the husband was not proposing to withdraw any of his criticisms of the wife. Accordingly, the trial proceeded, each of the parties being in the witness box for about a day. Mr Duffield was called on the husband's behalf and each of the parties relied upon a highly qualified forensic accountant to offer an opinion as to the value of the husband's New Star shares. Inevitably, the wife's expert advanced the high ground and the husband's the low ground.

[14] The submissions advanced by counsel were equally polarised. Mr Pointer QC, who then appeared for the husband, submitted that the wife was only entitled to be returned to her former position as a professional woman living in a flat with an income of about £50,000 a year net. Mr Pointer submitted that that could be achieved by allowing her £500,000 to purchase a flat and a £120,000 to cover 3 years of revenue shortfall whilst she worked her way back to her former level. Thus, he urged, the husband's offer of £1.3m was generous.

[15] Mr Mostyn asserted that as a consequence of the decision in *White v White* [2001] 1 AC 596, [2000] 2 FLR 981, the proper approach was to calculate the wife's award by reference to the marital acquest, that is to say the increase in the husband's fortune during the period of marriage. The extent of the acquest was much in dispute. Fundamentally, it was argued for the husband that the New Star shares were acquired before the marriage, since they were the subject of the gentlemen's agreement between the husband and Mr Duffield in May 2000. The obvious counter was that since they were not acquired by the husband until January 2001 they were the product of the years of marriage. We may add to that the differences between the wife's accountant (£20m) and the husband's accountant (£14m). From all that disputed territory Mr Mostyn drew his submission that the wife's award should be £7.2m, representing 37.5% of the marital acquest.

[16] The effect of Singer J's judgment can be broadly summarised as follows:

(1) He accepted the wife's evidence as to the circumstances of the marriage and its breakdown.

(2) He declined either to rule on the difference of opinion between the forensic accountants or to put a value on the New Star shares.

(3) He rejected the approach advocated by both Mr Pointer and Mr Mostyn.

(4) He held that the wife's half-share of the French villa should go to the husband but that the wife should have the London home valued at £2.3m.

(5) He added a lump sum of £2.7m to enable him to conclude his judgment with the following sentence:

'A global award equivalent to £5m (plus the furniture and chattels which have been agreed) seems to me a fair outcome irrespective of whatever value H in due course may achieve for the N Ltd shares.'

The appeal

[17] In his grounds of appeal and skeleton argument Mr Marks contended:

(1) The judge erred in permitting the wife to adduce evidence as to the cause of the breakdown in the face of her FDR declaration.

(2) The judge erred in holding that the husband was to blame for the breakdown of the marriage and that this consideration shielded the wife from the husband's reliance on the short duration of the marriage.

(3) The judge was plainly wrong to justify his substantial award on the ground that the wife had a legitimate expectation that she would live at a higher standard of affluence than she had enjoyed prior to the marriage on a long-term basis.

(4) The judge wrongly rejected a clear line of authority that established the principle on which claims were to be determined in short marriage cases. In particular he relied upon *S v S* [1977] Fam 127; *H v H (Financial Provision: Short Marriage)* (1981) 2 FLR 392; *Robertson v Robertson* (1983) 4 FLR 387 and *Hedges v Hedges* [1991] 1 FLR 196.

[18] In his skeleton argument Mr Mostyn had skilfully developed a response to each of the appellant's grounds. However at the conclusion of Mr Marks' submissions he was asked to address only two questions, namely:

(a) was the judge's conclusion sufficiently explained and reasoned;

(b) was the judge's overall award plainly excessive?

[19] In a succinct oral submission he characterised the judgment as heavily nuanced, but submitted that it was possible to construct an adequate and clear rationalisation from a careful analysis of its key paragraphs. From those paragraphs it emerged that the judge was clearly impressed by the wife's commitment to the marriage. Its short duration was neutralised by the combination of that commitment and the wife's comparable innocence in its breakdown. Furthermore, the judge had had proper regard to the wife's needs.

[20]   As to the scale of the overall award, Mr Mostyn emphasised that it represented something between one sixth and one seventh of the husband's fortune. The product of the marriage was something between £12m and £16m. Taking a middle figure, £5m represented 34% of the marital acquest.

[21]   Finally, he submitted that, before we could interfere, it would not be enough for us to conclude that the judge's reasoning was too attenuated if we were satisfied that the overall award lay within the very wide ambit of his discretion. Only if we concluded that the award was plainly excessive, as well as inadequately reasoned, could we interfere.

Conclusions

The procedural point

[22]   Mr Marks' criticisms are, at least superficially, well directed. The case of *G v G (Financial Provision: Separation Agreement)* [2004] 1 FLR 1011 was decided in this court on 28 June 2000 but only reported some 4 years later. That report clearly led to a major readjustment of the wife's case. In her Form E she had reserved the right to rely on s 25(2)(g). In his questionnaire the husband required her to state her position if she intended to rely on conduct which it would be inequitable for the court to disregard. Her answer of 19 December 2003 stated:

> 'The marriage came to an end at the sole behest of the petitioner who had formed an adulterous relationship with another woman. The respondent says that she is an innocent wife. In such circumstances the petitioner should not be heard to use the argument that "this marriage only lasted a very short time" (*Brett v Brett* [1969] 1 WLR 487).'

[23]   That was, therefore, the case she declared that she had abandoned at the date of the FDR some 6 weeks later. However, the case revived by her solicitor's letter of 6 August was the very same case.

[24]   In my judgment, that analysis does not carry Mr Marks very far. A retreat from a clear declaration is generally to be deprecated and may in many cases result in a heavy costs penalty. But such a declaration cannot possibly override or circumscribe the trial judge's obligation to investigate whatever he conceives relevant and necessary to enable him to discharge his statutory duty. Ancillary relief proceedings are quasi-inquisitorial and the judge is never confined by what the parties elect to put in evidence or by whatever they may agree to exclude from evidence.

[25]   Singer J was indisputably right to rule, as he did on 11 October, particularly given that the declaration had to be weighed in the context of the contentious affidavits filed by the parties both before and after the making of the declaration.

[26]   Mr Marks sought to meet that difficulty by asserting that, as a matter of principle and construction, allegations of conduct in ancillary relief could only be advanced under s 25(2)(g) and if that subsection was excluded by agreement or concession, then conduct could not be introduced as an aspect of any other of the statutory criteria. Thus it was not open to a party to disavow s 25(2)(g) and then contend that the other spouse's contribution, which s 25(2)(f) requires the court to assess, was valueless or devalued because of attitude or conduct. In support of this

submission he relied upon the case of *Wells v Wells* only reported at first instance in a note at [2001] Fam Law 656. The note could be read to record a conclusion that where a party alleges that the other has made a nil contribution to the welfare of the family the case must be advanced under s 25(2)(g). However, the note is ambiguous and without the judgment itself it is pointless to consider that authority further.

[27]   Mr Marks further submitted that it was not open to an applicant to finesse the other party's reliance on the short duration of the marriage by asserting that the breakdown was the consequence of the other's conduct. That case could only be mounted under s 25(2)(g), as the wife had here correctly recognised by her response to questionnaire.

[28]   Mr Marks contended that were we to hold otherwise, we would be flouting the principle established in the seminal case of *Wachtel v Wachtel* [1973] Fam 72 and opening the floodgates to ancillary relief trials that would be akin to the bitter defended divorce that flourished prior to the Divorce Reform Act 1969.

[29]   These submissions cannot be right, in my judgment. The statutory criteria are not to be rigidly characterised. The judge has an overriding obligation to regard and to reflect in his judgment 'all the circumstances of the case'. In my judgment, the language of s 25(2)(g) is intended to discourage allegations of conduct unless it is such that it would be inequitable to disregard. In other words, it is pointless, and in terms of costs, risky, to assert misconduct that does not measure high on the scale of gravity. But conduct that would not merit advancing under s 25(2)(g) is not, therefore, irrelevant or inadmissible. Often the court's assessment of the worth of the comparable contributions will require consideration of motives, attitudes, commitments and responsibilities.

[30]   As to the relevance of those factors in assessing the significance to be attached to the duration of the marriage, the proper approach is already settled by my judgment in the case of *G v G (Financial Provision: Separation Agreement)* [2004] 1 FLR 1011 with which the President and Wright J agreed. In presenting his appeal, Mr Pointer criticised Connell J for effectively relying on the husband's misconduct as a counter-balancing factor to the brevity of the marriage. My response to that submission is expressed in para [34] of the judgment when I said:

> 'A judge has to do fairness between the parties, having regard to all the circumstances. He must be free to include within that discretionary review the factors which compelled the wife to terminate the marriage as she did. The point was essentially taken as a defensive shield to the reliance upon the duration submission. There must surely be room for the exercise of a judicial discretion between the pole of a wife who is driven to petition by the husband's unfeeling misconduct and that of a wife who exits from a marriage capriciously and for her own advantage. It seems to me that the judge was doing no more than taking his bearings as to where he stood along that path.'

[31]   That passage seems to me to be fatal to Mr Marks' submission. He sought to distinguish the case by asserting that there the wife's case at trial had been both presented and found to be conduct inequitable to disregard within the meaning of s 25(2)(g). The judgment of Connell J in the Family Division was contemporaneously reported at [2000] 2 FLR 18. I do not consider that Connell J did so find. Further, even had he done so, I would not consider the distinction that Mr Marks seeks to draw as valid. On this aspect Singer J directed himself by reference to the decision of this court in *G v G* and he was clearly right so to do. Having seen and heard the parties extensively cross-examined, he was plainly entitled to conclude that the husband was to blame for the breakdown of the marriage. That finding entitled him to give much less weight to the duration of the marriage than he would have done had he found that the wife was to blame for its breakdown or that the parties had separated consensually,

each acknowledging unexpected incompatibility. Those conclusions lead to the rejection of Mr Marks' first and second grounds.

Principles

[32]   It is now convenient to consider Mr Marks' fourth ground in which he vigorously but vainly sought to argue that cases largely decided about 25 years ago settled the principle to be applied in determining claims arising out of brief marriages. The principle drawn from those early cases was that the award should be enough to get the unhappy applicant back on her feet. I think that characterisation is probably drawn from the judgment of Balcombe J in *Robertson v Robertson* (1983) 4 FLR 387 when at 392 he said:

> 'I also order a lump payment of £15,000 which seems to me more than adequate to enable the wife to get on her feet again.'

[33]   There are a number of very good reasons why that should no longer be the modern approach. First, it originated and developed during long years in which the yardstick for measuring the extent of the applicant's claim was an assessment of her reasonable requirements. Secondly, a marriage is not to be equated to a purely financial venture where the court may redress breach of contract or the disintegration of a partnership by an award of damages or other financial relief. Section 25 requires a more sophisticated evaluation of the extent of the wife's commitment to and investment in the marriage emotionally and psychologically. In some cases it may be necessary for the court to assess emotional and psychological damage and the extent to which the applicant's future capacity and opportunity to enter into a fulfilling family life has been blighted. What a party has given to a marriage and what a party has lost on its failure cannot be measured by simply counting the days of its duration.

[34]   Thirdly, Mr Marks' reliance on the old cases is clearly precluded by the decision of this court in *Foster v Foster* [2003] EWCA Civ 565, [2003] 2 FLR 299. Between that case and the present there is an obvious similarity in that the duration of each was approximately 2¾ years. In other respects, the cases are clearly distinguishable. In *Foster* the means of the parties were comparatively modest, the assets being approximately £400,000. Furthermore, during the marriage each had contributed to property dealing and development which had proved profitable. The wife had made the greater financial contribution to the dealing. The district judge decided to return to each what he or she had brought into the marriage as well as such post-separation contributions as he or she had made. The profits made during the marriage were to be divided equally between the parties. The result of that exercise left the wife with approximately 61% and the husband 39%. The wife appealed successfully to the circuit judge who increased her share to 70%. The husband's appeal succeeded and this court restored the order of the district judge. Since it was a second appeal caught by the provision of s 55 of the Access to Justice Act 1998 this court could not grant permission unless the husband demonstrated an important point of principle or practice or some other compelling reason. Hale LJ (as she then was) explained that the husband had cleared that hurdle thus:

> 'in our view the case does raise the important issue of the proper approach, in the light of *White v White* and later decisions of this court, to the parties' respective contributions in a short childless marriage where both are working. Accordingly, we gave permission to appeal.'

[35]   Accordingly, in her judgment Hale LJ considered the impact of the decisions in *White v White* [2001] 1 AC 596, [2000] 2 FLR 981, *Cowan v Cowan* [2001] EWCA Civ

679, [2002] Fam 97, [2001] 2 FLR 192 and *Lambert v Lambert* [2002] EWCA Civ 1685, [2003] Fam 103, [2003] 1 FLR 139. Counsel for the wife argued that those authorities were solely concerned with the problem of evaluating the very different contributions of breadwinner and homemaker over a long marriage where there have been children to bring up. They were of no relevance to a short, childless marriage where both parties had been working. Hale LJ rejected that submission emphatically. In para [19] she recorded counsel's eventual concession that where a substantial surplus had been generated by joint efforts it could not matter whether they had taken a short or long time to do so.

[36]   Although the facts of that case are very different and although much of the judgment is directed to the features of the particular case, it is clear that Hale LJ was signalling a fresh approach to measuring of awards in cases involving marriage of short duration. In my opinion, she says so expressly in the passages to which I have referred. Furthermore, she underlines that implicitly by omitting any reference to the old cases, cases which would, of course, have been very familiar to her.

The award

[37]   That leaves for consideration the husband's third ground, the only ground which, in my judgment, held substantial prospects of success. Was the judge right to found his award on the wife's legitimate expectation? Was his award plainly excessive? To answer these questions requires a careful analysis of the judgment.

[38]   The judge's explanation for the end result is by no means straightforward or clear. The case was extremely hard fought by the best available professionals on both sides. At its conclusion the husband was surely entitled to a clear explanation as to why the judge had opted for an award much closer to the submission of Mr Mostyn. Mr Mostyn effectively conceded the absence of a clear and simple explanation when he described the judgment, with customary advocacy, as heavily nuanced. I have read and re-read the judgment in a search for its true ratio. In the end I think that it can be discerned from the following significant paragraphs taken in combination.

[39]   First, in para [48] the judge explains his rejection of the old yardstick: what is required to get the wife on her feet. In para [48] he said:

> 'I can, therefore, accept that there may be cases – relatively extreme cases – where such an approach would remain valid. But I am satisfied that it would not be fair to apply it in this case. For what it ignores is the key element to my mind present here. That is that by virtue of this marriage, taken in its proper setting, both in terms of the way it was reached and the way it ended, H gave W a legitimate expectation than she would on a long-term basis be living on a higher economic plane than the rented flat and her £85,000 pa job had afforded her when she left them to live with him as his wife at the house he bought for that purpose. It would, in my judgment, quite simply be unfair to take the view as submitted by Mr Pointer that £500,000 for the purchase of a flat and £120,000 to cover 3 years of revenue shortfall until she could recoup her position in her specialist field would be adequate, and thus that H's £1.3m offer is very generous.'

[40]   This paragraph reveals that the decisive factor for the judge was that the marriage, taken in its full context, gave the wife a legitimate entitlement to a long-term future on a higher plane of affluence than she had enjoyed prior to marriage.

[41]   This then recurs in paras [64] and [65] when the judge said:

> 'This then, as it appears to me, is one of what may be a rare group of cases where the attempt to measure what the yardstick of equality should be set against is to beat the air or to hunt a chimaera. The game is simply not worth the very uncertain and extremely

expensive candle. Fairness can be better achieved, in my view, by carrying out the discretionary exercise ordained by the statute in recognition of all the relevant factors. Amongst those the short duration of the marriage, set in the context of its factual matrix as I have attempted to do, is undoubtedly very significant. Of course, I must strive to avoid a discriminatory approach based on outmoded concepts of differential financial and non-financial contributions. I must reflect what I believe is that modern approach by not limiting the award to an amount which will put this wife back where she was or which will, rather patronisingly, put her back on her feet.

[65] Rather, as it seems to me, the award should recognise that H has by this marriage, notwithstanding its short duration, given W a reasonable expectation that her life as once again a single woman need not revert to what it was before her marriage, and that she should be able to live at a significantly better standard in terms of accommodation and spendable income, even if at one which does not approach the level that H can afford for himself and his new family.'

[42]   Whilst I accept that in the context of this case the judge was entitled to regard as 'the key element' the wife's 'legitimate expectation' of living to a higher standard as the ex-wife of Mr Miller, I emphasise that it is a fact-dependent conclusion and it is not to be elevated into a principle or yardstick filling a vacuum created by the rejection of the restitutionary objective sought in the old cases.

[43]   Now it is necessary to cite in full the concluding four paragraphs under the subheading 'The Award':

'My conclusion is that W should have the opportunity to retain the former matrimonial home for as long as she chooses to live in it. Subject to any adjustment to the form of the order to accommodate her potential exposure to US tax, I intend that it should be transferred to her free of mortgage. That will involve H paying off the liability of about £500,000 secured on it or adding it to the lump sum payment to enable W to redeem it herself. The value of that property after deduction of notional sale costs has been taken as about £2.3m.

[71] In addition, a fair outcome to this case is that H will pay W a lump sum of a further £2.7m. If the *Duxbury* methodology is taken simply as a guide, then the computer programme *Capitalise* suggests that for a woman soon to be 36 a fund utilised in accordance with usual principles would generate an initial annual net income of about £98,000.

[72] That is very significantly less than the budget of well over £200,000 which W asserted was the sum of the costs met by H in the last year of cohabitation, suitably trimmed to reflect his departure. She will not be able to afford that standard, but with an income of that order, plus whatever she can earn, she will be able to live to a very tolerable standard in that house.

[73] A global award equivalent to £5m (plus the furniture and chattels which have been agreed) seems to me a fair outcome irrespective of whatever value H in due course may achieve for the N Ltd shares.'

[44]   It is possible to elaborate on the factors that emerged in those crucial paragraphs from the judge's earlier findings. First, as to 'the way (the marriage) was reached', the judge in paras [27]–[32] considered what weight should be given to the 5 years of intimate relationship immediately preceding the marriage. Essentially, he adopted the middle way. In para [29] he said:

'This rather tentative relationship, at least on H's part, until their engagement does not fit entirely happily to my mind with the epithets "exclusive" and "committed" which

Mr Mostyn invites me to apply. But it was certainly several grades more significant than H's rather dismissive description of it as one merely of "girlfriend and boyfriend".'

[45]   Then in para [32] he said:

'Into the balancing exercise I will put the fact, as I find, that there was no mutual commitment to make their lives together until their engagement in July 1999. Until then their ties were tentative, and their separate expectations did not accord. In this relationship there was no pre-engagement honeymoon to blend seamlessly into marriage. I tend, therefore, to favour Mr Pointer's submissions and treat this as a marriage of relatively short duration.'

[46]   As to 'the way (the marriage) ended', the judge left the middle ground to accept the wife's case. His essential findings are in paras [37] and [38] when he said:

'This marriage may well have been doomed, but my conclusions as an analysis of the explanations that I heard from both of them are these. H may well have developed an irritation with aspects of W's personality and behaviour. This reflects more his lack of adaptability than any shortcomings on her part. The sum of what he complains of is not marriage-breaking stuff. I do not subscribe to his view that his burgeoning relationship with the woman with whom he lives was a consequence rather than a cause of the breakdown.

[38]   None of this, to state the obvious, is conduct which it would be inequitable to disregard in arriving at a resolution of the financial dispute. But it has the result that it would be unfair to W to concentrate solely on the bare chronology of this marriage without acknowledging that she did not seek to end it nor did she give H any remotely sufficient reason for him to do so.'

[47]   In relation to their respective contributions, the judge's findings were again favourable to the wife. In considering their rival claims to the French villa he said:

'I have no doubt W is right that she was far more absorbed in the grand scheme as well as the minutiae of the property's conversion ...'

[48]   His overall conclusion is clear from para [43] in which he said:

'W's contributions to their family life were non-financial (save to the extent that she worked at the start of the marriage). She aspired to provide, as I have said, the domestic and social fabric in which they could both enjoy the fruits of H's success and the opportunities for leisure, relaxation and enjoyment which were available. A major contribution in this context was the planning and oversight she brought to the refurbishment, equipping and furnishing of the French property to which H has become so attached. Neither the modest period during which she was able to make this contribution, nor the very considerable scale of H's efforts and the rewards they brought him, affect the proposition, which I accept, that incommensurable though these contributions are as chalk and cheese, nevertheless no discriminatory attitude should be allowed to treat them as other than equivalent.'

[49]   Amplification of the paragraphs explaining the award is also capable of extraction from earlier paragraphs. As to the transfer of the former matrimonial home, a glancing reference in para [40] reveals that her objective in seeking to retain it was in part to use its extra space as an office for her projected future consultancy in interior design. It must also be balanced against [26], the paragraph in which the judge concluded that the fairer outcome was for the husband to have the outright ownership of the second home. Although there is no description of the matrimonial home in the judgment, during the course of argument we were shown the particulars prepared in the sale to the husband which demonstrate that it is a comparatively modest property with three bedrooms on four floors.

[50]   As to the judge's seeming reliance on the *Duxbury* methodology in para [71], he had earlier stated in para [40]:

'Although I shall refer as a point of reference only to a *Duxbury* calculation, I do not propose to decide this case upon the basis of any strict or even tangential reliance upon that to fix the award ...'

[51]   The reference to the wife's earning capacity in para [72] is apt, given that the judge had found in para [40]:

'But that she has and should exercise an earning capacity, given her age and aptitude, is incontestable, and I take it into account as one of the factors in the case.'

[52]   The reference in the final paragraph to 'whatever value the husband in due course may achieve for the N Ltd shares' is in, my judgment, significant. In his initial outline of the case the judge recorded the prospect of future sale of the New Star shares which might, subject to clearing a number of hurdles, 'net him something of the order of £24.44m'. There is another reference in para [41] when the judge said:

'In addition there is a good likelihood that at some stage the potential of his shares will be unleashed.'

[53]   It is easy and superficial to characterise this as a pay-off of £5m for a mere 2¾ years of marriage. In my judgment, the reality is very different. Although the judge did not attach much weight to the 4 years preceding engagement, the fact is that at the age of 26 the applicant committed herself to this man. The judge's findings show that during that period ambivalence was all on the husband's side. In para [28] he wrote:

'Until then W was hoping to marry H with more enthusiasm than he was demonstrating for that commitment, in my judgment.'

[54]   On engagement, she moved to London and found fresh employment. At the outset of the marriage, she worked to ensure the emergence of a primary home and a holiday home fit for his status as a leader in his chosen field. Once that was achieved, she tried for a family. The responsibility for the collapse of that endeavour must in part be ascribed to the husband's decision to end the marriage. Finally, it must not be forgotten that the net value of the award is, in reality, £4.5m, given the judge's decision that the wife's half-share in the villa was to go to the husband.

[55]   On that analysis, my ultimate conclusion is that the judge's award was both sufficiently, if obliquely, explained and that it cannot be labelled plainly excessive. In my judgment, it lies at the top end of the permissible bracket. Had I been sitting at first instance, I do not think that I would have gone so high. However, I would emphasise that the facts and circumstances of the case are highly unusual. The ambit of the judge's discretion in cases involving very large assets and a short childless marriage is particularly wide. Furthermore, Mr Mostyn rightly reminded us of the words of Lord Hoffmann in *Piglowska v Piglowski* [1999] 1 WLR 1360, [1999] 2 FLR 763 when he said:

'First, the appellate court must bear in mind the advantage which the first instance judge had in seeing the parties and the other witnesses. This is well understood on questions of credibility and findings of primary fact. But it goes further than that. It applies also to the judge's evaluation of those facts. If I may quote what I said in *Biogen Inc. v Medeva Plc.* [1997] R.P.C. 1, 45:

"The need for appellate caution in reversing the trial judge's evaluation of the facts is based upon much more solid grounds than professional courtesy. It is because specific findings of fact, even by the most meticulous judge, are inherently an incomplete statement of the impression which was made upon him by the primary evidence. His expressed findings are always surrounded by a penumbra of imprecision as to emphasis, relative weight, minor qualification and nuance ... of which time and language do not permit exact expression, but which may play an important part in the judge's overall evaluation."

The second point follows from the first. The exigencies of daily court room life are such that reasons for judgment will always be capable of having been better expressed. This is particularly true of an unreserved judgment such as the judge gave in this case but also of a reserved judgment based upon notes, such as was given by the district judge. These reasons should be read on the assumption that, unless he has demonstrated the contrary, the judge knew how he should perform his functions and which matters he should take into account. This is particularly true when the matters in question are so well known as those specified in s 25(2). An appellate court should resist the temptation to subvert the principle that they should not substitute their own discretion for that of the judge by a narrow textual analysis which enables them to claim that he misdirected himself.'

[56]   Although I have not found this an easy appeal, in the end I am firm in my conclusion that it must be dismissed. My judgment may well only serve to increase the husband's sense that the courts have been hard on him, but the limitations on the role of the appellate court are clearly spelt out.

WALL LJ

[57]   I agree. Like Thorpe LJ, whose judgment I have had the opportunity to read in draft, I have not found this an easy appeal. In the event, however, I have been persuaded by Mr Mostyn's skilful analysis of the judgment: (a) that the judge has sufficiently, if exiguously, explained his reasoning process; and (b) that the award is not so excessive as to be outside the band within which reasonable disagreement is possible.

[58]   It was, I think, unfortunate, that Mr Marks devoted so much of both his skeleton argument and his oral submissions to his first two grounds of appeal. These were: (1) that the judge erred in the exercise of his discretion by permitting Mrs Miller to adduce evidence as to the alleged cause of the breakdown of the parties' relationship, despite the parties having previously agreed that Mrs Miller would not be relying on any allegation of conduct which it would be inequitable for the court to disregard; and (2) that by conducting 'an inquisition into which party was more to blame for the breakdown of the relationship', and by finding that Mr Miller's 'fault in the divorce represented a shield to the assertion that this was a short marriage case', the judge conducted an exercise which was 'outside his discretion, the Matrimonial Causes Act 1973 (MCA 1973) having proscribed inquiry into the fault behind divorce save where there was conduct by one party which was such that it would be inequitable for the court to disregard it'.

[59]   In my judgment, these are bad points, for all the reasons Thorpe LJ gives in paras [22]–[31] of his judgment. I was equally unimpressed by Mr Marks' deployment of the 'floodgates' argument, expressed in his skeleton, in the following way:

'The court should not attempt to step into the shoes of one man and say that the straw that broke the camel's back in the relationship with his wife would not have broken the back of the court were the court in that relationship with that wife. Civil and criminal law dictate that you must take a man as you find him. The Family Division, however, pursuant to this judgment, must hereafter apply the test of an objective bystander in assessing where the fault for marital breakdown lies. The objective bystander, in this case the judge, stands loftily over the relationship and imposes his own moral perception of right and wrong in the midst of the enormous emotional upset of a marital breakdown.'

[60]   I recognise in this passage neither what Singer J did, nor what judges in short marriage cases will be required to do in the future. Nor do I agree with Mr Marks when he asserts of the judge:

'His view, set out over five short paragraphs of his judgment, attributes fault to the husband. Necessarily, that judgment is wholly flawed given the complexities of the human relationship, and is an exercise upon which he should never have embarked. Limited examination of the parties in cross-examination can only have provided the judge with the most superficial perspective of the parties and their marriage. Despite the obviously limited scope of the inquiry, the judge considered himself able to point the finger of blame for the breakdown of the relationship at the husband.'

[61]   The extravagance of Mr Marks' rhetoric can, I think, be tested both by what Singer J found, and how he went about it. In the first place, he was plainly right, in my judgment, to follow and apply paras [32]–[34] of Thorpe LJ's judgment in *G v G (Financial Provision: Separation Agreement)* [2004] 1 FLR 1011, para [34] of which Thorpe LJ has set out in para [30] of his judgment in the instant case, and which I will not repeat. I find it, however, an entirely accurate analysis of how a judge exercises a proper judicial discretion when dealing with s 25(2)(d) of the Matrimonial Causes Act 1973 (MCA 1973) in a short marriage case.

[62]   Secondly, an important factor for the judge (and manifestly one of the circumstances of the case) was Mrs Miller's commitment to the marriage. We know that Mrs Miller miscarried in August 2002. In para [36] of his judgment, Singer J said:

'Until only a few months before their separation these spouses were both hoping to have a child. He disengaged from that process at a time when he may well have sensed at least the beginnings of the relationship that led him to leave (her).'

[63]   The issue was not complex. Part of Mrs Miller's case, as found by the judge, was that the breakdown of the marriage was 'largely if not entirely attributable to an intimate relationship H formed with the woman with whom he now lives, the physical separation having occurred the day after he revealed the association' to his wife. The judge had taken the view that:

'... W's evidence could not be circumscribed as to preclude her from airing this issue without which it would be impossible to gauge the strength and impact of the catalogue of complaints about her conduct during cohabitation advanced by H to seek to justify (as I find was his intention) his decision that the marriage had no future and/or to dilute what W asserts was the destructive impact of his adultery. His case is clear: he maintains that his new association was a consequence of an unhappy marriage rather than a cause of its breakdown.'

[64]   Moreover, the investigation had proved valuable. The judge commented:

'... I do, as a result of hearing this evidence, regard myself as better able to position myself fairly in relation to W's claims than otherwise would have been the case. I am, moreover, satisfied that H was not put at a disadvantage by this ruling. W did not seek to go beyond what she had already said on the topic in her affidavit evidence. I do not believe that H's case on these issues would have been improved by any more intensive preparation than had already been devoted to it.'

[65]   It is to be noted that the judge embarked on this fact finding exercise by reference to the particular facts of the case. This is, of course, what the profession would call a 'big money/short marriage' case. On the particular facts of this case, the reasons for the breakdown of the marriage were relevant. That does not mean that they will be relevant in every case, nor does it mean that, if they are, there will need to be a disproportionate amount of time and costs spent investigating them. In this respect,

I agree with and adopt the following passage from Mr Mostyn's and Ms Bailey-Harris' skeleton argument:

'49.16   Mr Marks raises the spectre of Pandora's Box if the route that Singer J took is allowed to stand. He says that if the judgment is approved there would be merit in undertaking that assessment in every case. He says that it would open the floodgates to an inquiry that has been dead for 30 years. He says that an *"inevitable consequence would be the rebirth of the defended divorce"*. This is all so much rhetoric.

49.17   In the vast majority of cases established principles will guide the court to its conclusion without any need for consideration to be given to the reasons for the breakdown of the marriage. In all cases where the assets are insubstantial the predominant criterion will be the parties' respective needs, principally for accommodation. In a long marriage case, where the assets are substantial, and where they have been built up during the marriage, the result will almost invariably be an equal division. In a medium length marriage, where the assets are substantial, there may be a modest departure from equality to reflect the principle that a domestic contribution is an accrual over time. In a short marriage case, where there are children and where the assets are substantial, amongst the s 25 considerations the court will give particular recognition to the needs of the wife as the primary carer and to her future contributions in that role.

49.18   The court is only likely to entertain evidence and argument as to the reason for the breakdown of the marriage in a tiny handful of cases, where the marriage is short and childless, and where the assets are substantial, so much so that it can be said that the order that fairness requires can be met without impinging on the payer's needs. Moreover the judge is only likely to entertain evidence as to the cause of the breakdown of a marriage (in a case where s 25(2)(g) conduct is *not* pleaded) where, as here, one party not only relies strongly on the durational argument but also unjustifiably blames the other party for the breakdown in circumstances where his own hands are not clean. In the majority of short childless big money marriages the court will recognise, and the parties will accept, that the failure is a mutual misfortune where attribution of blame simply does not arise. In such cases there are no *G v G* poles within which the judge can align himself.

49.19   It can therefore be seen the spectre of floodgates is misconceived. The facts of this case were exceptional, as they were in *G v G*.

49.20   In this case the parties had set out their cases as to the reason for the failure of the marriage in their affidavits. They were shortly cross-examined on the topic. H did not instruct Mr Pointer to hold back in his cross-examination of W. Having read and heard the evidence Singer J was able to make the finding that was blindingly obvious to anyone who had attended the trial (para [37]):

"The sum of what he complains of is not marriage-breaking stuff. I do not subscribe to his view that his burgeoning relationship with the woman with whom he lives was a consequence rather than a cause of the breakdown."'

[66]   Finally, in relation to these two grounds of appeal, Singer J saw each of the parties in the witness box for a day. I entirely reject Mr Marks' submission that for an experienced and perceptive judge of the Family Division this 'provided the judge with the most superficial perspective of the parties and their marriage'. As the passages which I have cited clearly demonstrate, the judge said the investigation had helped him. I am no doubt at all that it did.

[67]   In my judgment, Mr Marks had two powerful arguments, both capable of very simple expression. The first was that the judge had simply not explained himself. The second was that the award was so large that, in the absence of a proper rationalisation, it was simply outside the band of reasonable decisions, and must, accordingly, be plainly wrong.

[68]   I acknowledge that, in my initial reading of the judgment, I was struck by the first point. This led me to think that the judge, highly experienced as he is in 'big money' cases, may have stepped 'outside the band' in awarding Mrs Miller a total of £5m. On the one hand, the judge had, rightly in my view, rejected the 'needs' approach identified in the pre-*White* cases. He had, equally rightly in my view, rejected Mr Mostyn's 'matrimonial acquest' approach. He had, again rightly, attempted to achieve fairness, and avoid discrimination by 'carrying out the discretionary exercise ordained by the statute in recognition of all the relevant factors'. But what were the relevant factors? And how had he balanced them? These are not questions to which there are answers which stand out from the judgment.

[69]   And how had he arrived at £5m? He had plainly decided that Mrs Miller should be entitled to retain the former matrimonial home, and should give up her share in the French property. But those factors, as Mr Mostyn was minded to concede, only explain how he got to the lump sum of £2.7m. A judgment should tell the parties before the court why they have won or lost. Mr Miller is entitled to know why he has to write a cheque for £5m as opposed to some lesser amount. In my judgment, he has a reasonable complaint when the answer has to be teased out of the judgment by nuance, or when the judgment is skilfully unpicked and then repackaged by Mr Mostyn.

[70]   However, before turning to the judgment, the first question one has to ask, I think, is whether, as Mr Marks submitted, the line of pre-*White* short marriage cases such as *S v S* [1977] Fam 127, *Robertson v Robertson* (1983) 4 FLR 387, and *Attar v Attar (No 2)* [1985] FLR 653 remain good law. I am in no doubt at all that the answer to that question is 'no', and that the approach adopted in those decisions, both at first instance and in this court, cannot survive in the light of the decision of the House of Lords in *White*.

[71]   I am reinforced in that conclusion by the decision of this court in *Foster v Foster* [2003] EWCA Civ 565, [2003] 2 FLR 299 in which Hale LJ, giving the leading judgment, plainly applied the principles identified in *White* in a short marriage case. This is part of what she said:

> '[14]   As Thorpe LJ also said in *Cordle v Cordle*, at para [34], the only universal rule is to apply the criteria in s 25(2) of the Matrimonial Causes Act 1973 to all the circumstances of the case (giving first consideration to the welfare of any minor children) and to arrive at a fair result that avoids discrimination. In *White v White* [2001] 1 AC 596, [2000] 2 FLR 981, at 599–600/603–606 and 987 respectively, Lord Nicholls of Birkenhead explained that Parliament has declined to lay down any rules; it has given the courts a wide discretion to take account of all the relevant circumstances of the case; it has even repealed the original statutory objective of seeking to place the parties in the position in which they would have been had the marriage not broken down. Implicitly, the objective must be to achieve a fair outcome and there could be no presumption or starting point of equality of distribution. However, having conducted the statutory exercise:
>
>> "a judge would always be well advised to check his tentative views against the yardstick of equality of division. As a general guide, equality should be departed from only if, and to the extent that, there is good reason to do so. The need to consider and articulate reasons for departing from equality would help the parties and the court to focus on the need to ensure the absence of discrimination." (at 605 and 989 respectively)
>
> [15]   He also pointed out (at 605 and 989 respectively) that in seeking to achieve a fair outcome there was no room for discrimination between husband and wife and their respective roles. Whatever the division of labour chosen by the husband and wife, or forced upon them by circumstances, fairness requires that this should not prejudice or advantage either party when considering their respective contributions for the purpose of s 25(2)(f) of the Matrimonial Causes Act 1973. Section 25(2)(f) refers to the contribution

which each has made to the welfare of the family, including any contribution made by looking after the home or caring for the family. If in their different spheres each contributed equally to the family, then in principle it matters not which of them earned the money and built up the assets.

[16]   *White v White* [2001] 1 AC 596, [2000] 2 FLR 981 concerned a long marriage in which both parties had been engaged in breadwinning as well as homemaking and childrearing. The principle has recently been reaffirmed by this court in *Lambert v Lambert* [2002] EWCA Civ 1685, [2003] 1 FLR 139, where the parties' roles were more clearly demarcated, holding that it was unacceptable to place a greater value on the contribution of the breadwinner than that of the homemaker as a justification for dividing the product of the breadwinner's efforts unequally (although of course there might be other reasons for doing so, such as a disparity in the parties' needs).

[17]   Miss Boyd, on behalf of the wife, however, argues that these cases were concerned with the problem of evaluating the very different contributions of breadwinner and homemaker over a long marriage where there have been children to bring up. They are of no relevance to a short childless marriage where both parties have been working. The court has to consider the duration of the marriage under s 25(2)(d). Here the only contributions to be considered under s 25(2)(f) are those in money or money's worth and so the court is entitled to take account of the fact that one has contributed more than the other.

[18]   This is a surprising proposition ...'

[72]   *Foster v Foster* [2003] EWCA Civ 565, [2003] 2 FLR 299 was a case in which wealth had been accumulated during the marriage by the joint efforts of both husband and wife. The district judge decided, accordingly, that the right approach was to return to each party that with which they had entered the marriage and to share the wealth accumulated during the marriage equally between them. That approach was upheld in this court. The length of the marriage, in that case, was of very little relevance. As Hale LJ perceptively remarked, where 'a substantial surplus had been generated by their joint efforts, it could not matter whether they had taken a short or a long time to do so'. The case, in my view, is a warning of the dangers which can flow if there is a disproportionate emphasis on the brevity of the marriage.

[73]   The fact that the pre-*White* approach was discriminatory is, I think, well illustrated by looking at a case like *Gojkovic v Gojkovic and Another* [1992] Fam 40, [1991] 2 FLR 233, a decision now remembered more for this court's judgment on costs than for its facts. It was, however, a very short marriage, during which the parties built up a fortune in the region of £4m–£5m, all of which was in real property in the husband's sole name. He offered the wife a flat worth £295,000 and a lump sum on a *Duxbury* basis (she was 49) of £532,000 designed to provide her with a net income for life, index linked, of £30,000 pa. The judge awarded her £1.3m, and this court dismissed the husband's appeal.

[74]   It is now possible to see, with the wisdom of hindsight, that both the husband's offer (and, it must be said, the judge's award) were discriminatory. Had an applicant in Mrs Gojkovic's position applied for ancillary relief today, I have no doubt at all that the fair award for her would have been an equal division of the family fortune.

[75]   *Gojkovic v Gojkovic* was, of course, a contribution case *par excellence*, but it is nonetheless a good example of a case in which an unequal division of assets on a needs basis in a short marriage was, viewed with hindsight, both unfair and discriminatory.

[76]   In my judgment, the pre-*White* short marriage cases are all liable to attack on the basis that they are discriminatory. Mr Marks, in oral argument, sought to turn the point by suggesting that, after a short and childless marriage between young people, it was in reality patronising to give a woman more money than she needed to make herself economically independent, and to enable her 'to stand on her own feet'. It was a nice advocate's flourish, and his use of the word 'patronising' derived from para [64] of the judge's judgment, cited by Thorpe LJ at paras [41] of his. However, the judge's use of the word occurs in the context of the judge determining that 'he must strive to avoid a discriminatory approach based on outmoded concepts of differential financial and non-financial contributions'. The question, therefore, is whether, in the instant case, an award limited to enabling Mrs Miller to be economically independent and to 'stand on her own feet' is discriminatory. In my judgment, the answer to that question is plainly 'yes'.

[77]   Furthermore, I have to say I received no help on the difficult issue of quantum from Mr Marks' comparisons with awards for libel or professional negligence or personal injuries. Not only were such comparisons, in my judgment, irrelevant, but they seemed to me both to demean the status of marriage, and to take no account of the serious social, financial and psychological effects which irretrievable breakdown frequently has on those who suffer it.

[78]   So I am in no doubt at all that the judge was right to reject the pre-*White* cases. He was right to hold on to the terms of s 25 and the discretionary exercise, and to follow the guidance of Thorpe LJ in *McFarlane v McFarlane; Parlour v Parlour* [2004] EWCA (Civ) 872, [2005] Fam 171, [2004] 2 FLR 893 at [110]:

> 'The judges must remain focused on the statutory language, albeit recognising the need for evolutionary construction to reflect social and economic change. The statutory checklist and the overall circumstances of the case allow the judge to reflect factors which are said to be inherent in either the entitlement model or the compensation model. But to adopt one model or another or a combination of more than one is to don a strait-jacket and to deflect concentration from the statutory language. Clearly in the assessment of periodical payments, as of capital provision, the overriding objective is fairness. Discrimination between the sexes must be avoided.'

[79]   But the question abides: how did the judge reason his conclusion and reach his award? Mr Mostyn did not, of course, have the luxury of submitting that the judge was right because he had accepted counsel's submissions. There was no respondent's notice. Mr Mostyn played the width of discretion, fact specific, within the parameters cards, but readily acknowledged that they were not, as generalisations, enough. I searched his skeleton argument in vain for a specific answer to the question. Fortunately, Mr Mostyn provided it in oral argument.

[80]   Mr Mostyn began by acknowledging that he could not, as he put it, anatomise the one magnetic factor which had attracted the judge's award of £2.7m for the lump sum. The judge had, however, plainly and rightly taken account of the overall size of the husband's estate, which Mr Mostyn put as being in the order of £30m–£36m. The size of the matrimonial acquest was between £12m and £18m, and an award of £5m in total from such an estate was in no sense disproportionate. The judge had also been right to take account of Mrs Miller's commitment to the marriage, and had been entitled to use that factor to neutralise its brevity. When making an assessment of Mrs Miller's needs, the judge had been entitled to award her the former matrimonial home free of mortgage. He had also been right to make his finding, in para [65] of the judgment, that Mrs Miller had a 'reasonable expectation that her life as once again a single woman need not revert to what it was before her marriage'. Thorpe LJ has cited this paragraph in full in para [41] of his judgment.

[81]   Against that background, Mr Mostyn argued, the margin of appreciation inevitably remained at its widest in the big money, short and childless marriages cases.

Within such a wide discretion, it was impossible to say that the judge had misapplied it. The key factors, which the judge had identified, were fairness, non-discrimination and Mrs Miller's commitment to the marriage. Taken in the context of an estate of this magnitude, the judgment, whilst heavily nuanced, was not outside the band.

[82] I have had to consider very carefully whether or not Mr Mostyn's 'nuances' amount to an impermissible re-writing of the judgment, but I have come to the clear conclusion that they do not. On the facts of this particular case, I agree with Mr Mostyn that the award, whilst undoubtedly high, is 'within the band'. I add four short points which, in particular, reinforce my view.

[83] The first point is the house. It would have been open to the judge to give Mrs Miller a fund to purchase alternative accommodation rather than provide her with a mortgage-free property worth £2.3m. However, this seems to me a discretionary decision by the judge which, if properly reasoned, is one with which this court cannot properly interfere. There are three particular factors which, in my judgment, support the judge's decision on this point. The first, as Thorpe LJ has pointed out, is that whilst the property is undoubtedly in a fashionable part of London, it is not excessive in size, and has the potential to be used by Mrs Miller for her business, should she pursue a career in interior design. Secondly, Mr Miller has chosen for himself and his new family a property worth £6.25m, also in the same part of London. On that scale, the former matrimonial home appears quite modest. Thirdly, of course, the judge made her give up her half-share in the French property, which reduces the value of the house award by £500,000.

[84] My second point relates to the lump sum. Here, the point which strongly influences my perception of the award overall, is the scope of Mr Miller's wealth. The judge found that on any view he was worth £17.5m, leaving out of account the fact that the 200,000 shares in New Star were worth between £12.35m and £18.11m. On any view, Mr Miller is a very rich man. No doubt he has worked hard for, and deserves, his wealth. But against the scale of that wealth, a lump sum of £2.7m and an overall award of £5m cannot, in my judgment, be said to be excessive or disproportionate.

[85] Thirdly, there is also the point, not to be overlooked, that this is a 'clean break'. If, in 10 years' time Mr Miller is worth £50m or £100m, that will be his wealth to enjoy.

[86] Fourthly, it follows that, in my judgment, this is a case in which s 25(2)(a) is an important factor. Mr Mostyn accepts that there has to be a departure from equality to achieve fairness to Mr Miller, and whilst I do not, speaking for myself, think that this is a 'matrimonial acquest' case, the point on which one alights when departing from equality must be a matter of broad discretion. If equality on a very conservative approach would have been one half of £17.5m (ie ignoring the New Star shares), for the judge to have alighted at £5m does not seem to me remotely unfair when, on the facts found by the judge, the whole of the s 25(2) criteria are taken into consideration.

[87] Finally, I would, speaking for myself, advise caution about the use of this, or any other decision, as a template for others. I have been where Mr Marks stands in this case. Russell LJ began his judgment in *Gojkovic v Gojkovic and Another* [1992] Fam 40, [1991] 2 FLR 233 with the following words (at 49):

> 'In his opening submissions to this court, counsel for the husband invited us to lay down guidelines which would, he said, be of assistance to those charged with the responsibility of deciding what, after divorce, is the appropriate level of lump sum payments in cases where very substantial capital assets are available. I do not think that such an exercise is possible. The guidelines already exist. Section 23 of the Matrimonial Causes Act 1973 is the enabling provision for an order for the payment of a lump sum. Section 25, as

amended by the Matrimonial and Family Proceedings Act 1984, in terms, requires the court to have regard to all the circumstances of the case and subs (2), under no less than eight subparagraphs, sets out the matters to which the court in particular shall have regard.

In the individual case, some of those matters will assume greater importance than others and, indeed, the facts of this case well illustrate that proposition. In my judgment in this case we are concerned with a wholly exceptional set of circumstances ...'

[88]   If those words have a familiar ring, it is because they have been spoken by every judicial generation since s 25 of the MCA 1973 had its first expression as s 5 of the Matrimonial Proceedings and Property Act 1970. I first heard them in the well-known judgment of Ormrod LJ in *Martin (BH) v Martin (D)* [1978] Fam 12, (1977) FLR Rep 444 at 19 and 448 respectively, which I will not repeat. The consistent message from this court has been that the judge must apply the factors identified in s 25(2) to the facts of the individual case. The House of Lords in *White v White* [2001] 1 AC 596, [2000] 2 FLR 981 now tells us, and *Foster* in this court confirms, that the objective is a fair result that avoids discrimination. Proposed outcomes can be tested against the yardstick of equality. These are the guidelines which practitioners and the courts must strive to follow.

[89]   For the reasons I have attempted to give, I have come to the conclusion that the judge's order, examined against these criteria, passes the test. I would, accordingly, dismiss the appeal.

BLACK J:

[90]   I have had the opportunity of reading both judgments and I agree.

Appeal dismissed.

Solicitors: *Sears Tooth* for the petitioner
          Withers for the respondent

PHILIPPA JOHNSON
Law Reporter

MILLER v MILLER; McFARLANE v McFARLANE
[2006] UKHL 24

House of Lords

Lord Nicholls of Birkenhead, Lord Hoffmann, Lord Hope of Craighead, Baroness Hale of Richmond and Lord Mance

24 May 2006

Financial relief – Divorce – Principles to be applied by court – Conduct – Contributions – Assets – Clean break – Departing from yardstick of equality

Financial relief – Divorce – Short childless marriage – Principles to apply – Evidence as to causes of breakdown of marriage – 'Legitimate expectation' of wife as to standard of living post-marriage

Financial relief – Periodical payments – Capital element – Clean break – Substantial future surplus of income over expenditure – Whether periodical payments could include an element of capital – Joint lives or term order

The case of Miller concerned a short childless marriage, of less than 3 years' duration; at the time of the marriage the husband was an exceptionally successful fund manager, earning about £1m a year, the wife earned £85,000 a year. The husband purchased the matrimonial property for £1.8m, and, subsequently, bought a second property, in joint names, in the South of France. During the course of the marriage the husband moved firms, taking a huge reduction in basic salary, but acquiring a significant number of shares in the new firm, which subsequently proved extremely valuable; the wife gave up her job to concentrate on furnishing the matrimonial home and the property in the South of France. The marriage ended when the husband left the wife for another woman, whom he subsequently married. In the ancillary relief proceedings the judge awarded the wife £5m, taking the view that the husband could not rely on the short duration of the marriage because he was to blame for the breakdown, and that the wife had a legitimate expectation that she would live at a higher standard of affluence on marriage. The Court of Appeal, although critical of the lack of detail in the judgment, dismissed the husband's appeal, holding that the judge had been entitled to take into account the husband's responsibility for the breakdown of the marriage, and to take into account as the 'key element' the wife's legitimate expectation of living to a higher standard. The case of McFarlane concerned a husband and wife with three children, whose marriage had lasted effectively for 16 years. Both husband and wife were qualified professionals, and until shortly before the birth of their second child earned similar sums of money. Thereafter, the wife remained at home to care for the children, while the husband continued his professional career, with a salary increasing considerably year on year. The family had insufficient capital to achieve a clean break, but the husband now earned substantially more than would be needed to meet his own and the wife's budgeted household expenditure. The district judge made a periodical payment order of £250,000 a year to the wife (one third of the husband's current net income), against an estimated income requirement of £128,000, on the basis that fairness required that the wife should have a share of future earnings which had been made possible by her past contribution to the husband's career. The periodical payment was reduced on appeal to the Family Division to £180,000, but the Court of

Appeal allowed the wife's appeal in part, restoring the award to £250,000 a year but limiting the term to 5 years. The court held that in exceptional cases, and on the basis of term rather than joint lives orders, periodical payments could be used by the recipient to accumulate capital.

Held – dismissing the husband's appeal in Miller; allowing the wife's appeal in McFarlane, restoring the order of the district judge –

(1)   Under the English system, the redistribution of resources from one party to another following divorce was justified on the basis of: (1) the needs (generously interpreted) generated by the relationship between the parties; (2) compensation for relationship-generated disadvantage; and (3) the sharing of the fruits of the matrimonial partnership. These three principles, each of which looked at factors linked to the parties' relationship, rather than to extrinsic, unrelated factors, could guide the court in making an award; any or all of them might justify redistribution of resources, although the court must be careful to avoid double counting. Which of the three would be considered first would depend upon the circumstances of the case. In general it could be assumed that the marital partnership did not stay alive for the purpose of sharing future resources unless this was justified by need or compensation. The ultimate objective was to give each party an equal start on the road to independent living (see paras [10], [13], [15], [16], [29], [137] [138], [140], [141], [144]).

(2)   The court was to have regard to the parties' conduct only if it would be inequitable to disregard it. Where there was no conduct which it would be inequitable to disregard, the court should not seek to weigh the parties' respective conduct or attitudes in an attempt to assess responsibility for the breakdown of the marriage, or to attribute 'legitimacy' or 'reasonableness' to the wish of one party to continue the marriage against the wishes of the other. The lower courts had been wrong to take into account the husband's alleged responsibility for the breakdown of the marriage in Miller under the guise of having regard to all the circumstances of the case, given that it was conduct which fell far short of 'conduct which it would be inequitable to disregard' (see paras [63], [64], [65], [145], [164]).

(3)   The question of contributions should be approached in much the same way as conduct. Special contribution is to be regarded as a factor leading to a departure from equality of division only when it would be inequitable to disregard it (see paras [66]–[68], [146]).

Per Baroness Hale of Richmond: the contributions to be taken into account were contributions made and to be made to the 'welfare of the family', not contributions to accumulated wealth. Only if there was such a disparity in their respective contributions to the 'welfare of the family' that it would be inequitable to disregard it should this be taken into account in determining their shares (see para [146]).

(4)   A periodical payments order could be made to afford compensation as well as to meet financial needs. If capital had been equally shared and was enough to provide for need and compensate for disadvantage, there should be no continuing financial provision. A clean break was not to be achieved at the expense of a fair result; if a claimant was owed compensation, and capital assets were not available, the social desirability of a clean break would not be sufficient reason for depriving the claimant of that compensation. There was no reason to limit periodical payments to a fixed term in the interests solely of achieving a clean break. Given the high threshold which now applied to extending the term of a periodical payments order it was not appropriate to make an order intended to compensate the wife whose continuation the wife would have to justify, it should be for the husband to justify a reduction, at which stage the court could consider whether a clean break had become a realistic option (see paras [32], [39], [97], [134], [154], [155]).

(5)   While the standard of living enjoyed by the parties was to be taken into account, as one of the matters included on the statutory checklist, hopes and expectations were not an appropriate basis on which to assess financial needs. Claims for expectation losses did not fit comfortably with the notion that either party was free to end the marriage (see para [58]).

(6)   In Miller the needs generated by the relationship were comparatively small, as was the need for compensation, but the wife was entitled to some share in the assets, including the considerable increase in the husband's wealth during the marriage. Had the yardstick of equality been applied to all the assets which accrued during the marriage, the wife would have got more; there were, however, reasons to depart from the yardstick of equality, either on the basis that the substantial growth was attributable to contacts and capacities the husband brought to the marriage, or on the basis that the assets were business assets generated solely by the husband during a short marriage (see paras [69], [73], [158]).

(7)   McFarlane was a paradigm case for an award of compensation in respect of the significant future economic disparity sustained by the wife, arising from the way the parties conducted their marriage. Equal division of the capital was not enough to provide for needs or compensate for disadvantage but unusually the husband's very substantial earning power was far in excess of the family's financial needs after separation. The wife, having given up her own highly-paid career for the family, was not only entitled to generous income provision, including sums which would enable her to provide for her own old age and insure the husband's life, she was also entitled to a share in the very large surplus, on the principles both of sharing and of compensation. The Court of Appeal had been wrong to set a 5-year time limit on the order, on the basis that the wife would save the whole surplus above her requirements and that she would have the burden of justifying continuing payments at the end of the order, especially given the high threshold. The burden should be on the husband to justify a reduction, at which stage the court could consider whether a clean break was practicable, which would depend on the amount of capital generated by the husband (see paras [90], [91], [92], [93], [154], [155]).

Per Baroness Hale of Richmond, Lord Hoffmann agreeing: in a matrimonial property regime which started, as the English system did, with the premise of separate property, there remained some scope for one party to acquire and retain separate property which was not automatically to be shared equally between them. If assets were not 'family assets' that is not generated by the joint efforts of the parties, then the duration of the marriage might justify a departure from the yardstick of equality of division (in terms of a reduction to reflect the period of time over which the domestic contribution had or would continue, rather than in terms of accrual over time). The nature and source of the property and the way the couple had run their lives might be taken into account in deciding how it should be shared. However, these arguments would be irrelevant in the great majority of cases, and should not be taken too far (see paras [150], [152], [153]).

Per Lord Nicholls of Birkenhead: in relation to matrimonial property, ie the matrimonial home and property acquired during the marriage otherwise than by inheritance or gift, the equal sharing principle applied as much to short marriages as to long marriages, being no less a partnership of equals. However, in relation to non-matrimonial property, ie property which the parties brought with them into the marriage or acquired by inheritance or gift during the marriage, following a short marriage, fairness might well require that the claimant should not be entitled to an equal share. In a longer marriage non-matrimonial property represented a contribution made to the marriage by one of the parties whose weight would, in some circumstances, diminish, in others not. In all cases the nature and source of the parties' property were, as circumstances of the case, matters to be taken into account when determining the requirements of fairness, but the courts should be exceedingly slow to introduce or re-introduce a distinction between 'family' assets and 'business or investment' assets. Exceptional earnings were a contribution to marriage which could justify departure from equality of division only when it would be inequitable to proceed otherwise. Where it became necessary to distinguish matrimonial property from non-matrimonial property, the court might do so with the degree of particularity or generality appropriate in the case (see paras [17], [19], [20]–[25], [55], [68]).

Per Lord Mance: the duration of the marriage could not be discounted as a relevant factor, nor could the financial arrangements of the parties during the marriage. Once needs and compensation had been addressed, divorce itself would not justify the court disturbing principles by which the parties had chosen to live their lives while married. An established earning capacity, or very valuable acquired expertise and acumen would, if viewed as 'assets' brought into a marriage, not be easily or reliably measurable or comparable with other qualities. To the extent that the focus was on assets acquired during the marriage, rather than overall assets, it was natural to look at the period until separation (see paras [169], [170], [172], [174]).

Per Lord Hope: the Scottish system for financial settlement on divorce discriminated against women who had chosen motherhood over a career in the interests of the family and ought to be reconsidered as soon as possible. Compensation for significant future economic disparity arising from the way in which the parties had conducted the marriage was impossible under the Scottish system, which would have required the wife to adjust to a lower standard of living over 3 years or less. Instead of an absolute maximum period of 3 years for periodical allowances, the court should have a discretion to provide such allowances for a longer period where, in exceptional circumstances and applying the overriding criterion of fairness, the judge found that one party to the marriage whose contribution to the marriage had resulted in a reduction of his or her earning capacity ought to be compensated out of the other party's future income because the capital needed to provide such compensation was not available (see paras [117], [121]).

Statutory provisions considered
Matrimonial Causes Act 1866, s 1
Matrimonial Proceedings and Property Act 1970
Matrimonial Causes Act 1973, ss 23, 24(A)(B), 25, 25A, 25B, 28(1), 31(7), (7B), Part II
Divorce (Scotland) Act 1976, s 5(2)
Divorce Jurisdiction, Court Fees and Legal Aid (Scotland) Act 1983, s 1
Matrimonial and Family Proceedings Act 1984
Family Law (Scotland) Act 1985, ss 8(2), 9(1), 10(3)(b), 11(4)(e), 13(2)(a)
Pensions Act 1995
Family Law Act 1996, s 66
Welfare Reform and Pensions Act 1999
Family Law (Scotland) Act 2006, s 16

Cases referred to in judgment
Ackerman v Ackerman [1972] Fam 225 [1972] 2 WLR 1253, [1972] 2 All ER 420, CA
Attar v Attar (No 2) [1985] FLR 653, FD
B v B (Mesher Order) [2002] EWHC 3106 (Fam), [2003] 2 FLR 285, FD
Burgess v Burgess [1996] 2 FLR 34, CA
Cornick v Cornick (No 3) [2001] 2 FLR 1240, FD
Cowan v Cowan [2001] EWCA Civ 679, [2002] Fam 97, [2001] 3 WLR 684, [2001] 2 FLR 192, CA

Dipper v Dipper [1981] Fam 31, [1980] 3 WLR 626, (1980) 1 FLR 286, [1980] 2 All ER 722, CA

Fleming v Fleming [2003] EWCA Civ 1841, [2004] 1 FLR 667, [2003] All ER (D) 215 (Nov), CA

Foster v Foster [2003] EWCA Civ 565, [2003] 2 FLR 299, CA

G v G (Financial Provision: Equal Division) [2002] EWHC 1339 (Fam), [2002] 2 FLR 1143, FD

G v G (Financial Provision: Separation Agreement) [2004] 1 FLR 1011, CA

GW v RW (Financial Provision: Departure from Equality) [2003] EWHC 611 (Fam), [2003] 2 FLR 108, FD

H v H (Financial Provision: Short Marriage) (1981) 2 FLR 392, FD

Hedges v Hedges [1991] 1 FLR 196, CA

Jacques v Jacques (1997) SC (HL) 20, HL

Lambert v Lambert [2002] EWCA Civ 1685, [2003] Fam 103, [2003] 2 WLR 631, [2003] 1 FLR 139, [2003] 4 All ER 342, CA

Latter v Latter (1990) SLT 805, Ct of Sess

Leslie v Leslie [1911] P 203, PDAD

Little v Little (1990) SLT 785, Ct of Sess (1st Div)

McFarlane v McFarlane; Parlour v Parlour [2004] EWCA Civ 872, [2005] Fam 171, [2004] 3 WLR 1480, [2004] 2 FLR 893, [2004] 2 All ER 921, CA

Miller v Miller [2005] EWCA Civ 984, [2006] 1 FLR 151, [2005] All ER (D) 467 (Jul), CA

Minton v Minton [1979] AC 593, [1979] 2 WLR 31, (1978) FLR Rep 461, [1979] 1 All ER 79, HL

M v M (Financial Relief: Substantial Earning Capacity) [2004] EWHC 688 (Fam), [2004] 2 FLR 236, FD

N v N (Financial Provision: Sale of Company) [2001] 2 FLR 69, CA

O'D v O'D [1976] Fam 83, [1975] 3 WLR 308, (1975) FLR Rep 512, [1975] 2 All ER 993, CA

P v P (Inherited Property) [2004] EWHC 1364 (Fam), [2005] 1 FLR 576, FD

Page v Page (1981) 2 FLR 198, CA

Parlour v Parlour; McFarlane v McFarlane; [2004] EWCA (Civ) 872, [2005] Fam 171, [2004] 3 WLR 1481, [2004] 2 FLR 893, [2004] 3 All ER 921, CA

Preston v Preston [1982] Fam 17, [1981] 3 WLR 619, (1981) 2 FLR 331, [1982] 1 All ER 41, CA

R v R (Rape: Marital Exemption) [1992] 1 AC 599, [1991] 3 WLR 767, [1992] 1 FLR 217, [1991] 4 All ER 481, HL; affirming [1991] 2 WLR 1065, [1991] 2 All ER 257, CA; affirming [1991] 1 All ER 747

Robertson v Robertson (1983) 4 FLR 387, FD

S v S [1977] Fam 127, [1976] 3 WLR 775, [1977] 1 All ER 56, CA

SRJ v DWJ (Financial Provision) [1999] 2 FLR 176, CA

Wachtel v Wachtel [1973] Fam 72, [1973] 2 WLR 366, [1973] 1 All ER 829, CA

Wallis v Wallis (1992) SC 455, Ct of Sess (1st Div)

Wallis v Wallis (1993) SC (HL) 49, HL(S)

White v White [2001] 1 AC 596, [2000] 3 WLR 1571, [2000] 2 FLR 981, [2001] 1 All ER 1, HL

Wilson v Wilson (1999) SLT 249, OH

James Turner QC and Philip Marshall for the appellant Miller
Barry Singleton QC and Deepak Nagpal for the appellant McFarlane
Nicholas Mostyn QC, Tim Bishop and Rebecca Bailey-Harris for the respondent Miller
Jeremy Posnansky QC and Stephen Trowell for the respondent McFarlane

Cur adv vult

LORD NICHOLLS OF BIRKENHEAD:

[1]   These two appeals concern that most intractable of problems: how to achieve fairness in the division of property following a divorce. In *White v White* [2001] 1 AC 596, [2000] 2 FLR 981 your Lordships' House sought to assist judges who have the difficult task of exercising the wide discretionary powers conferred on the court by Part II of the Matrimonial Causes Act 1973. In particular, the House emphasised that in seeking a fair outcome there is no place for discrimination between a husband and wife and their respective roles. Discrimination is the antithesis of fairness. In assessing the parties' contributions to the family there should be no bias in favour of the money-earner and against the home-maker and the childcarer. This is a principle of universal application. It is applicable to all marriages.

[2]   In the *White* case the capital assets were more than sufficient to meet the parties' financial needs. The two appeals now before the House again involve large amounts of money but they raise different issues from those in the *White* case. The first appeal concerns the division of capital assets where the marriage was short-lived. The *White* case concerned a lengthy marriage, of over 30 years. The marriage between Alan and Melissa Miller lasted less than 3 years. The second appeal concerns the marriage between Kenneth and Julia McFarlane. This lasted for 16 years. The parties' capital was insufficient to enable an immediate clean break, but Mr McFarlane was a notably high earner. The principal issue in the McFarlane appeal concerns the role of a periodical payments order in this type of case.

[3]   The facts in both cases are unusual. But before summarising these facts and identifying the issues in these cases it will be convenient to consider some general principles.

The requirements of fairness

[4]   Fairness is an elusive concept. It is an instinctive response to a given set of facts. Ultimately it is grounded in social and moral values. These values, or attitudes, can be stated. But they cannot be justified, or refuted, by any objective process of logical reasoning. Moreover, they change from one generation to the next. It is not surprising, therefore, that in the present context there can be different views on the requirements of fairness in any particular case.

[5]   At once there is a difficulty for the courts. The Matrimonial Causes Act 1973 (the 1973 Act) gives only limited guidance on how the courts should exercise their statutory powers. Primary consideration must be given to the welfare of any children of the family. The court must consider the feasibility of a 'clean break'. Beyond this the courts are largely left to get on with it for themselves. The courts are told simply that they must have regard to all the circumstances of the case.

[6]   Of itself this direction leads nowhere. Implicitly the courts must exercise their powers so as to achieve an outcome which is fair between the parties. But an important aspect of fairness is that like cases should be treated alike. So, perforce, if there is to be an acceptable degree of consistency of decision from one case to the next, the courts must themselves articulate, if only in the broadest fashion, what are the applicable if unspoken principles guiding the court's approach.

[7]   This is not to usurp the legislative function. Rather, it is to perform a necessary judicial function in the absence of parliamentary guidance. As Lord Cooke of Thorndon said in *White*, at 615 and 999 respectively, there is no reason to suppose that in prescribing relevant considerations the legislature had any intention of excluding the development of general judicial practice.

[8]   For many years one principle applied by the courts was to have regard to the reasonable requirements of the claimant, usually the wife, and treat this as determinative of the extent of the claimant's award. Fairness lay in enabling the wife to continue to live in the fashion to which she had become accustomed. The glass ceiling thus put in place was shattered by the decision of your Lordships' House in the *White* case. This has accentuated the need for some further judicial enunciation of general principle.

[9]   The starting point is surely not controversial. In the search for a fair outcome it is pertinent to have in mind that fairness generates obligations as well as rights. The financial provision made on divorce by one party for the other, still typically the wife, is not in the nature of largesse. It is not a case of 'taking away' from one party and 'giving' to the other property which 'belongs' to the former. The claimant is not a suppliant. Each party to a marriage is entitled to a fair share of the available property. The search is always for what are the requirements of fairness in the particular case.

[10]   What then, in principle, are these requirements? The statute provides that first consideration shall be given to the welfare of the children of the marriage. In the present context nothing further need be said about this primary consideration. Beyond this several elements, or strands, are readily discernible. The first is financial needs. This is one of the matters listed in s 25(2) of the 1973 Act, in para (b): 'the financial needs, obligations and responsibilities which each of the parties to the marriage has or is likely to have in the foreseeable future'.

[11]   This element of fairness reflects the fact that to greater or lesser extent every relationship of marriage gives rise to a relationship of interdependence. The parties share the roles of money-earner, home-maker and childcarer. Mutual dependence begets mutual obligations of support. When the marriage ends fairness requires that the assets of the parties should be divided primarily so as to make provision for the parties' housing and financial needs, taking into account a wide range of matters such as the parties' ages, their future earning capacity, the family's standard of living, and any disability of either party. Most of these needs will have been generated by the marriage, but not all of them. Needs arising from age or disability are instances of the latter.

[12]   In most cases the search for fairness largely begins and ends at this stage. In most cases the available assets are insufficient to provide adequately for the needs of two homes. The court seeks to stretch modest finite resources so far as possible to meet the parties' needs. Especially where children are involved it may be necessary to augment the available assets by having recourse to the future earnings of the money-earner, by way of an order for periodical payments.

[13]   Another strand, recognised more explicitly now than formerly, is compensation. This is aimed at redressing any significant prospective economic disparity between the parties arising from the way they conducted their marriage. For instance, the parties may have arranged their affairs in a way which has greatly advantaged the husband in terms of his earning capacity but left the wife severely handicapped so far as her own earning capacity is concerned. Then the wife suffers a double loss: a diminution in her earning capacity and the loss of a share in her husband's enhanced income. This is often the case. Although less marked than in the past, women may still suffer a disproportionate financial loss on the breakdown of a marriage because of their traditional role as home-maker and childcarer.

[14]   When this is so, fairness requires that this feature should be taken into account by the court when exercising its statutory powers. The Court of Appeal

decision in *SRJ v DWJ (Financial Provision)* [1999] 2 FLR 176, at 182, is an example where this was recognised expressly.

[15]   Compensation and financial needs often overlap in practice, so double-counting has to be avoided. But they are distinct concepts, and they are far from co-terminous. A claimant wife may be able to earn her own living but she may still be entitled to a measure of compensation.

[16]   A third strand is sharing. This 'equal sharing' principle derives from the basic concept of equality permeating a marriage as understood today. Marriage, it is often said, is a partnership of equals. In 1992 Lord Keith of Kinkel approved Lord Emslie's observation that 'husband and wife are now for all practical purposes equal partners in marriage': *R v R (Rape: Marital Exemption)* [1992] 1 AC 599, [1992] 1 FLR 217 at 617 and 220 respectively. This is now recognised widely, if not universally. The parties commit themselves to sharing their lives. They live and work together. When their partnership ends each is entitled to an equal share of the assets of the partnership, unless there is a good reason to the contrary. Fairness requires no less. But I emphasise the qualifying phrase: 'unless there is good reason to the contrary'. The yardstick of equality is to be applied as an aid, not a rule.

[17]   This principle is applicable as much to short marriages as to long marriages: see *Foster v Foster* [2003] EWCA Civ 565, [2003] 2 FLR 299, at 305, para [19] per Hale LJ. A short marriage is no less a partnership of equals than a long marriage. The difference is that a short marriage has been less enduring. In the nature of things this will affect the quantum of the financial fruits of the partnership.

[18]   A different approach was suggested in *GW v RW (Financial Provision: Departure from Equality)* [2003] EWHC 611 (Fam), [2003] 2 FLR 108 at 121–122. There the court accepted the proposition that entitlement to an equal division must reflect not only the parties' respective contributions 'but also an accrual over time': at 122, para [40]. It would be 'fundamentally unfair' that a party who has made domestic contributions during a marriage of 12 years should be awarded the same proportion of the assets as a party who has made the domestic contributions for more than 20 years: para [43]. In *M v M (Financial Relief: Substantial Earning Capacity)* [2004] EWHC 688 (Fam), [2004] 2 FLR 236, at 252, para [55](7), this point was regarded as 'well made'.

[19]   I am unable to agree with this approach. This approach would mean that on the breakdown of a short marriage the money-earner would have a head start over the home-maker and childcarer. To confine the *White* approach to the 'fruits of a long marital partnership' would be to re-introduce precisely the sort of discrimination the *White* case was intended to negate.

[20]   For the same reason the courts should be exceedingly slow to introduce, or re-introduce, a distinction between 'family' assets and 'business or investment' assets. In all cases the nature and source of the parties' property are matter to be taken into account when determining the requirements of fairness. The decision of Munby J in *P v P (Inherited Property)* [2004] EWHC 1364 (Fam), [2005] 1 FLR 576 regarding a family farm is an instance. But 'business and investment' assets can be the financial fruits of a marriage partnership as much as 'family' assets. The equal sharing principle applies to the former as well as the latter. The rationale underlying the sharing principle is as much applicable to 'business and investment' assets as to 'family' assets.

Matrimonial property and non-matrimonial property

[21]   A complication rears its head at this point. I have referred to the financial fruits of the marriage partnership. In some countries the law draws a sharp distinction between assets acquired during a marriage and other assets. In Scotland, for instance, one of the statutorily prescribed principles is that the parties should share the value of the 'matrimonial property' equally or in such proportions as special circumstances may justify. Matrimonial property means the matrimonial home plus property acquired during the marriage otherwise than by gift or inheritance: ss 9 and 10 of the Family Law (Scotland) Act 1985. In England and Wales the Matrimonial Causes Act 1973 draws no such distinction. By s 25(2)(a) of the 1973 Act the court is bidden to have regard, quite generally, to the property and financial resources each of the parties to the marriage has or is likely to have in the foreseeable future.

[22]   This does not mean that, when exercising his discretion, a judge in this country must treat all property in the same way. The statute requires the court to have regard to all the circumstances of the case. One of the circumstances is that there is a real difference, a difference of source, between: (1) property acquired during the marriage otherwise than by inheritance or gift, sometimes called the marital acquest but more usually the matrimonial property; and (2) other property. The former is the financial product of the parties' common endeavour, the latter is not. The parties' matrimonial home, even if this was brought into the marriage at the outset by one of the parties, usually has a central place in any marriage. So it should normally be treated as matrimonial property for this purpose. As already noted, in principle the entitlement of each party to a share of the matrimonial property is the same however long or short the marriage may have been.

[23]   The matter stands differently regarding property ('non-matrimonial property') the parties bring with them into the marriage or acquire by inheritance or gift during the marriage. Then the duration of the marriage will be highly relevant. The position regarding non-matrimonial property was summarised in the *White* case, at 610 and 994 respectively:

'Plainly, when present, this factor is one of the circumstances of the case. It represents a contribution made to the welfare of the family by one of the parties to the marriage. The judge should take it into account. He should decide how important it is in the particular case. The nature and value of the property, and the time when and circumstances in which the property was acquired, are among the relevant matters to be considered. However, in the ordinary course, this factor can be expected to carry little weight, if any, in a case where the claimant's financial needs cannot be met without recourse to this property.'

[24]   In the case of a short marriage, fairness may well require that the claimant should not be entitled to a share of the other's non-matrimonial property. The source of the asset may be a good reason for departing from equality. This reflects the instinctive feeling that parties will generally have less call upon each other on the breakdown of a short marriage.

[25]   With longer marriages the position is not so straightforward. Non-matrimonial property represents a contribution made to the marriage by one of the parties. Sometimes, as the years pass, the weight fairly to be attributed to this contribution will diminish, sometimes it will not. After many years of marriage the continuing weight to be attributed to modest savings introduced by one party at the outset of the marriage may well be different from the weight attributable to a valuable heirloom intended to be retained in specie. Some of the matters to be taken into account in this regard were mentioned in the above citation from the *White* case. To this non-exhaustive list should be added, as a relevant matter, the way the parties organised their financial affairs.

Flexibility

[26]   This difference in treatment of matrimonial property and non-matrimonial property might suggest that in every case a clear and precise boundary should be drawn between these two categories of property. This is not so. Fairness has a broad horizon. Sometimes, in the case of a business, it can be artificial to attempt to draw a sharp dividing line as at the parties' wedding day. Similarly the 'equal sharing' principle might suggest that each of the party's assets should be separately and exactly valued. But valuations are often a matter of opinion on which experts differ. A thorough investigation into these differences can be extremely expensive and of doubtful utility. The costs involved can quickly become disproportionate. The case of Mr and Mrs Miller illustrates this only too well.

[27]   Accordingly, where it becomes necessary to distinguish matrimonial property from non-matrimonial property the court may do so with the degree of particularity or generality appropriate in the case. The judge will then give to the contribution made by one party's non-matrimonial property the weight he considers just. He will do so with such generality or particularity as he considers appropriate in the circumstances of the case.

[28]   I must mention a further matter where flexibility is important. In big money cases, the capital assets are more than sufficient to meet the parties' financial needs and the need for either party to be compensated when one party's earning capacity has been advantaged at the expense of the other party. In these cases, should the parties' financial needs and the requirements of compensation be met first, and the residue of the assets shared? Or should financial needs and compensation simply be subsumed into the equal division of all the assets?

[29]   There can be no invariable rule on this. Much will depend upon the amounts involved. Generally a convenient course might be for the court to consider first the requirements of compensation and then to give effect to the sharing entitlement. If this course is followed provision for the parties' financial needs will be subsumed into the sharing entitlement. But there will be cases where this approach would not achieve a fair outcome overall. In some cases provision for the financial needs may be more fairly assessed first along with compensation and the sharing entitlement applied only to the residue of the assets. Needless to say, it all depends upon the circumstances.

Periodical payments and the clean break principle

[30]   So far I have been almost entirely concerned with lump sum payments as distinct from periodical payments. I have, therefore, made only passing mention of an important principle now embodied in the statute: the clean break principle. This principle is relevant in the *McFarlane* appeal. Two issues arise in this regard. The first concerns the reach of periodical payments orders. The question is whether periodical payments orders may be made for the purpose of providing compensation as distinct from maintenance.

[31]   I see no difficulty on this point. There is nothing in the statutory ancillary relief provisions to suggest Parliament intended periodical payments orders to be limited to payments needed for maintenance. Section 23(1)(a) empowers the court, in quite general language, to order one party to the marriage to make to the other 'such periodical payments, for such term, as may be specified in the order'. In deciding whether, and how, to exercise this power the statute requires the court to have regard to all the circumstances of the case: s 25(1) of the 1973 Act. The court is required to have particular regard to the familiar wide-ranging checklist set out in s 25(2). These provisions, far from suggesting an intention to restrict periodical payments to the one particular purpose of maintenance, suggest that the financial provision orders in s 23 were intended to be flexible in their application.

[32]   In particular, I consider a periodical payments order may be made for the purpose of affording compensation to the other party as well as meeting financial needs. It would be extraordinary if this were not so. If one party's earning capacity has been advantaged at the expense of the other party during the marriage it would be extraordinary if, where necessary, the court could not order the advantaged party to pay compensation to the other out of his enhanced earnings when he receives them. It would be most unfair if absence of capital assets were regarded as cancelling his obligation to pay compensation in respect of a continuing economic advantage he has obtained from the marriage.

[33]   It was not always so. At its inception the court's power to order the husband to make periodic payments to the wife was expressly limited to payments for her maintenance and support: s 1 of the Matrimonial Causes Act 1866. The rationale underlying this power seems to have been the wife's necessity. At that time the husband owned the entirety of the wife's property: *Leslie v Leslie* [1911] P 203, at 205.

[34]   Times and attitudes have changed, and with them the content and language of the ancillary relief provisions. The history was conveniently summarised by Thorpe LJ in *McFarlane v McFarlane; Parlour v Parlour* [2004] EWCA Civ 872, [2005] Fam 171, [2004] 2 FLR 893 at 196–198 and 916–917 respectively, paras [87]–[99]. The wife's financial needs, or her 'reasonable requirements', are now no more a determinative or limiting factor on an application for a periodical payments order than they are on an application for payment of a lump sum. I agree with Charles J's observations to this effect in *Cornick v Cornick (No 3)* [2001] 2 FLR 1240, at para [106].

[35]   This leads me to the second issue regarding periodical payments orders. It concerns the impact of the clean break principle on periodical payment orders made to provide compensation to a disadvantaged party. There is, of course, a significant practical difference between providing compensation by appropriate division of existing capital assets and providing compensation by means of a periodical payments order. Of its nature a lump sum payment is once and for all. A lump sum payment represents, to that extent, the financial closure of a failed marriage. It draws a line under the past. Periodical payments represent the opposite. Future earnings and future payments lie in the future. They are a continuing financial tie between the parties. Today the undesirability of such continuing ties is regarded as self-evident. The modern approach was expressed succinctly by Lord Scarman in his familiar words in *Minton v Minton* [1979] AC 593, (1978) FLR Rep 461, at 608 and 472 respectively:

'An object of the modern law is to encourage [the parties] to put the past behind them and to begin a new life which is not overshadowed by the relationship which has broken down.'

[36]   So I turn to the statute. Section 25A of the 1973 Act provides:

'(1)   Where on or after the grant of a decree of divorce or nullity of marriage the court decides to exercise its powers under section 23(1)(a) [power to order periodical payments] ... in favour of a party to the marriage, it shall be the duty of the court to consider whether it would be appropriate so to exercise those powers that the financial obligations of each party towards the other will be terminated as soon after the grant of the decree as the court considers just and reasonable.

(2)   Where the court decides in such a case to make a periodical payments ... order in favour of a party to the marriage, the court shall in particular consider whether it would

be appropriate to require those payments to be made ... only for such term as would in the opinion of the court be sufficient to enable the party in whose favour the order is made to adjust without undue hardship to the termination of his or her financial dependence on the other party.'

[37]   This statutory statement of principle raises a question of a similar nature to that affecting the whole of s 25. By s 25A(1) and (2) duties are imposed on the court but the court is left with a discretion. The court is required to 'consider' whether it would be 'appropriate' to exercise its powers in a particular way. But the section gives no express guidance on the type of circumstance which would render it inappropriate for the court to bring about a clean break.

[38]   In one respect the object of s 25A(1) is abundantly clear. The subsection is expressed in general terms. It is apt to refer as much to a periodical payments order made to provide compensation as it is to an order made to meet financial needs. But, expressly, s 25A(1) is not intended to bring about an unfair result. Under s 25A(1) the goal the court is required to have in mind is that the parties' mutual financial obligations should end as soon as the court considers just and reasonable.

[39]   Section 25A(2) is focused more specifically. It is concerned with the termination of one party's 'financial dependence' on the other 'without undue hardship'. These references to financial dependence and hardship are apt when applied to a periodical payments order making provision for the payee's financial needs. They are hardly apt when applied to a periodical payments order whose object is to furnish compensation in respect of future economic disparity arising from the division of functions adopted by the parties during their marriage. If the claimant is owed compensation, and capital assets are not available, it is difficult to see why the social desirability of a clean break should be sufficient reason for depriving the claimant of that compensation.

[40]   Against that background I turn to the facts and particular issues raised by these appeals, starting with Mr and Mrs Miller.

The Miller marriage

[41]   Mr and Mrs Miller were engaged to be married in July 1999 and they married a year later, on 14 July 2000. They did not live together before their marriage. They separated in April 2003. So the marriage lasted two years and nine months. The marriage was childless. Sadly, the wife had a miscarriage. When they separated the husband was aged 39 and the wife was 33.

[42]   The parties' backgrounds can be summarised as follows. The wife was born and brought up in the USA. She acquired expertise in the field of public relations. In February 1995 she moved to.England to take up employment in Cambridge. She was in charge of investor relations at a pharmaceutical company. In March 2000, in anticipation of her marriage, she changed her job. She left her Cambridge flat and moved to London to work for a financial public relations firm as an associate partner earning £85,000 pa.

[43]   The husband was born and brought up in England. He married his first wife in 1987 and was divorced in 1992. He has had a highly successful career in asset management. After graduating from Birmingham University he trained as an accountant. In 1994 he joined Jupiter Asset Management. He was a senior fund manager and became a main board director. In 1995 Jupiter was taken over by Commerzbank. Commerzbank gave Jupiter's employees a share of the equity to be bought back in the year 2000 on the basis of a profits-related formula. Jupiter was extremely successful, and the profits-related formula required Commerzbank to pay the staff of Jupiter £500m. The husband's share was a cash payment of £13m net of tax. He received this in March 2000.

[44]   The founder of Jupiter was Mr John Duffield. Relations between him and Commerzbank deteriorated, and they parted company acrimoniously in May 2000. Mr Duffield commenced an action for wrongful dismissal. The husband saw that his future lay with Mr Duffield, but at that time both he and Mr Duffield were bound to Commerzbank by non-competition agreements. In late May they agreed between themselves that, subject to being released from these restrictions, the husband would join Mr Duffield in a new company, New Star Asset Management Group Ltd. The dispute between Mr Duffield and Commerzbank was settled in November 2000 on terms which included the release of the two men from their employment restrictions. The husband then left Jupiter and joined New Star as chief investment officer in January 2001. He brought with him the management of three funds having total assets of £240m. He paid £200,000 for 200,000 shares in New Star.

[45]   Mr and Mrs Miller separated in April 2003 on the day after the husband told the wife the marriage was at an end and that he had formed a relationship with the woman to whom he is now married. In July 2003 the husband petitioned for divorce, alleging unreasonable behaviour on the part of the wife. She refuted this allegation and cross-petitioned, alleging adultery. By consent the suit proceeded on the wife's petition and a decree of divorce nisi of 16 February 2004 was made absolute on 17 February 2005.

[46]   Meanwhile the wife sought financial ancillary relief. At the hearing before Singer J in October 2004, the husband's assets were worth about £17.5m, plus whatever value should be attributed to his 200,000 shares in New Star. This figure of £17.5m compared with £16.7m when the parties married in July 2000, and £17m when they separated in April 2003. The husband's basic salary at New Star was £181,000. His bonus for 2003 was £3m and for 2004 £1.2m.

[47]   The wife's financial circumstances contrasted sharply. At the time of the hearing she had assets worth £100,000, of which half were locked in pension funds. If she had paid her outstanding costs she would have been more than £300,000 in debt.

The hearing before the judge

[48]   The judge awarded the wife a capital sum of £5m, made up of the former matrimonial home in London, worth £2.3m, and a lump sum of £2.7m. In addition she received goods worth about £150,000.

[49]   It is impossible to do justice to Singer J's wide-ranging judgment in a brief summary. Three points can be noted. First, the judge found he could not place a firm value on the husband's New Star shares. He said their present value was inestimable and their future value unfathomable. Their current sale value was variously estimated by the parties' experts at £12m and £18m. In fact the shares were subject to restrictions which precluded their current sale. But the judge was reasonably confident that, unless the husband meanwhile triggered an obligation to sell his shares, in December 2006 he was likely to receive £6m for 75,000 out of his total holding of 200,000 shares.

[50]   Secondly, the judge had before him written and oral evidence from both parties about the reasons why the marriage had failed. The judge held that nothing either spouse alleged against the other remotely constituted conduct of such gravity that it would be inequitable to disregard it. But he added that, having heard this evidence, he regarded himself as better able to assess the wife's claims. He held it

would be unfair to concentrate solely on the bare chronology without acknowledging that the wife did not seek to end the marriage. Nor did she give the husband any remotely sufficient reason for doing so.

[51]   Thirdly, the judge considered the court's approach to cases where the marriage was short but wealthy. He held that in the present case the key feature was that the husband gave the wife a legitimate expectation she would on a long-term basis be living on a higher economic plane than the rented flat and her £85,000 job had afforded her when she left her flat and her job to live with the husband as his wife at the house he had bought for that purpose. The judge said, in para [65]:

> '... the award should recognise that H has by this marriage, notwithstanding its short duration, given W a reasonable expectation that her life as once again a single woman need not revert to what it was before her marriage, and that she should be able to live at a significantly better standard in terms of accommodation and spendable income, even if at one which does not approach the level that H can afford for himself and his new family.'

The judge concluded that a global award equivalent to £5m, plus the agreed furniture and other goods, was a fair outcome irrespective of whatever value the husband might in due course achieve for the New Star shares.

The hearing in the Court of Appeal

[52]   The husband appealed. The Court of Appeal, comprising Thorpe and Wall LJJ and Black J, dismissed the appeal. Thorpe LJ held that the judge's award could not be labelled plainly excessive, although it was at the top end of the permissible bracket. The judge was entitled to take into account that the husband was to blame for the breakdown of the marriage even though his conduct would not merit advancing under s 25(2)(g) of the Matrimonial Causes Act 1973 as amended. The husband's misconduct could be used as a counter-balancing factor to the brevity of the marriage. Further, the judge was entitled to regard the wife's legitimate expectation of living to a higher standard as the ex-wife of Mr Miller as the 'key element' in the case.

[53]   Wall LJ agreed that the reasons for the breakdown of the marriage were relevant in this case. His perception of the award overall was strongly influenced by the size of the husband's wealth. The husband was a very rich man. An overall 'clean break' award of £5m was not excessive or disproportionate. Black J agreed with both judgments.

The pre-White short marriage cases

[54]   Several issues arise from these judgments. The first concerns the relevance today of the approach to short marriages enunciated in the 1980s. In the 1980s and earlier there were several reported cases concerning short marriages. The facts vary widely, but in these cases the general approach to division of assets was to concentrate on making provision for the financial needs of the claimant, usually the wife, and on compensating her for any financial disadvantage she had suffered from the breakdown of the marriage. To greater or lesser extent this approach appears in *S v S* [1977] Fam 127, *H v H (Financial Provision: Short Marriage)* (1981) 2 FLR 392, *Robertson v Robertson* (1983) 4 FLR 387, *Attar v Attar (No 2)* [1985] FLR 653 and *Hedges v Hedges* [1991] 1 FLR 196.

[55]   On the present appeal, Mr Turner QC submitted this approach has not been invalidated by the decision in the *White* case. Both Singer J and the Court of Appeal declined to adopt this submission. They were right to do so. In the 1980s cases attention was directed predominantly at the wife's needs. There may be cases of short marriages where the limited financial resources of the parties necessarily mean that attention will still have to be focused on the parties' needs. That is not so in big money cases. Then the court is concerned to decide what would be a fair division of the whole of the assets, taking into account the parties' respective financial needs and any need for compensation. The court will look at all the circumstances. The general approach in this type of case should be to consider whether, and to what extent, there is good reason for departing from equality. As already indicated, in short marriage cases there will often be a good reason for departing substantially from equality with regard to non-matrimonial property.

'Legitimate expectation'

[56]   The next issue concerns the feature described by the judge as the key feature in the case. The judge said the key feature was that the husband gave the wife a legitimate expectation that in future she would be living on a higher economic plane.

[57]   By this statement I doubt whether the judge was doing more than emphasise the importance in this case of the standard of living enjoyed by Mr and Mrs Miller before the breakdown of their short marriage. This is one of the matters included on the statutory checklist. The standard of living enjoyed by the Millers during their marriage was much higher than the wife's accustomed standard and much higher than the standard she herself could afford.

[58]   If the judge meant to go further than this I consider he went too far. No doubt both parties had high hopes for their future when they married. But hopes and expectations, as such, are not an appropriate basis on which to assess financial needs. Claims for expectation losses do not fit altogether comfortably with the notion that each party is free to end the marriage. Indeed, to make an award by reference to the parties' future expectations would come close to restoring the 'tailpiece' which was originally part of s 25 of the 1973 Act. By that tailpiece the court was required to place the parties, so far as practical and, having regard to their conduct, just to do so, in the same financial position as they would have been had the marriage not broken down. It would be a mistake indirectly to re-introduce the effect of that discredited provision.

Conduct

[59]   Next is the question of the parties' conduct. The relevance of the parties' conduct in financial ancillary relief cases is still a vexed issue. For many years now divorce has been based on the neutral fact that the marriage has broken down irretrievably. Some elements of the old concept of fault have been retained but essentially only as evidence of irretrievable break down. As already noted, parties are now free to end their marriage and then remarry.

[60]   Despite this freedom, there remains a widespread feeling in this country that when making orders for financial ancillary relief the judge should know who was to blame for the breakdown of the marriage. The judge should take this into account. If a wife walks out on her wealthy husband after a short marriage it is not 'fair' this should be ignored. Similarly if a rich husband leaves his wife for a younger woman.

[61]   At one level this view is readily understandable. But the difficulties confronting judges if they seek to unravel mutual recriminations about happenings within the marriage, and the undesirability of their attempting to do so, have been rehearsed many times. In *Wachtel v Wachtel* [1973] Fam 72, at 90, Lord Denning MR led

the way by confining relevant misconduct to those cases where the conduct was 'obvious and gross'.

[62]   The Law Commission then considered the problem. The commission concluded that courts should be obliged to take account of conduct where to do otherwise would offend a reasonable person's sense of justice. To this end the court should be free to examine sufficient of the matrimonial history to enable the judge to 'get a feel of the case': see the Law Commission report on Family Law – *The Financial Consequences of Divorce* Law Com No 112 (HMSO, 1981), paras 36–39.

[63]   Parliament gave effect to this recommendation in para (g) in the new s 25(2) introduced by the Matrimonial and Family Proceedings Act 1984. One of the matters to which the court should have regard is 'the conduct of each of the parties, if that conduct is such that it would in the opinion of the court be inequitable to disregard it'. It is implicit in this provision that conduct outside this description is not conduct which should be taken into account.

[64]   This history is well known. I have mentioned it only because there are signs that some highly experienced judges are beginning to depart from the criterion laid down by Parliament. In *G v G (Financial Provision: Separation Agreement)* [2004] 1 FLR 1011, at 1017, para [34], Thorpe LJ said the judge 'must be free to include within [his discretionary review of all the circumstances] the factors which compelled the wife to terminate the marriage as she did'. This approach was followed by both courts below in the present case. Both the judge and the Court of Appeal had regard to the husband's conduct when, as the judge found, that conduct did not meet the statutory criterion. The husband's conduct did not rank as conduct it would be inequitable to disregard.

[65]   This approach, I have to say, is erroneous. Parliament has drawn the line. It is not for the courts to re-draw the line elsewhere under the guise of having regard to all the circumstances of the case. It is not as though the statutory boundary line gives rise to injustice. In most cases fairness does not require consideration of the parties' conduct. This is because in most cases misconduct is not relevant to the bases on which financial ancillary relief is ordered today. Where, exceptionally, the position is otherwise, so that it would be inequitable to disregard one party's conduct, the statute permits that conduct to be taken into account.

Contribution

[66]   A point of a similar nature concerns the approach to be adopted when evaluating the contributions each party made to the welfare of the family. Apparently, in this post-*White* era there is a growing tendency for parties and their advisers to enter into the minute detail of the parties' married life, with a view to lauding their own contribution and denigrating that of the other party. In the words of Thorpe LJ, the excesses formerly seen in the litigation concerning the claimant's reasonable requirements have now been 'transposed into disputed, and often futile, evaluations of the contributions of both of the parties': *Lambert v Lambert* [2002] EWCA Civ 1685, [2003] Fam 103, [2003] 1 FLR 139, at 117 and 152 respectively, para [27].

[67]   On this I echo the powerful observations of Coleridge J in *G v G (Financial Provision: Equal Division)* [2002] EWHC 1339 (Fam); [2002] 2 FLR 1143, at 1154–1155, paras [33]–[34]. Parties should not seek to promote a case of 'special contribution' unless the contribution is so marked that to disregard it would be inequitable. A good reason for departing from equality is not to be found in the minutiae of married life.

[68] This approach provides the principled answer in those cases where the earnings of one party, usually the husband, have been altogether exceptional. The question is whether earnings of this character can be regarded as a 'special contribution', and thus as a good reason for departing from equality of division. The answer is that exceptional earnings are to be regarded as a factor pointing away from equality of division when, but only when, it would be inequitable to proceed otherwise. The wholly exceptional nature of the earnings must be, to borrow a phrase more familiar in a different context, obvious and gross. Bodey J encapsulated this neatly when sitting as a judge in the Court of Appeal in *Lambert v Lambert*, at 127 and 163 respectively, para [70]. He described the characteristics or circumstances which would bring about a departure from equality:

> '... those characteristics or circumstances clearly have to be of a wholly exceptional nature, such that it would very obviously be inconsistent with the objective of achieving fairness (ie it would create an unfair outcome) for them to be ignored.'

Mr Miller's appeal

[69] I accept the husband's contention that both the judge and the Court of Appeal misdirected themselves on the 'conduct' issue. Even so I would dismiss Mr Miller's appeal, largely for two reasons. The first concerns the increase in the husband's wealth during the marriage. The husband brought substantial wealth into the marriage at its outset. That was non-matrimonial property. That was a major financial contribution he made to the marriage. But it would be wrong to suppose that during the period of the marriage the husband's assets increased only by the comparatively modest amount of £300,000 or so represented by his property other than his New Star shares.

[70] When the parties married New Star had not got off the ground, although some of the groundwork had been done. New Star then expanded and flourished, as a result of activities undertaken for the most part during the period of the marriage. New Star set itself to grow quickly, and it did so. By rights issues and placings spread over the period from March 2001 to December 2003 substantial numbers of shares were issued at prices ranging from £80 to £150 per share. As a result New Star paid out over £140m in acquiring management of funds having assets worth the staggering amount of £3.73 billion. It is in this context that the experts' valuations of £12m and £18m for the husband's New Star shares, if they could currently have been sold, have to be seen.

[71] Plainly the accretion to the husband's wealth during the marriage, as a result of work he did during the marriage, was very substantial indeed. Although the marriage was short, the matrimonial property was of great value. The gain in the husband's earned wealth during the marriage was huge.

[72] Secondly, the judge was entitled to regard the high standard of living enjoyed by the parties during the marriage as a key feature of this case. That was not a standard of living the wife would be likely to achieve for herself.

[73] Having regard to these two features I consider the sum of £5m awarded by the judge is appropriate in this highly unusual case. The midway figure between the experts' valuations of the New Star shares was £15m. Taking this as no more than some indication of the value of these shares, the husband's worth was of the very approximate order of £32m. An award of £5m, including in this the matrimonial home, represents less than one third of the value of the New Star shares and less than one sixth of the husband's total worth. An award of less than one half of the value of the

New Star shares reflects the amount of work done by the husband on this business project before the marriage.

The McFarlane marriage

[74]   Kenneth McFarlane and Julia Chocholowska married on 1 September 1984. They lived together for 2 years before then. There were three children of the marriage, a boy, Jamie, and two girls, Sarah and Helen. They are now aged 16, 15 and 9 years. They are being educated at private schools. During their marriage the parties lived in south west London. They separated in December 2000. So the marriage lasted effectively for 16 years. A divorce decree nisi was made on 22 February 2002 and this was made absolute on 28 May 2003. The parties are now 46 years old.

[75]   By the time they married both parties had qualified professionally, the wife as a solicitor and the husband as a chartered accountant. They had each served their traineeship with leading City firms. After the birth of Jamie the wife returned to work. At the end of 1989 she moved to Freshfields, the well-known City firm of solicitors, where she worked a 4-day week. In 1990 the husband became a partner in Touche Ross.

[76]   Until this time the wife earned as much as the husband. For a while she earned more than him. In 1991, before the birth of their second child, Sarah, the parties agreed the wife should abandon her career and bring up the children on a day by day basis. They agreed to concentrate on the husband's career. Subsequently the wife did not return to work as a solicitor. On two occasions she began to re-train, first as a teacher and next as an independent financial adviser. The husband remained with Touche Ross and then its successor, Deloittes. He was the breadwinner for the family. He worked very hard and was, and continues to be, very successful.

[77]   In addition to the matrimonial home in Barnes, south-west London, the parties had a holiday home in Devon. At the trial the matrimonial home was valued at £1.5m and the holiday home at £255,000. In June 2000 a flat in Clerkenwell, just north of the City, was bought in the husband's name for £415,000.

[78]   As to family income, the wife's income was minimal after she gave up work. In round figures the husband's gross partnership income rose from £455,000 in 1998–1999 to £972,000 in 2000–2001, the year of separation, and then to £1,286,000 in 2002–2003. The corresponding net figures are £272,000, £579,000 and £753,000. The parties' standard of living rose as the husband's earnings increased and then as the mortgage on the matrimonial home was paid off over a period of 5 years. The wife's evidence was that the amount they spent on living costs, excluding school fees and mortgage repayments, rose from £66,000 in 1995 to £138,000 in 2000.

The hearing before the district judge

[79]   After their separation the parties agreed on a broadly equal division of the capital assets of about £3m owned by them. This capital was accumulated during their marriage, apart from an inheritance of about £40,000 the wife received from her father's estate. The parties agreed the wife should retain the matrimonial home and live there with the children. The husband was to have the holiday home in Devon, the flat in Clerkenwell and his partnership current account with Deloittes.

[80]   Before District Judge Redgrave it was common ground there was insufficient capital available to achieve a clean break. Further, it was common ground that the wife was entitled to a maintenance award on a joint lives or further order basis. The only

substantial contentious issue was the level of the periodical payments for the wife and for the children. The parties gave oral evidence.

[81]   The wife estimated her income requirements at £215,000 pa. Broken down, this was £87,000 for the three children and £128,000 for herself. This included private health insurance and some life insurance premiums. The husband estimated his personal spending requirements, excluding housing costs and pension provision, at £60,000 to £80,000 a year.

[82]   The husband's proposal was that he should make payments of £20,000 for each child, plus school fees, and £100,000 for the wife on a joint lives or further order basis, plus extras such as insurance. The wife sought £70,000 for the three children, plus school fees, and £275,000 for herself.

[83]   The judge's findings and conclusions can be summarised in this way. The wife was the primary carer of the children. Her financial needs were to maintain a home for herself and the parties' three children. This should be in the former matrimonial home. The wife had an earning capacity, but it was severely depressed by the length of time she had been out of the job market. Additionally, she was the single parent of three children, of whom the youngest was only 6 years old. It was unreasonable to expect her to take steps to acquire or improve her earning capacity until, at the very least, the youngest child reached secondary school age.

[84]   As to contributions to the family life, there was not a scintilla of criticism of the wife, either as a partner or as a mother. The parties' contributions to the marriage were of different but equal value. The judge said:

'The agreed split of capital is a reflection of the equal but separate contributions that these parties made to a marriage which lasted 16 years and which produced three children.'

[85]   The judge noted that part of the overall circumstances was that the joint decision of the parties to concentrate on the husband's career in order to fund the family's lifestyle resulted in the greatest fruits of his endeavours being available towards the end of the marriage and after its breakdown. The spadework for these rewards was carried out over a long period, and it would be unfair to take the view that the wife had not contributed to the recent increases in the husband's earnings after the separation. The wife's contributions enabled the husband to create a working environment which had produced greater rewards, 'of which she should have her fair share'. She had continued to make a contribution to the family in the nurturing of the children in a single parent household. That contribution had not come to an end when the parties separated.

[86]   The judge concluded that £60,000 a year for the children's maintenance was reasonable and that the appropriate award for the wife was £250,000 a year. This was one third of the husband's current net income. This amount 'reflects [the wife's] needs, obligations and the contribution that she has made over the years of the marriage'.

The appeals to the judge and the Court of Appeal

[87]   The husband appealed. The appeal was heard by Bennett J. He held that the effect of an award of maintenance at the rate of £250,000 was to give the wife an amount of money 'way above' her needs. The reality was that the husband would be paying the wife money likely to be saved and accumulated. That would subvert the principle that the purpose of periodical payments is maintenance and an award of capital is made once and once only. On this the district judge fell into error and her award should be set aside. In the exercise of his own discretion Bennett J ordered

payment of £20,000 for each of the children and a reduced amount, of £180,000, for the wife. To that extent the husband's appeal succeeded. As before, the payments to the wife were to be made during the parties' joint lives or until the wife should remarry or further order.

[88]   The wife appealed to the Court of Appeal. She sought reinstatement of the district judge's order. The appeal was heard by Thorpe, Latham and Wall LJJ, in conjunction with an appeal from Bennett J in the case of Parlour: *McFarlane v McFarlane; Parlour v Parlour* [2004] EWCA Civ 872, [2005] Fam 171, [2004] 2 FLR 893. On the appeals the court disagreed with Bennett J on the sole ground on which Bennett J considered the district judge had misdirected herself. Contrary to the view of Bennett J, the Court of Appeal held that in exceptional cases periodical payments orders can properly be used as a means to enable a payee to accumulate capital.

[89]   Nevertheless, when restoring the district judge's periodical payments order of £250,000 a year, the Court of Appeal limited its duration to 5 years. The court adopted this course because it was concerned, of its own motion, that by making a joint lives order in the present case the court would not be giving due effect to the clean break principle. The court was uneasy that a periodical payments award as large as £250,000 should be made for an indefinite period. The parties' presentation of the case as one for a joint lives order had diverted attention from the opportunity to achieve a clean break 'years before either party approached retirement'. Thorpe LJ preferred an order for periodical payments for an 'extendable' term of 5 years. After 5 years the court could reassess the prospects of a clean break in the light of the husband's capacity to re-mortgage his new home, the extent to which the wife had built up a capital reserve from the surplus of income over expenditure in the intervening years, and the revival of the wife's earning capacity: see *McFarlane* at 192–193 and 918 respectively, para [70]. Wall LJ was of the same view. He said that 'indeterminate and unfocused joint lives orders very substantially in excess of needs' are not within the statutory objective: see para [138]. From that decision the wife appealed to your Lordships' House.

Mrs McFarlane's appeal

[90]   The starting point of any discussion of the McFarlane case is to recognise its unusual combination of features. The parties' capital assets were insufficient to make an immediate clean break possible. That is not unusual. What is unusual is that, side by side with this (comparative) insufficiency of capital, there was a substantial excess of income. The husband's annual income was far in excess of the financial needs of the husband and of the wife even after they had separated. The latter feature is unusual. Normally the family income is not enough to meet the financial needs of both the husband and the wife after their combined household has split into two separate households. That is not so here.

[91]   A third feature is that the high level of the husband's earnings after the breakdown of the marriage was the result of the parties' joint endeavours at the earlier stages of his professional career. The wife gave up her career to devote herself to making a home for them both and for the children. As Bennett J noted, the husband was able to reap the benefits of the wife's contribution not just during the marriage. He continued to do so after the separation and after the divorce.

[92]   A fourth feature is that the career foregone by the wife was a professional career as successful and highly-paid as the husband's. This is not a case where the wife's future success was a matter for speculation. Speculation of this character is seldom helpful. Here the wife had a proven track record when the parties agreed she

should give up her job. A fifth feature is that, as primary carer of the three children, the wife continued to be at an economic disadvantage and continued to make a contribution from which the children and, indirectly, the husband benefited. He was relieved of the day to day responsibility for their children.

[93]   Clearly in this situation the wife is entitled to a periodical payments order in respect of her financial needs. She needed money to live in the former matrimonial home which was to be the continuing home for her and the children. But it would be manifestly unfair if her income award were confined to her needs. This is a paradigm case for an award of compensation in respect of the significant future economic disparity, sustained by the wife, arising from the way the parties conducted their marriage.

[94]   With that in mind I have an initial difficulty with the approach of the Court of Appeal. Before the district judge the parties were agreed that the appropriate order was a joint lives order. The judge assessed the quantum at £250,000 a year. Although she did not quantify the two elements separately, it is clear that this amount was partly in respect of the wife's financial needs and partly in respect of what I have labelled compensation. Further, the district judge had the clean break principle well in mind. Having seen and heard the parties, she was 'satisfied that this is not a case where the wife could adjust, without undue hardship, to the termination of periodical payments in her favour'. Although contrary argument was not addressed to the district judge on this point, I can see no ground for disturbing this assessment. There is no reason to doubt this was her considered view. And she recognised that the joint lives award might well need to be revised in later years.

[95]   The Court of Appeal, however, seems not to have had the distinction between needs and compensation clearly in mind when considering the way ahead. The court appears to have treated the surplus of income over expenditure as simply a means whereby the wife could accumulate a capital reserve. But that would be to mistake the purpose of this part of the district judge's award.

[96]   This leads me to the point where I fundamentally disagree with the Court of Appeal: the replacement of a joint lives order with a 5-year order. I agree with the Court of Appeal that when the husband has repaid the mortgage on his new home, and the wife's earning capacity has revived, the time may be ripe for a reassessment of the parties' position to see if a deferred clean break is practicable. A clean break might then be achievable by the court exercising its power to order the husband to make a lump sum payment to the wife as consideration for discharging his liability to make further periodical payments. The court has this power under s 31(7A) and (7B) inserted into the 1973 Act by s 66 of the Family Law Act 1996.

[97]   That is something which will merit careful consideration at a suitably early date. But I do not see how this leads to the conclusion that the district judge's joint lives order should be set aside in favour of an extendable 5 years' order. The practice in the family courts seems to be that on an application for extension of a periodical payments order made for a finite period the applicant must surmount a high threshold: *Fleming v Fleming* [2003] EWCA Civ 1841; [2004] 1 FLR 667, at 670, paras [12]–[14]. In the present case it would be altogether inappropriate, indeed unjust, to make a 5-year order and place the wife in that position when 5 years has elapsed. In the present case a 5-year order is most unlikely to be sufficient to achieve a fair outcome. Further financial provision of some sort will be needed. So, far from compelling the wife to apply for an extension of a 5-year order, and requiring her to shoulder the heavy burden accompanying such an application, it is more appropriate for the husband to have to take the initiative in applying for a variation of a joint lives order when he considers circumstances make that appropriate. Certainly the district judge cannot be said to

have erred in principle in making a joint lives order, especially when this was common ground between the parties. I would allow this appeal and restore the order of District Judge Redgrave.

[98]   One final point should be mentioned. The amount of £250,000 substantially exceeds the wife's financial needs. The district judge said it was for the wife to decide whether to make pension provision for herself, and whether to insure herself and the children against the risk of the husband's premature death. The Court of Appeal disagreed. The wife, the court said, must invest the surplus sensibly, or take the risk that her failure to do so might count against her on an application for discharge of the order.

[99]   On this point I largely agree with the Court of Appeal, but not wholly. When a review takes place the court will consider, in the light of the prevailing circumstances, what further amounts should be paid to the wife by way of periodical payments, or capitalised and paid as a lump sum if that is practicable, in respect both of needs and compensation. As to needs, the claimant's resources are always a matter to be taken into account. And claimants for financial ancillary relief are expected to manage their financial affairs sensibly and responsibly. Thus far I agree with the Court of Appeal. But the wife's claim for compensation stands differently. Her compensation claim is not needs-related; it is loss-related. So the compensation element of her claim is not directly affected by the use she makes of her resources.

LORD HOFFMANN:

My Lords,

[100]   For the reasons given in the speech of my noble and learned friend Baroness Hale of Richmond I too would allow Mrs McFarlane's appeal and dismiss Mr Miller's appeal.

LORD HOPE OF CRAIGHEAD:

My Lords,

[101]   I have had the privilege of reading in draft the speeches of my noble and learned friends Lord Nicholls of Birkenhead and Baroness Hale of Richmond. I would find it very difficult to say to which of them I would give the award if, like Paris on Mount Ida, I were forced to pass judgment on which of them offered the better guidance. The fact is that they complement each other. The clarity and simplicity which is to be found in Lord Nicholls of Birkenhead's speech is matched by the immensely valuable account which Baroness Hale of Richmond gives of the law's development and of the way the principles on which it is based should be applied in practice. On all points that are relevant to the disposal of these appeals I am in full agreement with them both. For the reasons that they give I too would dismiss the appeal in Mrs Miller's case and allow the appeal in Mrs McFarlane's case.

[102]   I should like, however, to add some observations on the way the problem raised by these cases is currently dealt with in Scots law. This was referred to by counsel in both cases in the course of the argument. Mr Posnansky QC for the husband in Mrs McFarlane's case relied on the way the clean break principle is given effect to in the Family Law (Scotland) Act 1985. This was to support his submission that a fair outcome had been achieved by the order which the Court of Appeal made in her case. He said that the solution that Parliament thought appropriate in 1985 to achieve fairness in Scotland must be taken as a good guide to what the same Parliament had in

mind as fair when it passed the corresponding legislation for England one year earlier. I do not think that the comparison which Mr Posnansky sought to draw stands up to examination. I should like to explain why.

The Scottish approach to fairness

[103]   The report of the Scottish Law Commission on Family Law – Aliment and Financial Provision, Scot Law Com No 67 (HMSO, 1981) was submitted to the Lord Advocate on 17 July 1981 and ordered by the House of Commons to be printed on 4 November 1981. The report of the Law Commission on Family Law – The Financial Consequences of Divorce, Law Com No 112 (HC 68) (HMSO, 1981) was submitted to the Lord Chancellor on 26 October 1981 and ordered by the House of Commons to be printed on 14 December 1981. A study of these reports shows that, despite their close proximity in dates, they proposed very different solutions to the basic problem as to how to reconcile the requirements of fairness with the desire for certainty.

[104]   As the Law Commission put it in para 19 of its report:

> 'We believe the formulation of policy in this and indeed other areas of the law involves the resolution of two objectives, each intrinsically desirable, but perhaps mutually inconsistent. The first is that the law should be certain and predictable in its results. This objective is not only consistent with the popular concept of justice; it also means that it is easier for lawyers to advise their clients on the likely outcome of a dispute, so promoting the conclusion of reasonable settlements and minimising recourse to contested trials. The second objective is that the law should achieve justice and fairness between the parties; and it is said that this necessarily involves considerable flexibility of approach by reason of the widely varying facts of each case.'

In para 35 the Law Commission, who were no doubt well aware of what the Scottish Law Commission were proposing, acknowledged that it was clearly desirable that the laws between these two parts of the UK should be based on the same principles. But they went on to say that they did not think that it necessarily followed that the English and Scottish laws governing the financial consequences of divorce should be couched in identical terms.

[105]   The approach which was favoured by the Law Commission was loosely structured. They attached greater importance to flexibility than they did to certainty. In para 21 they said that they favoured a reasonable balance between these two objectives. In the summary of their recommendations in para 46 of the report they said that any future legislation dealing with the financial consequences of divorce should be subject to continuous monitoring and periodical reports to Parliament. Their recommendation as to how the guidelines in s 25(1) of the Matrimonial Causes Act 1973 should be revised avoided an approach that was too prescriptive. They said that the importance of each party doing everything possible to become self-sufficient should be formulated in terms of a positive principle. They said that 'weight' should be given to the view that, 'in appropriate cases', periodical financial provision should be 'primarily' concerned to secure a smooth transition from the status of marriage to the status of independence. They left the formulation of the legislation to give effect to this flexible approach to Parliament.

[106]   The approach which was favoured by the Scottish Law Commission, on the other hand, was the reverse of that which was recommended for England and Wales. It was the product of extensive research and consultation. It was worked out in very much greater detail. It produced a result which favoured certainty in place of flexibility. The report contained a draft Bill, complete with explanatory notes, which was designed to implement its recommendations. It was presented as a fully worked

out system. There was no recommendation that the legislation that was proposed should be subject to monitoring or to review. It was intended to establish the law not just for a generation. Like the Forth Bridge, it was built to last for a very long time.

[107] It has to be acknowledged that the law relating to financial provision on divorce in Scotland was without any clearly laid down structure or objectives when the Scottish Law Commission began to look at it in 1976. Section 5(2) of the Divorce (Scotland) Act 1976 enabled either party to apply for financial provision by way of a periodical sum or capital sum or both. The court was directed to make with respect to the application such order, if any, as it thought fit. The amount of any award, and the principles on which the award should be based, were left entirely to the court to determine. The court for its part refrained from laying down any clearly defined principles.

[108] There was no obvious disadvantage in this system so long as exclusive jurisdiction in all proceedings for divorce remained in the Court of Session. This was a court where members of the Faculty of Advocates had the exclusive right of audience. The business was concentrated in the hands of a relatively small number of judges. The relatively small number of advocates who practised regularly in this field were able to predict the awards that were likely to be made by the judges in any given case without any real difficulty. But it was clear that that this system could not survive an extension of jurisdiction in divorce cases to the sheriff court, which the Royal Commission on Legal Services in Scotland had recommended in 1980. This reform was effected by s 1 of the Divorce Jurisdiction, Court Fees and Legal Aid (Scotland) Act 1983. The sheriff court now has concurrent jurisdiction with the Court of Session in actions for divorce. It is in the sheriff court that almost all divorce actions are now brought.

[109] The draft Bill which accompanied the Scottish Law Commission's recommendations for reform passed into law almost unaltered as the Family Law (Scotland) Act 1985 (the 1985 Act). The general note which introduces the annotations to this Act in Current Law Statutes pays tribute to the fact that the Act attracted so little in the way of criticism during its passage through Parliament. This was in sharp contrast to the controversy generated in the previous year by the Matrimonial and Family Proceedings Act 1984, which made changes in the same area in relation to England and Wales in response to the Law Commission's recommendations.

The risk of injustice

[110] The law as enacted in the 1985 Act has remained almost unaltered for over twenty years. Apart from amendments which were introduced by the Welfare Reform and Pensions Act 1999 to provide for the sharing of pensions, the only significant change is that made by s 16 of the Family Law (Scotland) Act 2006. It amends the rule laid down s 10(3)(b) of the 1985 Act that the date on which matrimonial property is to be valued is the date when the parties ceased to cohabit. The fact that this rule could lead to injustice was revealed by the decision of the First Division of the Court of Session in *Wallis v Wallis* (1992) SC 455. That case is instructive. It illustrates how inflexible the 1985 Act's regime relating to the valuation and division of the matrimonial property is compared with that in the English legislation.

[111] In *Little v Little* (1990) SLT 785, at 787C–D, I said that division of matrimonial property under the 1985 Act was essentially a matter of discretion, aimed at achieving a fair and practicable result in accordance with common sense. Those comments were directed at the risk that treating each step in the process as raising an issue of law and not of discretion would open up decisions by the court of first instance for reconsideration on appeal: see also Lord Dunpark at 790J–K. But there was no getting

away from the fact that the directions in the 1985 Act were designed to reduce the scope of the court's discretion to the minimum that was consistent with enabling the court to deal with each case on its own facts. The Scottish Law Commission had rejected the unfettered discretion model that up to then had been part of Scots Law: see paras 3.37–3.39 of their report. There is almost no room here for what Lord Cooke of Thorndon referred to in *White*, at 615 and 999 respectively, as the development of general judicial practice.

[112] The sheriff who granted decree of divorce in *Wallis v Wallis* made an order for the transfer by the wife of her half-share in the matrimonial home to the husband as part of the division of the matrimonial property. The Court of Session held that the effect of s 10(3)(b) of the 1985 Act was that the whole of the wife's share of the increase in its value after the date of separation which passed to the husband as a result of the sheriff's order had to be left out of account in the computation of the amount of the matrimonial property that determined how much of it was to be paid by him to the wife: *Wallis v Wallis* (1992) SC 455. Dr Eric Clive, the principal architect of the legislation and a Scottish Law Commissioner said that the decision was wrong (*Financial Provision on Divorce – A Question of Technique* 1992 SLT (News) 241). Professor Joseph Thomson, then Regius Professor of law at Glasgow University, said that it was right (*Financial Provision on Divorce – Not Technique but Statutory Interpretation* 1992 SLT (News) 245). When it came here on appeal your Lordships' House affirmed the decision of the Court of Session: *Wallis v Wallis* (1993) SC (HL) 49. In *Jacques v Jacques* (1997) SC (HL) 20, the House held, again affirming a decision of the Court of Session, that the sheriff was entitled to give effect to the principle of equal division in a way that had not been contemplated by the statute. He thought that the spouses could share equally in the increase in the value of the matrimonial property after the date when they separated. That could not be done under the rules laid down by the statute. So he refrained from making any order for a financial provision.

[113] The effect of the amendment made by s 16 of the Family Law (Scotland) Act 2006 is that property transferred to one of the spouses by order is now to be valued, unless otherwise agreed, at the date of the making of the property transfer order, or, in exceptional circumstances, such date as the court shall determine: see Joe Thomson's general note on this section in *Current Law Statutes* (Sweet & Maxwell, 2004). But this amendment leaves untouched another problem which was mentioned in *Wilson v Wilson* (1999) SLT 249. At 253C–D Lord Marnoch drew attention, as he had done previously in *Latter v Latter* (1990) SLT 805, to the fact that the definition of matrimonial property was capable in other ways, on occasion, of producing very real injustice. He thought it had done so in that case, where much of the wealth created during the marriage was vested in a farming company and the husband's shareholding in the company was excluded from the matrimonial property because it had been either held by him prior to the marriage or inherited by him from his father.

The clean break principle

[114] The clean break principle lies at the heart of the argument in Mrs McFarlane's case about the effect of s 25A(2) of the Matrimonial Causes Act 1973. The Scottish approach to it is set out in s 9(1)(d) of the 1985 Act. In this paragraph the 1985 Act states that the principles which the court shall apply in deciding what order for financial provision, if any, to make under it include the principle that:

'a party who has been dependent to a substantial degree on the financial support of the other party should be awarded such financial provision as is reasonable to enable him to adjust, over a period of not more than three years from the date of the decree of divorce, to the loss of that support on divorce.'

This rule is reinforced by s 13(2)(a), which provides that the court shall not make an order for a periodical allowance under s 8(2) of the 1985 Act unless the order is justified by a principle set out in para (c) (the economic burden of caring for children), (d) (financial support for no more than three years) or (e) (likelihood of serious financial hardship) of s 9(1). Paragraph (b) (fair account to be taken of economic advantages and disadvantages) is omitted from this list. Section 11(4) sets out various factors to which the court shall have regard for the purposes of s 9(1)(d), including all the circumstances of the case: s 11(4)(e). But it does not allow the court to override the 3-year limit. It excludes compensation aimed at redressing a significant prospective disparity between the parties arising from the way they conducted their marriages.

[115]   A rigid application of the clean break principle, as enacted in s 9(1)(d), has the advantage of certainty. But it runs the risk of becoming outdated as social conditions change and the reasoning behind it no longer fits in with modern concepts of fairness. As Lord Nicholls of Birkenhead has explained, the concept of fairness is ultimately grounded in what people think. Social and moral values change from one generation to the next. Baroness Hale of Richmond's comment in para [127] that statutory statements of principle translated into rules can operate harshly in some cases, particularly where the resources consist largely of income rather than capital, shows where the problem lies. The flexibility which sheriffs and judges need to adapt the law to what would be regarded as fair today as compared with what was regarded as fair 25 years ago is denied to them.

[116]   The way that Mrs McFarlane's case would have to be dealt with if the case had arisen in Scotland illustrates the problem. It would not be possible to design an award under the Scottish system that provided her with an amount of income for the future that gave fair recognition to her entitlement. She is entitled to an award that reflects the agreement that she and her husband entered into, because in their case the capital assets that would be needed for this are not available. They decided that she should sacrifice her own high earning career in the interests of the family while her husband developed his ability to generate income. Under the Scottish system he would continue to enjoy the benefits of his high earning capacity. But she could not be compensated for her future economic disparity, due to his lack of capital. She would be required instead to adjust to a lower standard of living. And she would have to do this over a period of no more than 3 years.

[117]   The annotation to s 9(1)(d) in *Current Law Statutes*, based on para 3.107 of the report by the Scottish Law Commission, explains the purpose of that paragraph. The principle is intended to enable the court to cushion the blow of divorce by providing funds to enable a spouse 'to find employment or retrain, or to adjust to a lower standard of living'. I agree with Lord Nicholls of Birkenhead's observation, in para [94] of his speech, that the situation in which Mrs McFarlane finds herself is a paradigm case for an income award that will compensate her for the significant future economic disparity, sustained by the wife, arising from the way the parties conducted their marriage. That is impossible under the rules which apply in Scotland.

[118]   With the benefit of hindsight, it can be seen how unfairly the principle which s 9(1)(d) lays down (it adopts the statutory convention avoided by the English legislation of referring to 'him' not 'her') discriminates against women. It operates harshly in cases where a high earning wife, or the highly qualified wife with the prospect of high earnings – and it is, of course, almost invariably the wife, not the husband who does this – gives up a promising and demanding career in the interests of the family. Women today compete on equal terms with men in business and in the professions for high earnings. They are being encouraged to do so by the measures for equal pay and the removal of discrimination on the ground of sex. These measures were already in place by 1985, but had not begun to realise their full potential for

change by that date. Many more women than were foreseen in 1981 are now reaching the ranks of those who are highly paid for what they do. But many women are mothers too. The career break which results from concentrating on motherhood and the family in the middle years of their lives comes at a price which in most cases is irrecoverable.

[119]   As the district judge recognised in Mrs McFarlane's case, it is almost always impossible for a woman who has made that choice to achieve the same pattern of high earning on her return to work which she would have done if the progress of her career had not been interrupted by concentrating on her family. The price that her decision brings with it is made all the more severe by the difficulties which under current conditions couples are likely to experience in providing for a pension which will maintain their standard of living in the future.

[120]   These effects appear not to have been foreseen in 1981 when the Scottish Law Commission published their report. Achieving a clean break in the event of divorce remains as desirable now as it was then. But if this means that one party must adjust to a lower standard of living, the result is that a clean break is being achieved at the expense of fairness. Why should a woman who has chosen motherhood over her career in the interests of her family be denied a fair share of the wealth that her husband has been able to build up, as his share of the bargain that they entered into when that choice was made, out of the earnings that he is able to generate when she cannot be compensated for this out of capital?

Scots law in need of reform

[121]   I suggest that the time has come for taking a fresh look at this problem. The length of the period for which a periodical allowance should be awarded should no longer be confined to an absolute maximum of three years. The court should have a discretion to provide for a longer period where, in exceptional circumstances and applying the overriding criterion of fairness, the judge finds that one party to the marriage whose contribution to the marriage has resulted in a reduction in his or her earning capacity ought to be compensated out of the other party's future income because the capital needed to provide this is not available. This could be achieved by inserting a qualification to this effect into s 9(1)(d) of the 1985 Act and by inserting a reference to s 9(1)(b) in s 13(2)(a). There may be other ways of achieving this result. Whatever method is chosen, it seems to me that the principles on which current restrictions are based need to be reconsidered in the interests of fairness as soon as possible.

BARONESS HALE OF RICHMOND:

My Lords,

[122]   There is much to be said for the flexibility and sensitivity of the English law of ancillary relief. It avoids the straitjacket of rigid rules which can apply harshly or unfairly in an individual case. But it should not be too flexible. It must try to achieve some consistency and predictability. This is not only to secure that so far as possible like cases are treated alike but also to enable and encourage the parties to negotiate their own solutions as quickly and cheaply as possible. This latter aim will become even more important once the new costs regime comes into force on 3 April, as each party will usually have to bear his or her own costs. We must, therefore, strive to identify some principles, consistently with the task set for the court by ss 25 and 25A of the Matrimonial Causes Act 1973 (the 1973 Act).

The search for principle

[123]   English law starts from the principle of separate property during marriage. Each spouse is legally in control of his or her own property while the marriage lasts. But in real life most couples' finances become ever-more inter-linked and inter-dependent. Most couples now choose to share the ownership of much of their most significant property, in particular their matrimonial home and its contents. They also owe one another duties of support, so that what starts as individual income is used for the benefit of the whole family. There are many different ways of doing this, from pooling their whole incomes, to pooling a proportion for household purposes, to one making an allowance to the other, to one handing over the whole wage packet to the other (see Jan Pahl, *Money and Marriage* (Palgrave Macmillan, 1989)). Some couples adopt one or other of these systems and retain it throughout their marriage. But as the gender roles also become more flexible within the marriage, with bread-winning and home-making responsibilities being shared and changing over time, so too their financial arrangements may also become more flexible and change over time. It also becomes less and less relevant to ask who technically is the owner of what.

[124]   When the marriage comes to an end, the court's powers are also flexible. They are no longer based upon the assumption that there is one male breadwinner to whom all or most of the resources belong and one female home-maker in need of his support (and entitled to it only as long as she remains deserving). The court is directed to take into account all of their resources from every source. It is then given a wide range of powers to reallocate all those resources, be they property, capital or income. It is directed to take account of all the circumstances, and in particular the checklist of factors listed in s 25(2). But what, at the end of the day, is it supposed to do? What is it trying to achieve?

[125]   In its original form, s 25 of the 1973 Act directed the court to try and place the parties in the financial positions in which they would have been had the marriage not broken down and each had discharged their financial obligations towards the other. This made perfect sense when the assumption was that the financial obligations undertaken, mainly by the husband, at marriage endured for life even if the marital consortium came to an end (indeed, before the Matrimonial Proceedings and Property Act 1970 came into force, a rich man whose divorced wife married a poorer one might still have to support her in the manner to which she had become accustomed during their marriage). But it made less sense once the basis of divorce was that the marriage had irretrievably broken down, the law no longer drew formal distinctions between the obligations of husbands and wives, and the court had a wide range of powers to distribute their resources in such a way as to enable each to go his or her separate way.

[126]   Hence the assumption of lifelong-obligation was repealed by the Matrimonial and Family Proceedings Act 1984, following the report of the Law Commission on Family Law – *The Financial Consequences of Divorce* Law Com No 112 (HMSO, 1981). The Commission's reasoning (see para 17) was essentially pragmatic. In the great majority of cases, it simply was not possible to enable two households to continue to live as if they were one. Nor in many cases was it desirable to perpetuate their mutual interdependence. The whole point of a divorce is to enable people whose lives were previously bound up with one another to disentangle those bonds and lead independent lives. But at least the discredited objective had encouraged a sort of equality: if the marriage had not broken down, the couple would still be enjoying the same standard of living. The object, therefore, was to get as close as possible to that for both of them. John Eekelaar dubbed this the 'minimal loss' principle (I used to refer to it as the principle of 'equal misery').

[127]   The 1984 Act put nothing in its place. The Law Commission, in their previous discussion paper (The Financial Consequences of Divorce: The Basic Policy, A Discussion Paper, 1980, Law Com No 103), had discussed various models of financial provision after divorce and found all of them wanting. Thus they deliberately eschewed recommending any overall guiding principle or objective, other than the attempt to disentangle the spouses' mutual interdependence. The Commission may have been inhibited because they were only considering financial provision, still usually referred to as maintenance, and not property adjustment and capital. This is in contrast with the approach of the Scottish Law Commission, of whose work the Law Commission were well aware. The Scots' Report (Family Law – Aliment and Financial Provision, Scot Law Com No 67 (HMSO, 1981) resulted in statutory statements of principle translated into rules. As my noble and learned friend, Lord Hope of Craighead has demonstrated, these can operate harshly in some cases, particularly where the resources consist largely of income rather than property.

Three pointers in the 1973 Act

[128]   Although the 1973 Act, as amended in 1984, contains no express objective for the court, it does contain some pointers towards the correct approach. First, the court is directed to give first priority to the welfare while a minor of any child of the family who has not attained the age of 18: s 25(1). This is a clear recognition of the reality that, although the couple may seek to go their separate ways, they are still jointly responsible for the welfare of their children. The invariable practice in English law is to try to maintain a stable home for the children after their parents' divorce. Research indicates that it is more successful in doing this than in securing a comparable income for them in future (see, eg, Sue Arthur, Jane Lewis, Mavis Maclean, Steven Finch and Rory Fitzgerald, *Settling Up: Making Financial Arrangements after Divorce or Separation* (National Centre for Social Research, 2002). Giving priority to the children's welfare should also involve ensuring that their primary carer is properly provided for, because it is well known that the security and stability of children depends in large part upon the security and stability of their primary carers (see, eg, Professor Jane Lewis FBA, 'Debates and Issues regarding Marriage and Cohabitation in the British and American Literature' (2001) 15(1) Int JLPF 159, at 178).

[129]   Secondly, the checklist in s 25(2) is not simply concerned with totting up the present assets and dividing them in whatever way seems fair at that time. Despite the repeal of the statutory objective, the court is still concerned with the foreseeable (and on occasions more distant) future as well as with the past and the present. The court has to consider, not only the parties' present resources, but also those that they will have in the foreseeable future: s 25(2)(a). The 1984 Act included in these any increase in earning capacity which it was reasonable to expect either of them to achieve. Although clearly aimed at trying to get home-makers back into the labour market, it applies equally to each party. Breadwinners are not expected to give up work so as to diminish the claims of the home-maker and children. Changes introduced by the Pensions Act 1995 require the court to consider any benefits under a pension arrangement which either party has or is likely to have and in this case not just in the foreseeable future: see s 25B(1) of the 1973 Act. The checklist has always required the court to take account of any benefit which a party will lose the chance of acquiring because of the loss of marital status: see s 25(2)(h). But until pension attachment and, more recently, pension sharing were introduced, there was often not much they could do to reflect this other than through periodical payments. The court also has to consider the parties' needs, both now and in the foreseeable future: see s 25(2)(b). Finally, when considering the parties' contributions to the welfare of the family, the 1984 Act inserted a requirement to look, not only to the past, but also to the contributions likely to be made in the

foreseeable future: see s 25(2)(f). Principally, of course, these will be the continued caring responsibilities resulting from the relationship.

[130]   Thirdly, several provisions were inserted in 1984 to encourage and enable a clean break settlement, in which the parties could go their separate ways without making further financial claims upon the other. One such provision has already been mentioned: the expectation that each party would take reasonable steps to increase their earning capacity. Three others are now contained in s 25A, which was much debated in argument before us. Section 25A(1) provides:

> 'Where on or after the grant of a decree of divorce or nullity of marriage the court decides to exercise its powers under section 23(1)(a) [periodical payments], (b) [secured periodical payments] or (c) [lump sum], 24 [property adjustment], 24A [property sale] or 24B [pension sharing] above in favour of a party to the marriage, it shall be the duty of the court to consider whether it would be appropriate so to exercise those powers that the financial obligations of each party towards the other will be terminated as soon after the grant of the decree as the court considers just and reasonable.'

This applies to the whole range of the court's powers, not just to the power to award future periodical payments. It assumes that the court has decided that some award is appropriate (in practice, there are very few cases in which some readjustment of the parties' strict proprietary rights is not required, if they cannot agree it, in order to disentangle their previously entangled affairs). The court is then required to consider whether it could achieve an appropriate result by bringing their mutual obligations to an end. This is a clear steer in the direction of lump sum and property adjustment orders with no continuing periodical payments. But it does not tell us much about what an appropriate result would be.

[131]   Section 25A(2) provides:

> 'Where the court decides in such a case to make a periodical payments or secured periodical payments order in favour of a party to the marriage, the court shall in particular consider whether it would be appropriate to require those payments to be made or secured only for such term as would in the opinion of the court be sufficient to enable the party in whose favour the order is made to adjust without undue hardship to the termination of his or her financial dependence on the other party.'

I assume that the reference to 'such a case' is to a case in which the court has decided to exercise its powers under the listed sections rather than to a case in which it has decided that it would be appropriate to exercise those powers so as to terminate the parties' financial obligations as soon as possible after the decree. If it decides to make a periodical payments order, it must consider how quickly it can bring those payments to an end. It has, therefore, to consider fixing a term, although in doing so it must avoid 'undue hardship'. This is linked to two other powers: s 28(1) allows the court to specify the duration of a periodical payments order; generally, it is open to the recipient to apply to extend the term, provided this is done before it expires; but s 28(1A) gives the court power to prohibit any application for an extension. If there is an application for an extension, the court has the same duty to consider bringing the periodical payments to an end as soon as possible: s 31(7); and it now has power to order a lump sum, property adjustment or pension sharing instead: s 31(7B). Thus if there were not the capital resources to achieve a clean break at the outset, it may be achieved later if sufficient capital becomes available.

[132]   Section 25A(3) reverses the decision of the Court of Appeal in *Dipper v Dipper* [1981] Fam 31, (1980) 1 FLR 286 and allows the court to dismiss an application for periodical payments at the outset. The logical consequence of the previous tailpiece had been that such claims should be kept alive unless the claimant agreed to relinquish

them. The lifelong obligation might be revived by events which had nothing to do with the marriage.

[133]   Section 25A is a powerful encouragement towards securing the court's objective by way of lump sum and capital adjustment (which now includes pension sharing) rather than by continuing periodical payments. This is good practical sense. Periodical payments are a continuing source of stress for both parties. They are also insecure. With the best will in the world, the paying party may fall on hard times and be unable to keep them up. Nor is the best will in the world always evident between formerly married people. It is also the logical consequence of the retreat from the principle of the lifelong obligation. Independent finances and self-sufficiency are the aims. Nevertheless, s 25A does not tell us what the outcome of the exercise required by s 25 should be. It is mainly directed at how that outcome should be put into effect.

White v White

[134]   Hence, these three pointers do make it clear that a clean break is not to be achieved at the expense of a fair result. But the 1973 Act still leaves us without much help towards what the court should be trying to achieve by its reallocation of their resources and why it should be doing so. The great leap forward was achieved by this House in *White v White* [2001] 1 AC 596, [2000] 2 FLR 981.

[135]   In hindsight, *White* should have been a simple case. There was a long marriage in which the couple had been partners in both senses of the term. Both were farmers. There were two farms. Both wanted to carry on farming. One solution might have been to give one farm to one and one to the other; at all events, the resources were such that each could have been enabled to farm independently. But by that time practice had become entrenched: in cases where there was enough to provide for both, the wife was entitled to her 'reasonable requirements', preferably capitalised, and the husband got the rest (see, eg, *O'D v O'D* [1976] Fam 83, (1975) FLR Rep 512; *Page v Page* (1981) 2 FLR 198; *Preston v Preston* [1982] Fam 17, (1981) 2 FLR 331). On separate property principles, this was deeply discriminatory. Where the parties had collaborated, not only in the enterprise of living together and bringing up their children, but also in the enterprise of making their living, as this couple had, why should only one of them be entitled to the surplus? In such a case, it is clear that the yardstick should be equal capital division, although factors such as the source of some of the assets might justify some adjustment.

[136]   Thus were the principles of fairness and non-discrimination and the 'yardstick of equality' established. But the House was careful to point out (see *White* at 605F and 989 respectively) that the yardstick of equality did not inevitably mean equality of result. It was a standard against which the outcome of the s 25 exercise was to be checked. In any event, except in those cases where the present assets can be divided and each can live independently at roughly the same standard of living, equality of outcome is difficult both to define and to achieve. Giving half the present assets to the breadwinner achieves a very different outcome from giving half the assets to the homemaker with children.

The rationale for redistribution

[137]   So how is the court to operate the principles of fairness, equality and non-discrimination in the less straightforward cases? As Ward LJ has argued non-judicially ('Have the House of Lords abused Cinderella? Their Contribution to Divorce Law', lecture at King's College, London, 23 November 2004), given that we

have a separate property system, there has to be some sort of rationale for the redistribution of resources from one party to another. In my view there are at least three. Any or all of them might supply such a reason, although one must be careful to avoid double counting. The cardinal feature is that each is looking at factors which are linked to the parties' relationship, either causally or temporally, and not to extrinsic, unrelated factors, such as a disability arising after the marriage has ended.

[138]   The most common rationale is that the relationship has generated needs which it is right that the other party should meet. In the great majority of cases, the court is trying to ensure that each party and their children have enough to supply their needs, set at a level as close as possible to the standard of living which they enjoyed during the marriage (note that the House did not adopt a restrictive view of needs in *White*: see 608G–609A and 993 respectively). This is a perfectly sound rationale where the needs are the consequence of the parties' relationship, as they usually are. The most common source of need is the presence of children, whose welfare is always the first consideration, or of other dependent relatives, such as elderly parents. But another source of need is having had to look after children or other family members in the past. Many parents have seriously compromised their ability to attain self-sufficiency as a result of past family responsibilities. Even if they do their best to re-enter the employment market, it will often be at a lesser level than before, and they will hardly ever be able to make up what they have lost in pension entitlements. A further source of need may be the way in which the parties chose to run their life together. Even dual career families are difficult to manage with completely equal opportunity for both. Compromises often have to be made by one so that the other can get ahead. All couples throughout their lives together have to make choices about who will do what, sometimes forced upon them by circumstances such as redundancy or low pay, sometimes freely made in the interests of them both. The needs generated by such choices are a perfectly sound rationale for adjusting the parties' respective resources in compensation.

[139]   But while need is often a sound rationale, it should not be seen as a limiting principle if other rationales apply. This was the error into which the law had fallen before *White*. Need had become 'reasonable requirements' and thus more generous to the recipient, but it was still a limiting factor even where there was a substantial surplus of resources over needs: see *Page v Page* (1981) 2 FLR 198. Counsel would talk of the 'discipline of the budget' and suggestions that a wife's budget might properly contain a margin for savings and contingencies, or to pass on to her grandchildren, were greeted with disbelief.

[140]   A second rationale, which is closely related to need, is compensation for relationship-generated disadvantage. Indeed, some consider that provision for need is compensation for relationship-generated disadvantage. But the economic disadvantage generated by the relationship may go beyond need, however generously interpreted. The best example is a wife, like Mrs McFarlane, who has given up what would very probably have been a lucrative and successful career. If the other party, who has been the beneficiary of the choices made during the marriage, is a high earner with a substantial surplus over what is required to meet both parties' needs, then a premium above needs can reflect that relationship-generated disadvantage.

[141]   A third rationale is the sharing of the fruits of the matrimonial partnership. One reason given by the Law Commission for not adopting any one single model was that the flexibility of s 25 allowed practice to develop in response to changing perceptions of what might be fair. There is now a widespread perception that marriage is a partnership of equals. The Scottish Law Commission found that this translated into widespread support for a norm of equal sharing of the partnership assets when the marriage ended, whatever the source or legal ownership of those assets (Family Law –

Aliment and Financial Provision, Scot Law Com No 67 (HMSO, 1981) paras 3.66–3.68). A decade earlier, the English Law Commission had found widespread support for the automatic joint ownership of the matrimonial home, even during marriage (First Report on Family Property – A New Approach, Law Com No 52 (HMSO, 1973)). Earlier still, the checklist of factors accompanying the new powers of property allocation in the Matrimonial Proceedings and Property Act 1970 had introduced the contributions which each party had made to the welfare of the family, including the contribution made by looking after the home and caring for the children. Thirty years later, the authors of *Settling Up* (see para [128] earlier, p 56), found that 'there appeared to be a relatively widespread assumption that an 'equal' or 50/50 division was the normal or appropriate thing to do', alongside a recognition of needs and entitlements (but their respondents' views on entitlements might not be quite the same as the lawyers', a point to which I shall return).

[142]   Of course, an equal partnership does not necessarily dictate an equal sharing of the assets. In particular, it may have to give way to the needs of one party or the children. Too strict an adherence to equal sharing and the clean break can lead to a rapid decrease in the primary carer's standard of living and a rapid increase in the breadwinner's. The breadwinner's unimpaired and unimpeded earning capacity is a powerful resource which can frequently repair any loss of capital after an unequal distribution: see, eg, the observations of Munby J in *B v B (Mesher Order)* [2002] EWHC 3106 (Fam), [2003] 2 FLR 285. Recognising this is one reason why English law has been so successful in retaining a home for the children.

[143]   But there are many cases in which the approach of roughly equal sharing of partnership assets with no continuing claims one against the other is nowadays entirely feasible and fair. One example is *Foster v Foster* [2003] EWCA Civ 565, [2003] 2 FLR 299, a comparatively short childless marriage, where each could earn their own living after divorce, but where capital assets had been built up by their joint efforts during the marriage. Although one party had earned more and thus contributed more in purely financial terms to the acquisition of those assets, both contributed what they could, and the fair result was to divide the product of their joint endeavours equally. Another example is *Burgess v Burgess* [1996] 2 FLR 34, a long marriage between a solicitor and a doctor, which had produced three children. Each party could earn their own living after divorce, but the home, contents and collections which they had accumulated during the marriage could be equally shared. Although one party might have better prospects than the other in future, once the marriage was at an end there was no reason for one to make further claims upon the other.

The ultimate objective?

[144]   Thus far, in common with my noble and learned friend, Lord Nicholls of Birkenhead, I have identified three principles which might guide the court in making an award: need (generously interpreted), compensation, and sharing. I agree that there cannot be a hard and fast rule about whether one starts with equal sharing and departs if need or compensation supply a reason to do so, or whether one starts with need and compensation and shares the balance. Much will depend upon how far future income is to be shared as well as current assets. In general, it can be assumed that the marital partnership does not stay alive for the purpose of sharing future resources unless this is justified by need or compensation. The ultimate objective is to give each party an equal start on the road to independent living.

Conduct and contributions

[145] Is there any need to qualify these aims, considered in the light of all the circumstances and the factors listed in s 25(2)? Two which have emerged in later cases should, in my view, be firmly rejected: conduct and special contributions. Section 25(2)(g) is quite clear: the court has to have regard to the parties' conduct if it would be inequitable to disregard it. In the olden days, when all the assets were assumed to be the breadwinner's and he was making an allowance to enable his wife to live separately from him, the wife's conduct might reduce the allowance she would otherwise have needed or even extinguish it altogether. She had, therefore, to be 100% blameless in order to be sure of her conventional one third share of his income. In theory, if she were 50% to blame, her share might be halved, although in practice the divorce courts were more flexible than that (but see, for example, the approach in *Ackerman v Ackerman* [1972] Fam 1, where a wife who was assessed as 25% to blame for the breakdown of the marriage was subject to a 25% discount from what she would otherwise have received). But once the assets are seen as a pool, and the couple as equal partners, then it is only equitable to take their conduct into account if one has been very much more to blame than the other: in the famous words of Ormrod J in *Wachtel v Wachtel* [1973] Fam 72, at 80, the conduct had been 'both obvious and gross'. This approach is not only just, it is also the only practicable one. It is simply not possible for any outsider to pick over the events of a marriage and decide who was the more to blame for what went wrong, save in the most obvious and gross cases. Yet in *Miller v Miller*, both Singer J and the Court of Appeal took into account the parties' conduct, even though it fell far short of this. In my view they were wrong to do so.

[146] In my view, the question of contributions should be approached in the much the same way as conduct. Following *White*, the search was on for some reason to stop short of equal sharing, especially in 'big money' cases where the capital had largely been generated by the breadwinner's efforts and enterprise. There were references to exceptional or 'stellar' contributions: see *Cowan v Cowan* [2001] EWCA Civ 679; [2002] Fam 97, [2001] 2 FLR 192. These, in the words of Coleridge J in *G v G (Financial Provision: Equal Division)* [2002] EWHC 1339 (Fam); [2002] 2 FLR 1143, at 1154, opened a 'forensic Pandora's box'. As he pointed out, at 1155:

> 'what is "contribution" but a species of conduct? ... Both concepts are compendious descriptions of the way in which one party conducted him/herself towards the other and/or the family during the marriage. And both carry with them precisely the same undesirable consequences. First, they call for a detailed retrospective at the end of a broken marriage just at a time when parties should be looking forward, not back ... But then, the facts having been established, they each call for a value judgment of the worth of each side's behaviour and translation of that worth into actual money. But by what measure and using what criteria? ... Is there such a concept as an exceptional/special domestic contribution or can only the wealth creator earn the bonus? ... It is much the same as comparing apples with pears and the debate is about as sterile or useful.'

A domestic goddess self-evidently makes a 'stellar' contribution, but that was not what these debates were about. Coleridge J's words were rightly influential in the later retreat from the concept of special contribution in *Lambert v Lambert* [2002] EWCA Civ 1685, [2003] Fam 103, [2003] 1 FLR 139. It had already been made clear in *White* that domestic and financial contributions should be treated equally. Section 25(2)(f) of the 1973 Act does not refer to the contributions which each has made to the parties' accumulated wealth, but to the contributions they have made (and will continue to make) to the welfare of the family. Each should be seen as doing their best in their own sphere. Only if there is such a disparity in their respective contributions to the welfare of the family that it would be inequitable to disregard it should this be taken into account in determining their shares.

The source of the assets and the length of the marriage

[147]   Nevertheless, such debates are evidence of unease at the fairness of dividing equally great wealth which has either been brought into the marriage or generated by the business efforts and acumen of one party. It is principally in this context that there is also a perception that the size of the non-business partner's share should be linked to the length of the marriage: see, eg, Eekelaar, *Asset Distribution on Divorce – the Durational Element* [2001] 117 LQR 552; and *Asset Distribution on Divorce – Time and Property* [2003] Fam Law 828; and *GW v RW (Financial Provision: Departure from Equality)* [2003] EWHC 611 (Fam), [2003] 2 FLR 108.

[148]   The strength of these perceptions is such that it could be unwise for the law to ignore them completely. In *White*, it was recognised that the source of the assets might be a reason for departing from the yardstick of equality (see 610C–G and 994 respectively). There, the reason was that property had been acquired from or with the help of the husband's father during the marriage, but the same would apply to property acquired before the marriage. In *White*, it was also recognised that the importance of the source of the assets will diminish over time (see 611B and 995 respectively). As the family's personal and financial inter-dependence grows, it becomes harder and harder to disentangle what came from where. But the fact that the family's wealth consists largely of a family business, such as a farm, may still be taken into account as a reason for departing from full equality: see *P v P (Inherited Property)* [2004] EWHC 1364 (Fam); [2005] 1 FLR 576. So too may be the nature of the assets, where these are businesses which will be crippled or lose much of their value, if disposed of prematurely in order to fund an equal division: see *N v N (Financial Provision: Sale of Company)* [2001] 2 FLR 69.

[149]   The question, therefore, is whether in the very big money cases, it is fair to take some account of the source and nature of the assets, in the same way that some account is taken of the source of those assets in inherited or family wealth. Is the 'matrimonial property' to consist of everything acquired during the marriage (which should probably include periods of pre-marital cohabitation and engagement) or might a distinction be drawn between 'family' and other assets? Family assets were described by Lord Denning in the landmark case of *Wachtel v Wachtel* [1973] Fam 72, at 90:

> 'It refers to those things which are acquired by one or other or both of the parties, with the intention that there should be continuing provision for them and their children during their joint lives, and used for the benefit of the family as a whole.'

Prime examples of family assets of a capital nature were the family home and its contents, while the parties' earning capacities were assets of a revenue nature. But also included are other assets which were obviously acquired for the use and benefit of the whole family, such as holiday homes, caravans, furniture, insurance policies and other family savings. To this list should clearly be added family businesses or joint ventures in which they both work. It is easy to see such assets as the fruits of the marital partnership. It is also easy to see each party's efforts as making a real contribution to the acquisition of such assets. Hence it is not at all surprising that Mr and Mrs McFarlane agreed upon the division of their capital assets, which were mostly of this nature, without prejudice to how Mrs McFarlane's future income provision would be quantified.

[150]   More difficult are business or investment assets which have been generated solely or mainly by the efforts of one party. The other party has often made some contribution to the business, at least in its early days, and has continued with her agreed contribution to the welfare of the family (as did Mrs Cowan). But in these non-business-partnership, non-family asset cases, the bulk of the property has been generated by one party. Does this provide a reason for departing from the yardstick of equality? On the one hand is the view, already expressed, that commercial and domestic contributions are intrinsically incommensurable. It is easy to count the money or property which one has acquired. It is impossible to count the value which the other has added to their lives together. One is counted in money or money's worth. The other is counted in domestic comfort and happiness. If the law is to avoid discrimination between the gender roles, it should regard all the assets generated in either way during the marriage as family assets to be divided equally between them unless some other good reason is shown to do otherwise.

[151]   On the other hand is the view that this is unrealistic. We do not yet have a system of community of property, whether full or deferred. Even modest legislative steps towards this have been strenuously resisted. Ownership and contributions still feature in divorcing couples' own perceptions of a fair result, some drawing a distinction between the home and joint savings accounts, on the one hand, and pensions, individual savings and debts, on the other (*Settling Up*, para [128] above, chapter 5). Some of these are not family assets in the way that the home, its contents and the family savings are family assets. Their value may well be speculative or their possession risky. It is not suggested that the domestic partner should share in the risks or potential liabilities, a problem which bedevils many community of property regimes and can give domestic contributions a negative value. It simply cannot be demonstrated that the domestic contribution, important though it has been to the welfare and happiness of the family as a whole, has contributed to their acquisition. If the money maker had not had a wife to look after him, no doubt he would have found others to do it for him. Further, great wealth can be generated in a very short time, as the *Miller* case shows; but domestic contributions by their very nature take time to mature into contributions to the welfare of the family.

[152]   My lords, while I do not think that these arguments can be ignored, I think that they are irrelevant in the great majority of cases. In the very small number of cases where they might make a difference, of which *Miller* may be one, the answer is the same as that given in *White* in connection with pre-marital property, inheritance and gifts. The source of the assets may be taken into account but its importance will diminish over time. Put the other way round, the court is expressly required to take into account the duration of the marriage: s 25(2)(d). If the assets are not 'family assets', or not generated by the joint efforts of the parties, then the duration of the marriage may justify a departure from the yardstick of equality of division. As we are talking here of a departure from that yardstick, I would prefer to put this in terms of a reduction to reflect the period of time over which the domestic contribution has or will continue (see Bailey-Harris, comment on *GW v RW (Financial Provision: Departure from Equality)* [2003] EWHC 611 (Fam), [2003] Fam Law 386, at 388) rather than in terms of accrual over time (see Eekelaar, 'Asset Distribution on Divorce – Time and Property' [2003] Fam Law 828). This avoids the complexities of devising a formula for such accruals.

[153]   This is simply to recognise that in a matrimonial property regime which still starts with the premise of separate property, there is still some scope for one party to acquire and retain separate property which is not automatically to be shared equally between them. The nature and the source of the property and the way the couple have run their lives may be taken into account in deciding how it should be shared. There may be other examples. Take, for example, a genuine dual career family where each party has worked throughout the marriage and certain assets have been pooled for the benefit of the family but others have not. There may be no relationship-generated needs or other disadvantages for which compensation is warranted. We can assume that the family assets, in the sense discussed earlier, should be divided equally. But it

might well be fair to leave undisturbed whatever additional surplus each has accumulated during his or her working life. However, one should be careful not to take this approach too far. What seems fair and sensible at the outset of a relationship may seem much less fair and sensible when it ends. And there could well be a sense of injustice if a dual career spouse who had worked outside as well as inside the home throughout the marriage ended up less well off than one who had only or mainly worked inside the home.

Application in the McFarlane case

[154]   There is obviously a relationship between capital sharing and future income provision. If capital has been equally shared and is enough to provide for need and compensate for disadvantage, then there should be no continuing financial provision. In *McFarlane*, there has been an equal division of property, but this largely consisted of homes which can be characterised as family assets. This was not enough to provide for needs or compensate for disadvantage. The main family asset is the husband's very substantial earning power, generated over a lengthy marriage in which the couple deliberately chose that the wife should devote herself to home and family and the husband to work and career. The wife is undoubtedly entitled to generous income provision for herself and for the sake of their children, including sums which will enable her to provide for her own old age and insure the husband's life. She is also entitled to a share in the very large surplus, on the principles both of sharing the fruits of the matrimonial partnership and of compensation for the comparable position which she might have been in had she not compromised her own career for the sake of them all. The fact that she might have wanted to do this is neither here nor there. Most breadwinners want to go on breadwinning. The fact that they enjoy their work does not disentitle them to a proper share in the fruits of their labours.

[155]   She does, of course, have to consider what she will do in the future. The children will eventually take up much less of her time and energy. She could either return to work as a solicitor or retrain for other satisfying and gainful activity. She cannot, therefore, rely upon the present level of provision for the rest of her life. But the Court of Appeal was wrong to set a limit to it on the basis that she would save the whole surplus above her requirements with a view to providing for herself once the time limit was up. They were wrong to place the burden upon her of justifying continuing payments, especially now that they have set a high threshold for doing so: see *Fleming v Fleming* [2003] EWCA Civ 1841; [2004] 1 FLR 667. On any view she will continue to be entitled to some continuing compensation, even if the needs generated by the relationship diminish or eventually vanish (although that cannot be guaranteed, despite her best endeavours, given the length of time she has been out of the labour market and the difficulties of repairing her pension position). The burden should be upon the husband to justify a reduction. At that stage, the court will again have to consider whether a clean break is practicable, as it could be if the husband has generated enough capital to make it realistic.

[156]   Accordingly, I would allow Mrs McFarlane's appeal and restore the order of the district judge.

Application in the Miller case

[157]   In *Miller*, the needs generated by the relationship are comparatively small. The wife will be able to re-establish herself in life within a relatively short time. But she was for some time the fiancée and then the wife of a very rich man. Much of that wealth accrued during the marriage. The New Star shares could not sensibly be

valued, but that the husband stood to gain at least £6m and probably a great deal more from them in the readily foreseeable future was undeniable. The company had been deliberately grown very quickly with a view to disposing of it advantageously in the relatively short term. Mrs Miller never sought to claim a half. The judge eschewed the yardstick of equality because the assets had not been generated by their joint efforts (cf *Foster v Foster*) but by the husband using his pre-marriage assets and expertise to generate substantial extra profits during the marriage. The judge quantified her claim without reference to the unfathomable value of the New Star shares acquired during the marriage, but in such a way as to give her a permanent income upon which she could live in the former matrimonial home albeit at a lower standard than she had been accustomed to during the marriage.

[158]   That is undoubtedly more than she would need to get herself back to where she would have been had the marriage not taken place. But that has never been the express objective of the law, even in the 1970s and 1980s when the Court of Appeal supported such an approach in short childless marriages. Even without the former statutory objective, the court has to take some account of the standard of living enjoyed during the marriage: see s 25(2)(c). The provision should enable a gentle transition from that standard to the standard that she could expect as a self-sufficient woman. But she is also entitled to some share in the assets. The couple had two homes and there is no reason at all why she should not have a share in their combined value, together with other assets obviously acquired for the benefit of the family. She is also entitled to some share in the considerable increase of the husband's wealth during the marriage. Had the yardstick of equality been applied to all the assets which accrued during the marriage, she would have got much more than she did. In my view the judge was wrong to take account of the reasons for the break-up of the marriage, but there was a reason to depart from the yardstick of equality because those were business assets generated solely by the husband during a short marriage. Whether one puts this as the result of the contacts and capacities he brought to the marriage or as the result of the nature and source of the assets generated (or, put another way, whichever the rationale one chooses from *GW v RW*), it comes to much the same thing.

[159]   Together her shares in the home and the other assets would amount to something so close to what the judge awarded that it would not be right to disturb the figure which he, with his unrivalled experience as a trial judge in such cases, considered fair. Accordingly, I would dismiss Mr Miller's appeal.

LORD MANCE:

My Lords,

[160]   I have had the benefit of reading in draft the speeches of my noble and learned friends Lord Nicholls of Birkenhead and Baroness Hale of Richmond. Happily, as Lord Hope has observed, there is very substantial common ground, with which I also concur, in the two comprehensive speeches of Lord Nicholls and Baroness Hale, and it would be wrong to venture on a third full speech covering the same ground. The main difference between the two speeches relates, as I see it, to the area covered by Lord Nicholls of Birkenhead in paras [17]–[19] and [54] and by Baroness Hale of Richmond in paras 148–152.

[161]   I would, however, add some observations on particular points, including that area, relating to the appeal in *Miller v Miller* [2005] EWCA Civ 984, [2006] 1 FLR 151. First, I agree that both the courts below decided the case on an erroneous legal ground, insofar as they accepted the wife's contention, based on the Court of Appeal's decision in *G v G (Financial Provision: Separation Agreement)* [2004] 1 FLR 1011, that the

husband's supposed bad conduct, falling short of the threshold stated in s 25(2)(g) of the Matrimonial Causes Act 1973 (the 1973 Act), could be taken into account 'as a significant counterbalancing factor to the point made on behalf of the husband that this was a short marriage'.

[162]   In this connection, Singer J said:

> '37   This marriage may well have been doomed, but my conclusions ... are these. H may well have developed an irritation with aspects of W's personality and behaviour. This reflects more his lack of adaptability than any shortcomings on her part. The sum of what he complains is not marriage-breaking stuff. I do not subscribe to his view that his burgeoning relationship with the woman with whom he lives was a consequence rather than a cause of the breakdown.

> 38   None of this, to state the obvious, is conduct which it would be inequitable to disregard in arriving at a resolution of the financial dispute. But it has the result that it would be unfair to W to concentrate solely on the bare chronology of this marriage without acknowledging that she did not seek to end it nor did she give H any remotely sufficient reason for him to do so.'

[163]   The Court of Appeal followed its reasoning in *G v G (Financial Provision: Separation Agreement)*, and held that Singer J was entitled to 'give much less weight to the duration of the marriage than he would have done had he found that the wife was to blame for its breakdown or that the parties had separated consensually each acknowledging unexpected incompatibility' (per Thorpe LJ, in *G v G (Financial Provision: Separation Agreement)*, para [31]). Thorpe LJ went on in paras [39]–[40] to cite para 48 of the judge's judgment as showing that:

> 'the decisive factor for the judge was that the marriage, taken in its full context, gave the wife a legitimate entitlement to a long term future on a higher plane of affluence than she had enjoyed prior to marriage.'

[164]   There can be few who marry believing that their marriage will be short-lived, however likely this may be on the statistics. Reasonable expectation of a long marriage cannot itself justify ignoring the reality if it is short-lived. Where there is no conduct which it would be inequitable to disregard, the court should not seek to weigh the parties' respective conduct or attitudes in an attempt to assess responsibility for the breakdown of a marriage, or to attribute 'legitimacy' or 'reasonableness' to the wish of one party to continue the marriage against the wishes of the other. One problem about any such attempt is evident from the first sentence of para 37 of Singer J's judgment, quoted in para [162] above. If 'this marriage may well have been doomed', what significance can there be in the fact that one party recognised this earlier than the other? How is one to judge between harsh realism and wishful thinking? More fundamentally, s 25(2)(g) recognises the difficulty and undesirability, except in egregious cases, of any attempt at assessing and weighing marital conduct. I now recognise the same difficulty in respect of marital contributions – conduct and contributions are in large measure opposite sides of a coin: see, eg, *G v G (Financial Provision: Equal Division)* [2002] 2 FLR 1143, per Coleridge J at para [34].

[165]   Both decisions below, therefore, involved a potentially significant error of approach. The error requires reconsideration of the judge's and Court of Appeal's conclusions as to the appropriate award. The error was obviously material to their reasoning in arriving at their decisions.

[166]   Secondly, the course of this litigation has to my mind been complicated by the fluctuating stance taken on the part of the respondent, Mrs Miller, in relation to what has been described as the matrimonial acquest, the increase in value of the

parties' assets during the marriage. Before Singer J, Mrs Miller claimed a share of such increase. But Singer J, having heard expert evidence on both sides, found difficulty in ascertaining its size to the point where, as I read his judgment, he effectively abandoned the search for such a measure altogether: see paras 49–64 of his judgment. The respondent did not seek to revisit this aspect until the appeal to your Lordships' House, when in her written case and oral submissions she argued that more specific account should have been taken of the matrimonial acquest, and sought to demonstrate that certain conclusions could safely be drawn about its size.

[167]   Thirdly, this is the area where the approaches of Lord Nicholls of Birkenhead and Baroness Hale of Richmond diverge in some measure, at least in principle. On the one hand, on Lord Nicholls of Birkenhead's approach, non-matrimonial property is viewed as all property which the parties bring with them into the marriage or acquire by inheritance or gift during the marriage (plus perhaps the income or fruits of that property), while matrimonial property is viewed as all other property. The yardstick of equality applies generally to matrimonial property (although the shorter the marriage, the smaller the matrimonial property is in the nature of things likely to be). But the yardstick is not so readily applicable to non-matrimonial property, especially after a short marriage, but in some circumstances even after a long marriage.

[168]   On the other hand, Baroness Hale of Richmond's approach takes a more limited conception of matrimonial property, as embracing 'family assets' (cf *Wachtel v Wachtel* [1973] Fam 72 per Lord Denning MR, at 90) and family businesses or joint ventures in which both parties work (cf *Foster v Foster* [2003] EWCA Civ 56, [2003] 2 FLR 299 per Hale LJ, at 305, para [19]). In relation to such property she agrees that the yardstick of equality may readily be applied. In contrast, she identifies other 'non-business-partnership, non-family assets', to which that yardstick may not apply with the same force particularly in the case of short marriages; these include on her approach not merely: (a) property which the parties bring with them with into the marriage or acquire by inheritance or gift during the marriage (plus perhaps its income or fruits); but also (b) business or investment assets generated solely or mainly by the efforts of one party during the marriage.

[169]   Baroness Hale of Richmond acknowledges that the difference between the two approaches will in the great majority of cases be irrelevant. Further, it seems to me that after a short marriage it may in reality often be difficult to determine precisely what assets (other than family assets) were generated during the marriage. The present case is an example, with arguments about whether Mr Miller can be said (by reason of his contacts, his gentleman's agreement with Mr Duffield and/or his experience) to have brought into the marriage any asset relating to his potential interest in New Star. To take into account the shortness of a marriage could enable a court to cut through some of these more intricate arguments in a manner consistent with s 25(2)(d) of the 1973 Act. More fundamentally, to allow the duration of a marriage as a relevant factor would cater for the considerations that, while some people may make a large amount of money in a short time, the nature of their work or other factors may mean that they do not do so at a consistent rate over their lives as a whole or for more than a short period of their lives, and furthermore, as Baroness Hale has pointed out, that there may be long-term risks in relation to non-business-partnership, non-family assets which remain with those directly involved in generating them. The longer the marriage, the less likely these are to be significant considerations. In a short marriage, the timing of which may or may not coincide with a period of significant increase in the value of non-business-partnership, non-family assets, such considerations argue in favour of some further flexibility in the application of the yardstick of equality of division. I see force in and would agree with the views expressed by Baroness Hale of Richmond in paras [152]–[153] of her judgment to the effect that the duration of a marriage,

mentioned expressly in s 25(2)(d) of the 1973 Act, cannot be discounted as a relevant factor.

[170]   Fourthly, and whatever the position on the third point, I agree with what Baroness Hale of Richmond has said in para [153], which is, as I see it, also consistent with the last sentence of para [25] of Lord Nicholls of Birkenhead's speech. The present marriage had what one might call a traditional aspect. Mr Miller worked, and Mrs Miller gave up work to look after him. But there can be marriages, long as well as short, where both partners are and remain financially active, and independently so. They may contribute to a house and joint expenses, but it does not necessarily follow that they are or regard themselves in other respects as engaged in a joint financial enterprise for all purposes. Intrusive inquiries into the other's financial affairs might, during the marriage, be viewed as inconsistent with a proper respect for the other's personal autonomy and development, and even more so if the other were to claim a share of any profit made from them. In such a case the wife might still have the particular additional burden of combining the bearing of and caring for children with work outside the home. If one partner (and it might, with increasing likelihood I hope, be the wife) were more successful financially than the other, and questions of needs and compensation had been addressed, one might ask why a court should impose at the end of their marriage a sharing of all assets acquired during matrimony which the parties had never envisaged during matrimony. Once needs and compensation had been addressed, the misfortune of divorce would not of itself, as it seems to me, be justification for the court to disturb principles by which the parties had chosen to live their lives while married.

[171]   Fifthly, Singer J was inclined to assimilate to property inherited or brought into a marriage property which was generated by one spouse 'using his or her pre-marriage assets or on the back of his or her pre-marriage 'fledged' experience' (see para 69). The word 'fledged' arises from the reasoning of Mr Nicholas Mostyn QC in a judicial capacity in *GW v RW (Financial Provision: Departure from Equality)* [2003] EWHC 611 (Fam), [2003] 2 FLR 108, para [51], where he treated 'a developed career, existing high earnings and an established earning capacity' as 'as much a non-marital asset as the provision of hard cash' and as 'a contribution unmatched by any comparable contribution by W'. In the present case, Mr Mostyn QC representing Mrs Miller was accordingly prepared before the judge to discount any claim by Mrs Miller relating to the matrimonial acquest (from 50% to 37.5%) to take into account that Mr Miller 'brought very valuable acquired expertise and acumen to this marriage'.

[172]   A possible difficulty about this approach is that it reintroduces, at the commencement of the marriage, a requirement to attempt to assess and compare the value of the contributions which each party is or would be likely to make during or apart from the marriage. I am not very confident that an established earning capacity or very valuable acquired expertise and acumen would, if viewed as 'assets' brought into a marriage, be easily or reliably measurable or comparable with other qualities, or indeed how far would one carry the inquiry into expertise and acumen. The concept of 'fledging' is probably anyway one which would diminish in relevance, the longer the marriage, so that, in the light of the answer I would give to the third point above, the answer to this fifth point may be correspondingly less important.

[173]   On the other hand, where at the beginning (or end) of the marriage an actual transaction is under way or in view which in due course yields a considerable new asset, there is no difficulty in principle (even if there may be some difficulty in valuation) in accepting that part of that asset may have to be excluded from any assessment of the matrimonial acquest or included in what the parties brought into the marriage. In the present case, Mr Miller already had, at the marriage date, real connections in the form of the Jupiter funds which he later took to New Star and real

prospects under the gentleman's agreement made with Mr Duffield of acquiring, as he subsequently did, valuable shares in New Star. I would regard these as real contributions brought into the marriage, which should on any view be taken into account accordingly.

[174]   Sixthly, if account is taken of the increase in the value of the parties' assets during the marriage (the matrimonial acquest), a question may arise about the date up to which one should measure it. Should this be up to date when the parties ceased effectively to live as married partners (here April 2003), as Mr Mostyn QC considered in his judicial capacity in *GW v RW* at para [34]? Or should it be up to a later date such as the date of trial, or even, in a case where an appellate court thinks it right to re-exercise the discretion, up to the date of the appellate decision? Reference was made by Mr Mostyn QC to my remarks in *Cowan v Cowan* [2002] Fam 97, [2001] 2 FLR 192 paras [130]–[135]. The matters to which the court must have regard under s 25 include several which exist or appear likely as at the date the court has regard to them (cf s 25(2)(a), (b), (f) and (h)). Others of the listed matters require the court to look back at the past (eg s 25(2)(c), (f) and (g)). To the extent that the focus is on the matrimonial acquest, the period during which the parties were making their different mutual contributions to the marriage has obvious relevance. The present may be viewed as a case (paralleling the then unreported decision of Coleridge J in *N v N (Financial Provision: Sale of Company)* [2001] 2 FLR 69 to which I referred in *Cowan v Cowan*) where the increase in value of the New Star shares between separation in April 2003 and trial in October 2004 or judgment in April 2005 was contributed to by the husband's further investment of time and effort, independently on its face of any contribution by the wife. Further, Mrs Miller had here no right to, and could not have been given, any part of Mr Miller's New Star shareholding in relation to which Mr Miller carried the risk. Mrs Miller has at all times been living in the house, which has now been formally transferred to her. Her only further claim was to a sum of money, assessed by the judge at £2.7m (which Mr Miller paid in two instalments in May and June 2005). Mr Miller cannot easily be said in this case to have been holding on to any asset which should have been Mrs Miller's, or to owe anything other than money. Assuming that the focus is on assets acquired during the marriage, rather than on the husband's overall means, it seems to me, therefore, natural in this case to look at the period until separation.

[175]   Seventhly, so far as concerns the resolution of this appeal, Mr Miller was a very wealthy man both before and at the end of the marriage. Leaving on one side the New Star shares, he had brought into the marriage in July 2000 assets of £16.7m and he had at the time of separation in April 2003 assets of £17m and at the time of trial assets of £17.7m. The New Star shares had been promised to Mr Miller by Mr Duffield under the gentleman's agreement of May 2000, whereby Mr Miller would, if he could, move from Jupiter and would join, and receive shares, in a new company – New Star – which Mr Duffield in fact established in June 2000. The realisation of this gentleman's agreement depended on Mr Duffield arranging for Commerzbank to release Mr Miller. Mr Duffield was able to arrange this on 22 November 2000, and Mr Miller was allotted 200,000 shares for £200,000 on 31 January 2001.

[176]   Of the 200,000 shares, 75,000 were subject to an option agreement, and Mr Miller was subject to restrictions precluding him from realising any immediate value in respect of any of them. He was also subject to 'share leaver' arrangements, whereby he could, in certain circumstances (eg dismissal for cause), be obliged to dispose of all 200,000 shares at par, ie for £200,000. On a number of occasions after January 2001, New Star raised money by issuing further shares, subject to differing rights or restrictions (the effect of which was not explored before the House), at prices varying from £80 for E shares in March 2001, to £150 for G shares in December 2001, to £80 for A shares in September 2003 and £90 in October 2003. Moneys so raised were

used to expand the business and to acquire the rights to manage further funds. Funds under management increased from £300m in January 2000 to £8.5 billion at trial in October 2004, gross annual income grew from £17.58m to £83.5m, and annual income before interest, tax, depreciation and amortisation was minus £8.8m in New Star's initial trading period but had become a positive £23.77m by trial.

[177]   The experts put before the judge widely varying figures for the value of Mr Miller's shares at trial, ranging from £12.35m to £18.11m on a notional sale between willing vendor and purchaser, in each case after allowing a discount to reflect the possibility that Mr Miller's employment might be terminated in circumstances requiring him to dispose of the shares at par. At the end of the day, all that Singer J was confident enough to say was that there was 'a good likelihood that at some stage the potential of his shares will be unleashed' (see para 41) and, more specifically, that unless Mr Miller was unlucky enough to trigger an obligation to sell his shares at par, he was 'likely to receive £6M gross upon the exercise by the end of December 2006 of the option he was required to enter into to sell 75,000 of his shares for £80 each' (see para 63).

[178]   In the event, Singer J concluded simply that Mrs Miller should, for as long as she might wish, have the opportunity to continue to live in the former matrimonial home, the value of which was £2.3m, and that in addition Mr Miller should transfer to her the sum of £2.7m, which should generate a net annual income of about £98,000 pa, making her 'able to live to a very tolerable standard in that house'. He concluded his judgment by saying in para 73:

> 'A global award equivalent to £5m (plus the furniture and chattels which have been agreed) seems to me a fair outcome irrespective of whatever value H in due course may achieve for the New Star shares.'

[179]   As I have already indicated, the reasoning which led to this conclusion cannot be sustained, so that the House must reconsider the appropriateness of the judge's award afresh.

[180]   The relevance of the value of the New Star shares at the date of trial is in the context of this case also open to question (cf my sixth point above). But even at the date of separation in April 2003, the 125,000 shares not subject to any option must have had a sterling value running into eight figures. Against this could be set the value of the contribution that Mr Miller brought into this short marriage, in the form of the Jupiter funds which he took to New Star and real prospects under the gentleman's agreement of acquiring, as he did, valuable shares in New Star (the fifth point above).

[181]   Within 3 months of the Court of Appeal's judgment, New Star was floated on the Alternative Investment Market in a transaction which Mrs Miller maintains would on any view enable a value to be attached to Mr Miller's shareholdings (by then converted from 200,000 into 20m shares, by a one for 100 share substitution). Within 3 months of the hearing before the House, your Lordships are told, Mr Miller (under commercial pressure by reason of alleged investment under-performance) has had to agree to revise his share arrangements so that in respect of either 6.05m or 6.55m shares (depending on further investment performance) he will now not receive more than his money back (ie 1p per share). But, at the same time, the stringency of the 'share leaver' arrangements to which he was subject has been somewhat relaxed; and the value of each share has, we are told, continued to climb. For my part, I do not think that these developments can or should affect the outcome of this appeal. They do not bear on what I have called the matrimonial acquest. They do not do anything to alter the conclusion that the amount now awarded to Mrs Miller will, however substantial in itself, have no major impact on Mr Miller's very substantial wealth or life.

[182]   Taking into account all the above observations, I might by myself have arrived at an award in Mrs Miller's favour of less than £5m, but I shall not carry my doubts on this aspect to the length of dissent in the case of *Miller v Miller*. In the case of *McFarlane v McFarlane*, I have nothing to add to what is said by my noble and learned friends, Lord Nicholls of Birkenhead and Baroness Hale of Richmond, with which I agree.

Appeal in Miller v Miller dismissed; appeal in McFarlane v McFarlane allowed.

Solicitors: *Sears Tooth* for the petitioner Miller
        Family Law In Partnership for the petitioner McFarlane
        Withers LLP for the respondent Miller
        Levison Meltzer Pigott for the respondent McFarlane

PHILIPPA JOHNSON
Law Reporter